Rural Mississippi Highway 61 headed north near Hollansworth, Mississippi. Photo by Brandonrush.

61 Highways Revisited

—ıʬ—

The Albums of Bob Dylan

Mr. Manmade Manufactured Mistaken Messiah, Mercilessly
Muttering Man of Miraculous Musical Mayhem, Maniacally
Moody Masquerading Minstrel, Meandering Misunderstood
Master Musician, Monumentally Mysterious Melodious Mystic,
Momentarily Modest Moralist, Mesmerizing Immortal Missing
Motorcyclist, Marvelously Mercurial Musical Magician,
Magnificently Marketed Mad Minister of Americana

Bob Shiel

ISBN: 1511980257
ISBN 13: 9781511980258

Table of Contents

Preface

Welcome, and please pass out all the syllabi so that we're all on the same page and we can get started. Oh, I forgot, I retired last summer.

61 Highways Revisited is actually not about Bob Dylan, or even his music. It's Saturday night, and Mommy just got home from the filling station, and she left the keys in the car. This book is about fun, fun, fun till Daddy takes the T-bird away. Therefore, the only way to "f" this up is to take it too seriously. So, take a deep breath, and let all that brain chatter go, but don't look at the tilt-a-whirl while you're riding the roller coaster. If you're not sure what that means, don't ask.

Having said that, mission impossible, which I not only choose to accept, but embrace pro-actively: To write a book about the albums of Bob Dylan whose title and manuscript are like a Bob Dylan song. Daunting task? You betcha. Intellectual candy? Bingo.

By the way (I invite you to get used to such parenthetical tangents, larks, and fun-filled diversions), if 61 albums are not easy to wrap your head around, consider the mind-boggling thousands of albums, thousands of artists, and even more thousands of cover versions of copyrighted Dylan songs that are known to have been recorded! Imagine the royalties Bob has reaped. Then, there are the hundreds of unofficial Dylan LPs released in foreign countries under labels that might or probably not be above board, if you know what I mean. I have personally filtered through Dylan sections in music stores in places like Guam, Fiji, New Zealand, Ireland, Mexico, Brazil, and Italy and come across Dylan LP animals from outer space. This is not to mention the redundant handful of Columbia Dylan LP releases omitted from the 61 in this book with titles like *The Essential Bob Dylan*, *The Best of Bob Dylan*, *The 50th Anniversary Collection*, *The Complete Album Collection Volume 1*, *Dylan* (a 2007 3 disc greatest hits up to *Modern Times*), and *The Original Mono Recordings*. Anyhoo, if 61 is a number that astounds you, please consider that this number is drastically pared down in the scheme of things in Bob Dylan album land.

By the way once again, please forgive the plug, but a worthy album and cause when it comes to covers of Dylan songs would be the 2012 *Amnesty International Chimes Of Freedom: The Songs Of Bob Dylan Honoring 50 Years of Amnesty International*. Here you'll find 4 discs with 73 tracks recorded by 73 different artists/bands with all proceeds going to this worthy cause. Not all, but about a dozen of these versions are in the signature department and as good as it gets.

Occasionally, it'll get wordy, for verbosity mirrors a Dylan song, does it not? How better tip the proverbial hat to Bob than to turn out a 104,204-word effort (Who's counting?) aimed at entertaining, educating, cajoling, provoking, annoying, humoring, uplifting, and otherwise stimulating its readers?

Why is this book important for others? After all, it won't, unless I'm wrong, change the evil on the 6 o'clock news tonight. It lacks significance to any degree whatsoever in the scheme of things. Yet, as our friend Mohatma Mohandas Gandhi pointed out, oh so crystal clearly, what we ought to be doing, meditating, is not significant at all, but it is extremely paramount that it be done anyway. Unless you stop reading right now, you are about to indelibly and permanently change your mind, and to Gandhi's point, that's all we got.

If happiness is the result of learning, and I presume it is, human suffering is the offspring of ignorance. Wisdom is about realizing precisely the knowledge bases about which one is ignorant. Ignorance, on the other hand, is not even being cognizant of the depths or content of one's frailties in scholarship, academic expertise, and mental awareness.

May we all realize how little we comprehend about the music of Bob Dylan? The size of this subject matter alone is intimidating enough. Its content is all the more daunting. Others, so many others, have undertaken the task, but not quite in the manner which you are about to witness. Let my obituary, hopefully somewhere around 2046, state that I did my part in the longstanding legacy of Bob Dylan mythology identification, an endeavor that surely will gain traction and endure long after he fixes to die, we lose Bob to the afterlife, he dies in his footsteps, his time of dyin' knocks, and the living are left to keep his grave clean.

There are countless books about Bob Dylan, and obviously his music. Yet, as I read these works, some casual and others more scholarly, I cannot help but notice that I keep having this gnawing feeling, "I am the album man." His records, which started out on vinyl, graduated to audio cassettes, morphed to CDs, and eventually made the move to MP3s and ipods have always been a focus of my fascination. In 1997 in the *Newsweek* story just before Bob performed for Pope John Paul deuce, I was heartened to read Bob's counsel, "Look to the songs. They are my lexicon." Thus, you will find **song titles in bold**, for that's Bob's lexicon, where he himself says it's at.

So, off we go meandering through Dylan's original text, source, lyrics, and music. They don't ever lie. Enough of the ignorance. Suffering may be part of the human condition, but that is a given, so accept it, like our friend Buddha. How many souls have healed in response to Dylan's lonely heart's magical musical muse?

There will be no footnotes or bibliography. And there may even be errors in fact, spelling, or God knows what (heaven forbid a typo), which while wholly unintentional, are undeniable, and in the spirit of academic enlightenment, I welcome friendly correction. Although prone to ignorance, I am not so ignorant to claim otherwise. This book is intentionally shot from the hip. We are all learning. An academic work this is not. The only source I can claim is consistent, casual, scholarly fandom since 1970. Given that I can't remember yesterday so well anymore, I don't know where I come up with this stuff. I'm just going through the albums, and what comes out comes out. I am less sure or concerned with whether others will care to delve into this monster than I am that if they do, they will be entertained and educated for having done so.

I can only speak for myself, which in this book I not only shall do, but that is ALL I do. Having, like Dylan, grown up in the Midwest, some say my reception to Bob's radio station ain't too bad, but you can be the judge of that. I wouldn't know and am not concerned.

In Bob Dylan's own heritage, this book is about medicating unnecessary pain caused by resistance to being in the present moment, which causes all sorts of suffering I won't go into, but my next book just might. Bob Dylan is a sort of eternal now guru who, while reverential towards those who showed him the way, is never nostalgic, never stuck in the same ole, same ole mind stuff of the past. Rather, our friend Bob is really perpetually thriving in a lifelong everlasting spontaneous wellspring of creativity, busy being born into the next galaxy of original thinking. Thus, he almost always appears to be light years ahead of his time, a tendency that has been annoying to no end and cost him countless fans, which in Bob's mind is nothing. This cosmic brainchild, if you will, is Bob Dylan's and his alone, but he has been reminding us on 61 albums going back to 1962 that it is also an inventive labor of love to which we all have access.

All this has been taken into great consideration while writing this book ever since the thought ever occurred to me. Otherwise, I would have spent years writing it, not just six months, but that would have been most anti-Dylan of me. After all, Bob's definition of rehearsing a song is merely knowing what key it's in, not that it matters.

Hence, I stuck to the original time framework of four months of writing and two months of editing, though proofreading had its way of taking on a life of its own. No rehashing, regretting, or looking back. Done deal, like it or not.

Enjoy the ride. You might be a casual Dylan observer, might have written him off eons ago, might never have been on the train in the first place, might be a sincere follower, might be a veteran of one, two, dozens, or even hundreds of live concerts. But you *stiiiiill* gotta give it up for Zimmy, Bobby, Archie, Ray, no matter what you say.

For all human beings, but particularly Americans, Dylan's work, and hopefully this book, provide a deep glimpse into the heart of America, Americana, and the heritage of pursuing a dream that is beyond the American dream. It is the human dream. To remember that, even though we feel alone on our paths SOMETIMES, we are not.

We are connected to the land. The literature. The music. The highways. The rivers. The small towns and urban jungles. Freedom. Justice. All that is evil which serves to nourish our better natures.

We humans are blessed with immense knowledge, which is utterly useless without a spiritual bond with a divine presence that goes by many names, depending on one's religious beliefs or non-beliefs, which is a great misnomer since a non-belief is a belief on some level. Each of Dylan's 61 albums crisscross in and out of spiritual themes running over and throughout them all. Just don't ask Bob to tell you what name to call Him, Her, or It. I reckon he'd tell ya to just go with it and not undertake swimming upstream against it.

Bob Dylan is a genuine American, and patriot, in the truest sense. He is a one of a kind that has inspired billions of others in every nation on earth to follow suit. Why else would his image grace a commemorative postage stamp in godforsaken Djibouti, where injustice, corruption, and hopelessness are a way of life? Dylan's reach knows no bounds.

Regardless, let's step back and look at the only evidence that matters, that which Bob Dylan himself has incessantly emphasized, even though many never take heed. The music. Thus, the albums. One by one. In chronological order, but in no particular hurry.

Any mention of the name Bob Dylan nowadays is likely to be met with the initial, "Is he still alive?," immediately followed by the mandatory, "He is such a great songwriter." True enough, and songwriting will no doubt lead the parade of accolades in the second paragraph of Bob's obituary the day after he leaves us for a better place. In fact, by that mournful, fateful day when Dylan's obituary hits the headlines, he might well have already received a Nobel Prize in Literature. Blah, blah, blah.

However, in paragraph 3 or 4 of said obituary will be little-known fodder for constructing the Dylan mythological legend beyond the more obvious. For example, his legacy as a live performer, bolstered for the past 27 years and counting by a staggering 100 plus live concerts a year, a pace that has not lessened well into Dylan's 70s. Did Frank Sinatra do almost 4,000 live concerts? Did B.B. King, a Sinatra nut galore, constantly reinterpret his compositions, whether obscure or classic in the judgments of others, to the point that they were sometimes unrecognizable by even avid fans? To these astonishing questions, it is only Bob Dylan that can answer, "Yes." Evidence to the contrary, at least over the long run, James Brown was *not* the hardest working man in show business.

Furthermore, how many realize that Bob is a painter whose hundreds of works have been displayed in galleries located on four continents? Or that this kid from a town which boasts the planet's largest iron ore pit is a welder and sculptor of three dimensional art also worthy of gallery exhibits far and wide?

This book is about none of that. It started out being about just the 29 studio albums of Bob Dylan exclusively containing previously unreleased original songs, and its focus ended up never wavering from that. However comma, as I approached the end of the first and really rough draft of that manuscript well within my original deadline parameter, I noticed how much f-ing fun I was having, and I decided to take on 32 more albums that generally speaking fall into categories like movie soundtracks, live albums, greatest hits, cover albums, and official bootleg releases. Keep in mind the theme we are dancing with – that fun and games are the by-product of having thoughts we have never had before. Education. Learning. This book is my teacher and a 300 level course in happiness.

Lots of synchronicity has been involved. For example, since the day after Labor Day 2014, when I set out on this trek to destinations unknown, Dylan has rolled into Chicago and given the best concert I have seen since about 2002, and that is going back about 20 shows. Bob's live band is currently on fire amidst his carefree croon. Simultaneously, *The Complete Basement Tapes* came out. *Shadows In The Night* hit records stores during this adventure, and at the Grammy ceremony this year, Dylan got some muckety-muck award that brought dozens of stars to the party. The man is 74 years old.

In the process of writing this monster, I have enjoyed the luxury of time to dwell on what brings me the most joy in life, pondering the myriad of infinite ways word combinations and obscure collocations might be put to bad-ass music, and countless epiphanies have occurred to me. One example will suffice. We all can dig the way Dylan turns a phrase. That he is surely a linguistic maestro, we can all agree.

However, personally, one of my dirtiest secrets, which heretofore I was absolutely adamant about taking to my grave, is that I have always relished Dylan's under-appreciated artistic contribution to human civilization of having inserted four and even five syllable words into rock and roll song titles. Temporary. Subterranean. And my all-time favorites, namely adverbs of degree. Absolutely. Positively. Approximately. In 1955 Little Richard gave us **Tutti Frutti**. In 1965 Sam the Sham and the Pharaohs raised the bar all the way to **Wooly Bully**. However, by 1966 Dylan's mesmerizing, enlightening effect on Donovan resulted in **Mellow Yellow**. Think about it.

How glad I am that I get to write this prior to Bob's death. While he is still a working, prolific artist in his 70s running circles around performing artists of all walks, cultural icons, and millions of creative unknown nobodies born five decades after him. With joy in my heart, my gratitude for the music of Bob Dylan, not Bob Dylan, is absolutely and truly infinite.

May my readers intellectually, bio-energetically, spiritually, and/or emotionally feel even a slice, and if only for a nanosecond, of the happiness, albeit insane, Bob has gifted this fan, writer, and ever-teachable student.

Highly suggested: Take on *61 Highways Revisited* in doses such as a couple chapters at a time, ideally listening to the albums you are reading about. Otherwise, much, if not the majority, will be missed. Start by first preparing your ears and eyes by opening your mind. Or, at least focusing it. Again, turn on some Bob Dylan music in the background as you read, ideally about the album you're listening to. Or, another suggestion is to, as you read along, listen to my audio companion to this here book, the 2 CD *61 Highways Revisited* (same title), which contains 32 songs either by or covered by Bob Dylan at some point in the past 54 years. Those songs were recorded sometime in the four years before I started writing this book, and are arranged on an acoustic disc of 17 tracks and an electric disc with 15 tracks (available through the lovely amazon.com on hard disc and cdbaby.com in digital MP3 format).

Another thing. Keep in mind, the English language is not shaped or delimited by dictionaries, but by its everyday users.

I ain't trying to persuade you, convince you, or change yer mind. All I'm trying to do is baby write a book, educate you, and entertain you. If yer lookin' for an expert, someone who knows it all, who's tryin' t' be right and make you wrong, someone who will look down his nose at you – well, it ain't me babe, it ain't me you're lookin' for.

The point is not that I am in Dylan's inner circle nor have access to it. I'm just writing a book that has wanted to be written since *Time Out Of Mind*.

As for Bob, he's still on the road, headed for another joint. Welcome to Dylan Music 301, where the only requirement is to always agree, even though we all see it from a different point of view. We're all tangled up in blue.

Acknowledgements

Dylan specific. Many thanks to Mike Stillman and Janet Fleming of Chicago for home hospitality and sharing lots and lots of bootleg audio and video recordings of live shows. I thank my brother John for leaving a worthy collection of 60s Dylan on vinyl hanging around our bedroom. Karl Erik Anderson in Norway has operated the best web site on the Internet, period (www.expectingrain.com), concerning all things Dylan for 20 some-odd years, and I am a grateful daily reader. Bill Pagel's current updates (www.boblinks.com) on Bob's live tours and postings of fan reviews continue to be a joy in my life. Dylan writers who I respectfully salute include Clinton Heylin, Peter Stone Brown, Greil Marcus, Michael Gray, Howard Sounes, Anthony Scaduto, David Browne, Jonathon Cott, David Kinney, and Jenny Ledeen. Oscar Montes, your enthusiasm is contagious. Special Rider Music for permission to raise money for charity by selling my double CD of homemade recordings of Bob Dylan copyrighted songs.

Just because. Gratitude to the Mankind Project and the thousands of good men in roughly 15 countries who have helped me take the gift of life by the throat. Men like Satpurkha DeRigne of Kansas City, who enthusiastically responded to daily cell phone readings in the oral tradition. Chicagoan Tim Goldich (check out his book series on gender politics, man) role modeled author weirdness I could live up to. Poet Jonno Kinsella of Glengarriff in County Cork, Ireland. Spiritual path partners Dave Lindgren and the thousands he has touched. Sycamore, tall Tom Weaver of Minnesota, don't you know. Walkers of the talk like Jeff Robins of Peoria. Loving Latvian Ed Feldmanis. Asa Baber, deceased *Playboy* columnist, 1990 right angel at the right time, and writing cheerleader from the other side. Hundreds of men who, due to their humility, would prefer their names not be mentioned. Accountability sergeant Luke Howe of Chicago. David C. and Don C. and all friends of Bill W. Rock of Ages Chuck Skelton. Big brother Dr. James Kinder of Waynesboro, Virginia. Chicagoans Scott Wills, Stu Frank, Andy Mitran, Bob Koehler, and Dawi Opara of The Men's Art Forum. My friends at Truman College in Uptown. Stuart Malone at Create Space. My wonderful family in Indiana, California, Arizona, Kentucky, Massachusetts, and Illinois, for starters. My parents Jody and John in that big house in the sky. And la-de-da, on and on.

Thank you Robert Allen Zimmerman. Thanks to your mother Beatrice's ancestors from Lithuania, and your father Abraham's father's Ukrainian family and Abraham's mother's Turkish heritage. We are all related.

1

Bob Dylan (eponymous first album)

Self-titled *Bob Dylan*, the first album resulted from an inexplicable "sound" that erupted in public and private performances, commencing somewhere in the vicinity of May 1961. This was only roughly 90 days after Bob's arrival in the city that never sleeps, which was apparently enough time to go from pretty good hack (I ought to know) to, well, holy crap! Prior to this, his guitar playing and voice quality were no more than worth listening to, not something one would likely yearn to ever hear again.

One could point to his February 1961 meeting of his sickly mentor and idol at the time, Woody Guthrie, his brushings with Tin Pan Alley legends such as John Lee Hooker and Dave Van Ronk, or any number of other mere guesses as to why he, and not any number of other musicians over the ages, rose to tower over the sounds inspiring him to stay up until dawn on amphetamines and red wine, scribbling lyrics and compiling melodies that will remain in the halls of Americana generations after his death. Yet, as his spring '61 Minnesota tapes and Greenwich Village concerts now reveal, right after Bob rolled into New York in late January of '61 something happened, and something changed.

Thus, when Robert Shelton caught Bob's live act in September of 1961, his now famous *New York Times* review catapulted Dylan into public consciousness and the office of Columbia records producer extraordinaire John Hammond, Sr. When Hammond told Dylan (whose last name was really still Zimmerman) his parents were required to sign his record contract because Bob wasn't legally an adult yet, he gullibly swallowed Bob's claim to be an orphan. Merely six weeks later, in roughly 48 hours of marathon session work the third week of November 1961, Bob's underselling first album was inexpensively (as in a few hundred dollars) recorded without fanfare in studio A at Columbia. With Bob sporting his early folkie fixture, his Dutch boy hat, on its cover, *Bob Dylan* was subsequently released into stores nationally March 19, 1962.

The sound on *Bob Dylan* was partly blues-laced Sonny Boy Williamson, Huddy Leadbetter, Robert Johnson, and Blind Willie McTell, yet somehow rooted in the folk tradition of the time popularized by the Clancy Brothers, Kingston Trio, the Weavers, and, of course, Woody Guthrie. **Talkin' New York** and **Song To Woody**, the only self-composed tunes on the song list, were vastly outnumbered by covers of Blind Lemon Jefferson, Jesse Fuller, Eric Von Schmidt, and a handful of traditional folk songs arranged in Dylan's old bluesman voice quality so infamous his first year in the Big Apple. Talent-dripping, death-obsessed, and gripping in its salute to American musical roots, the album surprisingly stayed within boundaries that Bob was crossing constantly outside the recording studio.

Songwriting was already a constant passion by the first album, and it would soon become a 24/7 obsession once a deal got sealed for publishing rights. Bob seemed to write lyrics and melodies effortlessly at all hours of the day and night. Stockpiling the best for his second album, almost but not all of these tunes remained outtakes of studio albums and have since been released either on *Biograph* in 1985 or in the *Bootleg Series*, which commenced in 1991.

None of *Bob Dylan* really points to the social commentary that would follow it in subsequent releases in 1963 and '64. The lyrics are honest and introspective, but do not reflect any influence of Bob's affair with Suze Rotollo, with whom he began to live only two months after recording. Suze's left wing communist leanings and that of her parents had only just begun to simmer in the mind of the young Minnesotan as he showed legendary Columbia records producer John Hammond, Sr. (a Robert Johnson revivalist and the so-called discoverer of talents like Benny Goodman, Billy Holiday, Count Basie, and Pete Seeger) what he could do in a recording studio with just a 1949 Martin 00-17 and a harmonica on a holder around his neck.

About the only song on his first album that reflects world events is the deeply touching **Song To Woody** (Guthrie). It underscores Bob's concern about the rat race on planet earth, no doubt, but more to the point, his realization of the failing health of the author of *Bound For Glory* and a heartfelt expression of love and admiration for one of his countless heroes. The first album, for this and other reasons such as its overall tone, can be described as an innocent-enough deeply personal projectile as opposed to social commentary.

What was going on in the personal life and inner landscape of the mind of Bob Dylan in 1961? Well, confirmed data points to an end-less series of couches and sleeping arrangements in Greenwich Village. Keeping late night hours, Bob would typically show up at afternoon or evening hootenannies and pass-the-hat open mikes at the likes of Café Wha? and Gerdes Folk City before penning melodies of his own until the wee hours. It was here that he quickly met countless personal influences that would go on to be influenced by him and where, in a matter of months, he went from stranger to somebody who had what everybody else wanted.

Call him rip off artist, arrogant nobody hick, or whatever you like, but in 1961 Bob was blending his own artistic amalgam with a pinch of late night radio from his Hibbing, Minnesota childhood here and a sprinkle of Greenwich Village influences like John Lee Hooker and Dave Van Ronk there. And wallah, he began to find all those voices, which became THE voice. This mystifying mojo, incomprehensible to be sure, coalesced merely a few months prior to recording that first album for one of the biggest record companies on the planet.

His ambition, although not overt at the time, was privately unquestion-able. "I'm gonna be big, really, big," he was repeatedly heard saying whenever the subject was broached with his beloved Suze, who would go on to grace the iconic cover of *Freewheelin'*. His ego was somehow a combination of overinflated and unnoticeable. The mindboggling achievement (or character defect, or both, depending on which light is shined on the matter) of the teenage Robert Zimmerman is that between his 16th and 21st birthdays he thoroughly reinvented himself by lying to himself and others to the point that the lines between fantasy and reality were non-existent. The psychic recklessness this displayed, in retrospect, seems unimaginably horrifying. It did, however, lay the groundwork for endless wellsprings of creativity in the decades to come.

Certainly in 1961 Bob was nothing short of a walking jukebox and musical sponge, soaking off of virtually every act he encountered at the time, which is saying a lot given the countless musicians he personally met and witnessed perform as he rapidly developed a reputation towering above his peers. His musical acuity ought never be minimized given the sheer quantity of styles he ripped off unabashedly on his march toward his unmistakable vibe that was soon to give birth to his own personal musical genre, coined folk rock but immediately copied by so many others that Bob never did ever admit to what he had done. It is nothing short of staggeringly implausible how any human being could have produced the quality of music in as many different styles that Bob mastered his first year in New York.

His debut album begins with the rollicking **You're No Good** (Jesse Fuller), which gives an inkling of the excellent guitar strumming, vocals, and especially harmonica licks that continue throughout the record. **Talkin' New York** contains compellingly wordy lyrics written by a hillbilly from Hibbing, Minnesota commenting on his first trip to Manhattan, sort of in the vein of the John Voigt character in *Midnight Cowboy*. **Talkin' New York** constituted Bob's promising first original song ever on record, but more importantly it foreshadowed his rising talent as a performer of his original material, a looming nuance that would eventually forever transform the entire music industry as we once knew it.

The traditional **In My Time of Dying** follows, and here Bob delivers his first old bluesman aching vocal that must have startled all listeners, particularly those that knew that Bob was merely twenty years old. **Man of Constant Sorrow** is Bob's take on a traditional ballad featuring a rambling character, like Woody Guthrie, seemingly aimless on his search for nothing and to nowhere. In **Fixin' To Die** (Bukka White) Bob's returns to the theme of death for the third (count 'em) time in a row, again sounding like an aging black Mississippian groaning out the pain of the privilege of getting old, since so many are not afforded the opportunity.

Peggy-O (again traditional) suddenly and singlehandedly lightens the mood, chronicling the beauty of a fair yellow-haired Irish maiden, a village known as Fennario, and the fate of a few restless characters known as the lieutenant and our captain, all the while playfully ripping out blistering harmonica solos in what seems to be a children's nursery rhyme. **Highway 51** (Curtis Jones) solidifies the first album's salute to American roots by mythologizing one of the nation's most-storied north-south two lane thoroughfares.

Gospel Plow is a traditional tune arranged in Bob's now familiar urgent elder screech and begins side two. **Baby Let Me Follow You Down** is done in the arrangement of Eric Von Schmidt, who Bob kindly credits in the opening talking verse and then goes on to grab the listener by the throat with killer harmonica licks. Then comes **House of the Rising Sun**, which he recorded prior to asking Dave Van Ronk for permission, which oddly led to Dave's version becoming long-forgotten and many believing that Dylan wrote this traditional ballad about the dangers of living the hard life in New Orleans, at least until mid-60s rock and roll fans incorrectly assumed the tune was penned by the Animals. **Freight Train Blues** (John Lair) features Bob both yodeling in stellar fashion and impressing one and all with his harmonica again.

Then, **Song To Woody,** a melodic mimic of Guthrie's **1913 Massacre**, delivers another little clue that some fabulous song-writing ability laid latent in the elder adolescent habitual liar, Bob Zimmerman, who had folks believing he actually grew up in Gallop, New Mexico and joined the circus as a teenager. Closing out the first album is Blind Lemon Jefferson's **See That My Grave Is Kept Clean,** a startling request that one's grave site is given its proper respect once the dirt is shoveled, the church bells have tolled, the heart stops beating and the hands have turned cold. Whew, what a chilling termination to a career-launching release. Alrighty then.

Given the mere two days Bob spent recording his first album, it makes sense that only four known outtakes exist. Three, **House Carpenter**, **He Was A Friend Of Mine**, and **Man On The Street** appeared 30 years later on the first volume of the official bootleg series. In addition, a Woody Guthrie tune, **Ramblin' Blues**, was recorded but remains unreleased. Though these are all covers, due to Bob's still emerging confidence as a songwriter, John Hammond, Sr. fully sensed that the quantity and qual-ity of Bob's songwriting in 1961 held infinite promise, despite some in the press and echelons of Columbia who referred to Dylan as "Hammond's folly" and a commercial bust. Granted, 2,500 or so initial LP sales earned Columbia and Bob personally in the neighborhood of chump change.

Nevertheless, between the recording and release of *Bob Dylan*, Hammond hooked his folly up with Lou Levy at music publisher Leeds Music, and Bob inked his first publishing contract during a lunch date at Jack Dempsey's restaurant at 50th and Broadway, a fabled music industry hangout. Though he didn't have many original compositions to show for himself other than the two which appeared on his first album, this was not the case for long, and he was far more excited about having a publish-ing deal than a recording contract, which is saying a lot. Thus began in earnest Bob's obsession with taking old melodies, tweaking them a hair, adding his brilliant poetry, and wallah – we were about to witness a rise to the pinnacle of the music industry by the most unlikely of characters.

Humanity has Columbia's wise John Hammond, Sr., who at the time was 51 years old and had three illustrious decades in the music busi-ness on his resume, to thank for patiently nurturing Dylan and not rushing out album number two. Things very easily could have gone in a completely different direction. Thankfully, Dylan's career did not commence in the quick-cash music industry of the 21st century and he was afforded the opportunity to nurture his craft as his first album's sales sputtered, or else, well, let's not go there.

#2

The Freewheelin' Bob Dylan

After more than 14 months of relentless songwriting and recording, mostly once again in studio A at Columbia, *The Freewheelin' Bob Dylan* was sprung on an unsuspecting public on May 27, 1963. Given that a whole book could and ought to be written about this album on its own merit, suffice it to say that it was gracefully executed, and its seismic impact was arguably later equaled on numerous Dylan studio albums, but it was never topped.

Outside the recording studio, between Bob's first and second albums, as a matter of course, much else was occurring, developing, and being distilled. The velocity of his personal existence and career quickened from 60 to 90 miles per hour, and his songwriting not only raised the roof, but rocketed through it. In May of 1962 he contractually agreed to the shark, hustler, and cold-blooded Albert Grossman becoming his manager. Consequently, in July 1962 Bob left Leeds and signed over his publishing business to M. Witmark and Sons. Meanwhile, furthermore, and of lasting importance, he legally turned his back on the name Robert Allen Zimmerman.

In December 1962, after concluding his last recording session with the late great John Hammond, Sr., Bob went off to London and performed at a handful of clubs, including the Troubador, which Pete Seeger had suggested as a place to plug into the London folk scene and where he met an enormous influence on his early 60s songwriting, Martin Carthy. He also performed a musical role in a British television play called *Mad House On Castle Street*. He then proceeded to rendezvous with Odetta in Rome, where he managed to write **Girl From The North Country** and **Boots Of Spanish Leather**, both highly inspired by Carthy's version of **Scarborough Fair**. While in Europe he also spent quite a bit of time hanging out with American folk artists Dick Farina and Eric Von Schmidt, who both admired Bob's incredible new songwriting such as **Don't Think Twice, It's Alright** and provided him feverish inspiration with the stuff they were doing at the time.

In addition, Dylan maintained a rather hectic live touring pace, highlighted by a radio performance on Cynthia Gooding's folk music show in New York in February 1962, a July 2, 1962 gig at the Finjian Club in Montreal, and an October 1962 appearance at the Gaslight in New York. His first solo concert at a major venue, New York's Town Hall, on April 12, 1963, was concluded with a reading of his *Last Thoughts On Woody Guthrie*, which eventually got released on *Bootleg Series Volume 1* in 1991. On April 25, 1963 he performed at the Bear Club in Chicago, where he first met and jammed with blues guitar god Michael Bloomfield, an experience Dylan will vividly recall until the day he dies. He also made illustrious, heralded appearances at a May 10, 1963 folk festival at Brandeis University and at Carnegie Hall on October 26, 1963.

The solo acoustic Gaslight, Brandeis, and Carnegie shows were commercially released more than 40 years later as part of Columbia's official bootleg series, along with his Halloween 1964 Philharmonic Hall show and the Witmark demos covering 1962 to 1964. Because these dizzying releases came out so many years later in a non-chronological fashion, it becomes difficult, if not impossible, without finicky analysis, to accurately trace the intense development of Dylan's early 60s characteristics as a songwriter, recording artist, performing artist, and otherwise two-legged human being.

More than a full year before *Freewheelin'*, none other than Pete Seeger was already acknowledging in Billboard magazine that Dylan was the most prolific songwriter around. Pete had heard Dylan's stunningly

lovely and inexplicably insightful March 1962 composition **Blowin'
In The Wind**, which was debuted at Gerdes Folk City in Greenwich
Village with an abbreviated two-verse version in April 1962, and he
immediately realized that Bob Dylan was no ordinary songwriter.
Commercially it would eventually be covered by upwards of 50 known
artists in English alone, but more importantly would become, along
with **We Shall Overcome**, a primary anthem of the U.S. civil rights
movement.

Melodically the song has its origins in a Negro spiritual, **No More
Auction Block**, which Dylan later covered, and lyrically it may have
sprung from Woody Guthrie's *Bound For Glory*, which describes Woody's
political affections as being like newspapers blowing in the wind in
New York City alleys. **Blowin' In The Wind** opens *Freewheelin'* with
the sound of guitar strumming and raspy vocals belting out a message
of peace and justice to an unjust American society still struggling with
racial harmony 100 years after *The Emancipation Proclamation*. Suffice
it to say that Dylan's permanent legacy in music, American, and world
history was implausibly, but indisputably and indubitably secure as of
song one on album two.

The romantic **Girl From The North Country,** portraying either Echo
Helstrom, a girl (literally) from the other side of the tracks in Hibbing,
Bonnie Beecher, a Minnesota co-ed still in Bob's inner circle, or Suze
Rotolo, Bob's main but not only squeeze at the time the song was written. Perhaps it was some combination thereof, as it was composed while
Bob was in Rome (with Odetta) and probably longing for the compan-
ionship of all three of these muses. In any case, for the first but certainly not the last time, Bob was displaying an uncanny ear for slightly
adjusting what he heard others (Martin Carthy) doing and effortlessly
transforming that into an original masterpiece. With *Freewheelin's*
third song, **Masters of War,** aimed at the evil industrial military complex President Eisenhower warned about in his exit speech, the 1960s
were conceived. Eleven months later, of course, when the Beatles appeared on Ed Sullivan, they were born.

Blowin' In The Wind would go on to make Dylan millions by being covered by artists as diverse as Stevie Wonder and Peter, Paul, and Mary. Pops Staples was quoted as saying he could not believe a white man had the sensitivities to come up with a song that told the story of a black man. It had an intuitive tone as if it had come from another world, had written itself, or was channeled through an immortal source. **Girl From The North Country** likewise seemed the perfect arrangement of melody and lyrics and has gone on to influence untold numbers of songwriters for generations. The acerbic snarling twang, vengeance, and plainspoken storytelling in **Masters of War** made it an immediate anthem for peace activists and anti-war protesters alike. Bob's follow up to his first album, in just its first three songs, had already begun to rock the foundations of the music industry.

Not bad for a college dropout, and his two-year high school English teacher in room 204 at Hibbing High, B.J. Rolfzen, must have been one proud peacock. From 1957-59 the rather shy yet uninhibited Robert Zimmerman had sat in the front row three seats from the door, right under his Navy veteran and bookworm literature instructor, apparently soaking up every word and more, however discreetly. In 1963, before his not-to-be college graduation would have presumably taken place, Zimmerman had written, recorded, and released a literary and musical LP masterpiece judging from the first three songs alone. Plus, he was just getting warmed up!

Inconceivably, counter-intuitively, and most improbably, **A Hard Rain's A-Gonna Fall** was composed about a month or two prior to the Cuban missile crisis of October 1962, notwithstanding *Freewheelin'* liner notes stating that it was written in response to heightened fears of nuclear warfare. In any case, whether world events were influencing Bob's lyrics or the public's perception of phenomena such as the culmination of racial relations in America, exactly 100 years after the Civil War, was being sculpted by what Bob was driving at, there is no question that his second album catapulted him above his folk contemporaries. If one thought **Blowin' In The Wind** was a 20th century poetic prophecy, **A Hard Rain's A-Gonna Fall** left no question that this lad, chap, Jewish cowboy, and/or beatnik (take your pick), clearly no chump, blockhead, dolt, or knucklehead, had something to say to both musicians and human beings that plainly could not be ignored.

This is certain in terms of both melodies and lyrics. Video footage of Dylan's performances at the Newport Folk Festival in the summer of 1963, immediately on the heels of *Freewheelin'* hitting record stores, indicate that folk luminaries such as Pete Seeger, Roscoe Holcomb (a favorite of Eric Clapton), and Doc Watson were gladly stepping aside to avoid the tidal wave of public devotion to Bob as the intellectual leader of the political left, a role he would eventually come to ardently resist but find unavoidable. Again, Seeger, as early as 1963, conceded that nobody had ever achieved what Dylan had done musically and lyrically on *Freewheelin'*. Pete had passed Woody's hat to Bob.

Rounding out the 5 folk anthems written right before, around, or after Bob was eligible to vote, destined to become elevator music for the ages, **Don't Think Twice It's Alright** featured Bob's first studio attempt at a country crooning vocal quality, for lack of a better word, that oddly would not occur again until *Nashville Skyline* a full six years later. On **Don't Think Twice** we also are treated to Dylan's adept talent for a rather complex finger-picking style credited to Merle Travis.

However, if you will kindly permit me, the real legacy of *Freewheelin'* persevering to this day was, is, and forever shall be the role it played in the emergence of thoughtful, thought-provoking poetry as a weapon in the arsenal of songwriters. I mean, Elvis may have freed our bodies, but Bob freed up our minds. The beat poets, led by Alan Ginsburg and Jack Kerouac, were now held in higher esteem as Dylan legitimized their auspicious literary genre through melody and verse. With or without LSD, uppers, downers, and in-between baby boomers stifled by middle class sensibilities tuned in, turned on, took in, turned against, took part, took off, tripped out, and/ or turned to Bob Dylan for his adroit, amusing, articulate, absurd, acidic, astonishing ability to write and record songs for the ages, especially the 1960s. Dylan's coronation as anti-establishment king was the inadvertent collective repercussion of forces, once begun, Bob could never have predicted, did not seek, and unquestionably could not control or put a halt to, even though he and he alone caused them, if that makes any sense.

Not to flabbergast you or anything, but in the 15 months Dylan spent recording songs leading into *Freewheelin'*, Columbia amassed enough material for three (or more) albums of superlative quality. Half or more of this material falls in a category that can be described as beyond unreleased. More like unknown. Of the 16, **yes 16**, known outtakes from *Freewheelin'*, six were covers and ten Bob wrote. It is likely that these 16 rejects constitute a drop in the bucket of all Dylan's musical explorations going on in Columbia's studio A from November 1961 to March of 1963.

Freewheelin' outtake covers included Arthur Crudup's hit that launched Elvis, **That's Alright Mama**, Robert Johnson's **Milk Cow Calf's Blues**, Big Joe Williams' **Baby Please Don't Go**, Hank Williams' **I Heard That Lonesome Whistle Blow**, and the traditionals **Wichita** and **Going To New Orleans**.

A parade of stellar originals had to be discarded simply due to lack of audio space. In the case of **Mixed Up Confusion**, it actually was briefly released as a single just prior to the *Freewheelin'* release. Bob and an electric quartet labored long and hard at nailing a 1956 Johnny Cash choo-choo train-driven country rock sound that was on a different planet from the sound of *Freewheelin'*. Until **Mixed Up Confusion** appeared on *Biograph* in the mid-80s, who knew Dylan was up to stuff like this in December of 1962?

The remaining documented list of original *Freewheelin'* rejects, undoubtedly incomplete, rendered the following pearls mere throwaways in the annals of American music: **Baby, I'm In The Mood For You**, **Talkin' Bear Mountain Picnic Massacre Blues** (a lyrical farce put to the melody of Woody Guthrie's **Talkin' Dust Bowl Blues**), **Talking Hava Negiliah Blues**, **Rocks and Gravel**, **Sally Gal**, **Talking John Birch Paranoid Blues**, **Rambling Gambling Willie**, **The Death of Emmit Till**, and **Let Me Die In My Footsteps**. Correct me if I'm mistaken, but that mouthful for all practical purposes constitutes one of the best folk music albums in American history. Nevertheless, almost thirty years would pass as diehard Dylan bootlegging bandits scurried to steal away on the black market before some of this stuff saw the legal light of day.

That occurred only when the official bootleg series started coming out, when eventually all surfaced except **The Death of Emmit Till**, a little-known civil rights narrative Bob put to chord sequencing resembling **House Of The Rising Sun** mostly known only to bootlegging diehard Dylan network fanatics just since Bob played it in early 1962 when he sat down with Cynthia Gooding on her New York radio show. On this occasion Cynthia commenced to exhibit Webster's dictionary definition of sucking up to a celebrity, while Bob played her like a fiddle by making up preposterous tales about his past as the gullible Cynthia perfectly played the "Ahwww, shucks" role, obviously much to Bob's delight. As outstanding as Bob's music sounded that night, let's just say his playful, uncanny, convincing knack for publicly combining fiction with the truth was not limited to the musical arena. Check out this Cynthia/Bob bootleg for the essence of Bob Dylan's Charlie Chaplin shtick. Apparently, it worked on Cynthia well enough (I don't blame her!) that she subsequently and repeatedly had Bob perform at gatherings in her New York apartment, and somewhere on God's green earth there exist recordings to prove this. As for **The Death** (or sometimes **Ballad**) **of Emmit Till**, Bob had the musical acumen to realize that the words were a bit mawkish and that he had thinly disguised this particular precocious attempt to carry on the folk music protest song tradition. Thus, he wisely scrapped it, knowing, and proving, he could do better on *The Freewheelin' Bob Dylan*.

Other *Freewheelin'* era recordings that made the cut were Bob's original compositions of **Down The Highway,** containing a glimpse into Bob's irrefutable, deep, and artistically inspiring sadness over Suze having moved to Italy for 6 months, **Bob Dylan's Blues**, which publicly introduced Bob's private comical propensity echoing the ghost of Charlie Chaplin, **Bob Dylan's Dream**, a sincere, tender melodic salute to Martin Carthy's sentimental **Lord Franklin**, the bereavement of friendships gone by, and the fantasy/delusion of suppressing the pain of it all, **Oxford Town**, a backhandedly lovely account of the grizzly ordeal of James Meredith in the height of Jim Crow Mississippi, **Talking World War III Blues**, a sarcastic sneer at Cold War paranoia in contrast to the absence of cynicism in **A Hard Rain's A-Gonna Fall**, **Corrina, Corrina**, a reworked traditional tale which showcased a sweet backing quintet of studio musicians Bob was hesitant to employ, clinging to poverty as his excuse, **Honey, Just Allow Me One More Chance**, a light-hearted cover inclusion trumpeting the futile buoyant expectancy of the love search, and last but not least, **I Shall Be Free**, the fourth and final *Freewheelin'* preposterous, witty ditty detailing a clever chain of amusing events making fun of everything and everybody from capitalism to racism to romance to politics to Hollywood to the entire album the listener has just lent an ear.

Whew, if that 400-something-word sentence just exhausted me, in 1962 and early 1963 what do you think Dylan felt like doing amphetamines and red wine till all hours, writing, rehearsing, and recording original songs 24/7, constantly filling notebook and scraps of paper with poetic lyrics, and all the while still living in pretty much a state of poverty? And keeping this up for the next four years? Where in the heck did he come up with all those words? And, how did he then and does he still now keep inventing and reinventing those wonderful melodies that remain timeless and pass the test of time to this day? Whatever Dylan was channeling in those early years in studio A at Columbia, and managed to maintain especially for the duration of 1961 to 1966, every songwriter yearns to collide with, even if for only an instant. Name an American songwriter not influenced by Dylan in the past 50 years, and my house, car, and life savings are yours.

A couple weeks before the scheduled release of *Freewheelin'*, Bob was to have appeared on *The Ed Sullivan Show*. However, to his credit Bob chose to cancel the gig at the last minute due to CBS television's fear that the song Dylan intended to play on live television, the hysterical satire **Talkin' John Birch Paranoid Blues**, might unleash a law suit by the John Birch Society, which might not take too kindly to being sarcastically ridiculed for its over-the-top fear of commies. Sullivan's people had likely already gotten wind of the fact that Columbia records had nixed this particular song from *Freewheelin'* over similar concerns.

Even prior to the Sullivan debacle, with Tom Wilson as his new studio recording producer instead of John Hammond, Dylan had made eleventh-hour recordings of **Girl From The North Country, Masters of War, Bob Dylan's Dream**, and **Talkin' World War III Blues** to replace the legally risky **Talkin' John Birch Paranoid Blues**, the traditional **Rocks and Gravel**, and originals **Ramblin' Gamblin' Willie** (just love that one, man) and **Let Me Die In My Footsteps**. You gotta hand it to Bob for having some heavyweight substitutions on hand in a pinch there. One is wont to reckon that Bob's obsession with death on his first album led to the probably prudent decision to drop **Let Me Die In My Footsteps** from *Freewheelin'* lest his articulation of cold war anxieties cross the line into over-the-top, maudlin morbidity.

The Freewheelin' Bob Dylan had begun to change the parameters of popular music by emphasizing poetry and clever literary devices as the intellectual focuses of popular music. Upon its release Dylan immediately started to tower over his contemporary competition, and this obvious gospel truth nobody could deny. His sheer songwriting and performing virtuosity had started to commit involuntary manslaughter on Tin Pan Alley. A Hibbing hillbilly hick had accomplished the highly improbable, unheard of, and hitherto unfathomable by self-composing and recording five 1960s folk anthems, as I cherry pick from the dozens of *Freewheelin'* era gems, **Blowing In The Wind, Girl From The North Country, Masters of War, Don't Think Twice It's All Right**, and **A Hard Rain's A Gonna Fall**, prior to his 22nd birthday.

Take that, Gershwin. Bravo, Bob.

3

The Times They Are A Changin'

Upon release in January 1964, Bob's third solo acoustic record, *The Times They Are A Changin'*, took the acerbic **Masters of War** and stretched it into a concept album extolling the virtues of the civil rights movement, social change, and the ascension of folk music. His fame from the *Freewheelin'* record had detonated to the tune of a $5,000-a-month paycheck (in 1963 dollars!) with 100,000 copies sold and another 100,000 on backorder. An onslaught of pressure from Columbia, his fans, his friends, his parents, his girlfriend, and his own ambition drove Bob to hide within a self-imposed mind guard made up of an inner circle the likes of Victor Mamudes, Allan Ginsburg, Suze Rotolo, then-mistress Joan Baez, and Dave Van Ronk and his wife, Terri Thal. I've always reckoned that on the nitty-gritty level, the most momentous modification in Bob's lifestyle resulting from his early commercial good fortune was the end of his Manhattan couch surfing.

The album had already long since sowed a few seeds at the '63 Newport Folk Festival, where Bob's presence catapulted him to the throne of folk royalty, a crowning that came as a double-edged sword. Feeling trapped by the political left, which demanded he be their mouthpiece, underneath his slightly spasmodic irrepressible comical body language, anger oozed out of each and every pore of Bob's artist within. In addition, his annoyance at being found out to be the product of a middle class Minnesotan upbringing, causing the press (none other than Newsweek magazine) to unjustly accuse Bob of plagiarizing the lyrics to **Blowin' In The Wind**, induced Bob's legendary reputation, proclivity, and go-to propensity to mask himself by going underground. The spring '63 *Freewheelin'* release and the summer '63 Newport so-called success evidently slapped Bob into a panic over the prison of the traps of stardom, gradually giving birth to the recluse we have come to know and love/hate.

To begin with, no fewer than 15 exceptional *The Times They Are A-Changin'* outtakes must be noted, lest we fail to recognize the 1963 Bob Dylan songwriting assembly line. These include, but by no means are limited to the following worthy gems: **Seven Curses, New Orleans Rag, Farewell, Eternal Circle, Walls of Red Wing, Paths of Victory, Hero Blues, Moonshiner Blues, Only A Hobo, Ain't Gonna Grieve, John Brown, Lay Down Your Weary Tune, Percy's Song,** and **Who Killed Davey Moore**. For the record, these super-lative jewels comprise what otherwise would constitute 1.5 albums worth of more-than-commercially viable material. Such random data legitimizes our topic, Bob Dylan, due to his literary as well as musical exploits, as a peerless, miraculous, freakish, peculiar prodigy in the hallowed halls of Americana. I mean, who's counting, but on albums 2 and 3 we are already talking about no fewer than 31 known out-takes comprising roughly 2.5 albums worth of high quality, brilliant material destined for the history channel of the obscure and pertineer long forgotten.

Having said that, the melodies making the cut contain not a single dud. Undamming the locks, as it were, **The Times They Are A Changin'** was a deliberate, successful attempt to create an anthem for social change, despite that fact that it turned Dylan into a reluctant poster boy and staunch rebel dedicated to the cause of preserving his own artistic liberty. This song perhaps more than any other is to blame for Bob being placed on a pedestal that he would come to forever reject and regret. It was musically profoundly molded by Irish and Scottish bal-lads Bob was exposed to on his first trip to the U.K. in 1962. Lyrically, it brilliantly spoke to Christians of all ilks when Mark 10:31 was ref-erenced in the first-shall-be-last-and-the last-first line. When all was said and done, on the personal level, **The Times They Are A Changin'** unbeknowingly (utilitarian non-word), unintentionally, and unexpectedly shot Bob Dylan in the foot.

Most auspicious of all, however, is that it was composed prior to the assassination of President John Kennedy on November 22, 1963. Countless fans and even historians have understandably assumed the opposite. How counterintuitive of Dylan to write songs intuitively foretelling the course of events before the fact. In retrospect, it is now 20/20 hindsight apparent that Bob Dylan, not society itself, was changing at the speed of light, so he was capable of spotting that which he himself got. It seems that neither he nor the Beatles could go wrong in the 60s. Double sixes turned up at just about every roll of the dice. Social change seemed to be a half step behind transformations of both Dylan and the Fab Four.

The album title and Bob's eerie Woody Guthrie lookalike appearance on the album cover gave the impression of a second-class billboard or poster, fueling the baby boom rejection of middle class materialism, on one hand, and natural, understandable suspicions that Bob was a fraud, on the other. As for the latter accusation, on some level, there is without question no doubt. *The Times They Are A-Changin'* album cover is an early case in point.

Even Abraham Zimmerman himself was dumbfounded and found it impossible to wrap his head around people's willingness to swallow hook, line, and sinker the fictitious Bohemian character his son had promulgated upon the masses. Hence, my constant references to Bob's wizardry. I mean, no Hollywood actor I know of has ever jumped from the big screen to real life the way Dylan the illusionist has and hoodwinked more over a longer period of time. Speaking for myself, this hoodwink-ee has enjoyed (almost) every minute of the mirage and regrets not a penny of the roughly $10,000 I have contributed over the years to Dylan's royal, persuasive, relentless, rollicking flight-from-reality ruse. When I come across Bob's dad, Abe, someday in that big house in the sky, he probably still won't be capable of seeing it from my point of view.

Yes, I said each and every word of that.

In any case, sticking to the point, the opening track, **The Times They Are A-Changin'**, nearly singlehandedly epitomizes the label of Bob Dylan as the trumpet of youth yearning to unshackle themselves from parental bondage. Simultaneous with the January 13, 1964 release of *The Times They Are A-Changin'*, the 1960s were just about to explode, as the February 9, 1964 Beatles appearance on the Ed Sullivan Show was just about to change, well, everything. Little did Dylan know that George Harrison, in particular, was paying close attention to *Freewheelin'*, and Bob was only months away from getting bored with the folk music scene, from which he would soon irreversibly move on.

As the album unfolds, its lack of humor and musical diversity, in contrast to *Freewheelin'*, somehow flows magnificently from one stark, sparsely arranged dirge to another. **Ballad of Hollis Brown**, a melodic descendant of the traditional murder ballad **Pretty Polly** and a chord sequence going back hundreds of years to both the British Isles and Appalachia, is frankly a shocking grim rural Gothic fable about a father executing his own starving family backed by a lilting, hypnotically cadenced acoustic double drop D sharp minor chord echoing after each line of each verse. More than 50 years later this one still sends chills down yer spine, man. **With God On Our Side** utilizes a politically and historically savvy voice merged with a tone of generational ingenuousness while borrowing a melody from the Irish folk ballad, **The Patriot Game**. Here we find Bob pretty much re-writing his own naïve version of American history from the point of view of a pacifist, or idiot, in the minds of those who never bother to read between the lines of history books.

The soft and understated studio rendition of **One Too Many Mornings**, more remembered for its spring '66 live cacophony rocked out interpretation, is narrated by a lover grown too independent to consider a reunion and too smitten by love to harbor regrets. Closing side one, Bob's first foray into writing from the female perspective, **North Country Blues,** sternly depicts the outsourcing of iron ore mining operations in a place resembling the Mesabi Iron Range community (Hibbing) where Bob lived from age 7 to 18, again anchored in a soothing, trance-inducing minor chord, this time B sharp minor.

Side Two commences with the psychologically and socially shrewd **Only A Pawn In Their Game**, first revealed in public at a summer 1963 voter registration drive in Greenwood, Mississippi. Here the murder of Medgar Evers ironically and cleverly exposes poor southern whites as victims of the cunning, baffling, and powerful nature of the insidious institution of racism. **Boots Of Spanish Leather**, yet another spinoff of Martin Carthy's take on **Scarborough Fair**, was penned in Italy as Bob searched in vain for Suze Rotolo, who, unbeknownst to him, had returned to Long Island after completing a stint studying abroad.

In a fit of indignation **When The Ship Comes In**, yet another early Dylan enchanting merging of music and words, wrote itself over the course of a sleepless night in a hotel room after an impertinent hotel clerk had denied Bob occupancy only to be persuaded by his companion, Joan Baez, that the disheveled Dylan was in fact an upstanding citizen and reputable artist. Baez, to this day, cannot get over how effortlessly and efficiently Bob came up with this musical monument to hope eternal. A February 3, 1963 newspaper article inspired **The Lonesome Death of Hattie Carroll**, a stunning assault on the hypocritical criminal justice system that slapped the hand of a second degree murderer of an immigrant Baltimore hotel barmaid. Just another death knell for Dylan's artistic liberty in that the political left immediately cast him in bronze as their anti-establishment troubadour and social injustice whistle blower. Bob, obviously, would have none of this.

Concluding the record is **Restless Farewell**, epitomizing the expression of hateful wrath Bob harbored for those who would just as soon box him into a safe, comfortable womb to withhold from him his passionately-held right to creative license. Carefully recorded over several hours, Dylan is conceivably responding to unmerited **Blowin' In The Wind** plagiarism charges in the final verse, "The dirt of gossip blows into my face and the dust of rumor covers me – so I'll make my stand

and remain as I am, and bid farewell, and not give a damn." You tell 'em, Bob.

The Times They Are A Changin' may have lacked the comical absurdity woven into the penetrating intellectual intuition on *Freewheelin'*, yet it left Bob Dylan peerless as both a budding and fully-realized genius in the world of popular American music. Having virtually invented a musical genre he could call his own, his influence on musicians was becoming unbounded as it even spread to global proportions. His effect on society, for lack of a better term, was evidenced on every song on *The Times They Are A-Changin'* except the romantic paragons, **One Too Many Mornings** and **Boots Of Spanish Leather**. 1963 concert performances in England began what would turn into greater popularity across the pond, a trend that has persisted to this day. At home in America Peter, Paul, and Mary's rendition of **Blowin' In The Wind** and Bob's performance of **When The Ship Comes In** and **Only A Pawn In Their Game** at the March on Washington August 28, 1963 were crowning events in his rise to poster boy of the civil rights movement, whether he liked it or not.

He really could not concern himself with such weighty burdens. He was more concerned with staying up all night on amphetamines, drinking Beaujolais, writing brilliant pieces of American music that will likely stand the test of eternity, and sticking to his own artistic vision. Dylan already had outgrown *The Times They Are A-Changin'* by the time, just one month after its release, the Beatles commenced waging the British invasion of America when they broke into **All My Loving** on The Ed Sullivan Show at 8 p.m. eastern standard time Feb. 9, 1964. The slow-moving cogs of the music record industry simply could keep up with neither The Beatles nor Bob Dylan.

The 1960s were busy being born.

Dylan at the August 28, 1963 March On Washington. Photo taken by Rowland Scherman on assignment from the U.S. Information Agency.

#4

Another Side of Bob Dylan

L ess socially conscious than the superior folkie rhetoric on *The Times They Are A Changin'*, *Another Side of Bob Dylan* constructed a bridge that would eventually lead to Bob's troika of electric rants on the ensuing three albums. Six of the eleven all-original compositions would bolster Dylan's financial independence for life by being covered by music artists crisscrossing genres from gospel to country to blues to folk to rock to rhythm and blues. His record deal with Columbia was beginning to pale compared to profits flowing from his Witmark music publishing contract.

Although the album is arranged solely of Bob performing alone on guitar, harmonica, and piano (on **Black Crow Blues** Bob's ability to pound the 88s being revealed publicly for the first time), *Another Side Of Bob Dylan* can actually be more aptly characterized as a rock album without electric guitars. This is directly be attributable to the February 1964 splash of the Beatles on American radio airwaves. **I Want To Hold Your Hand**, in particular, with its outrageous chords and refreshingly novel and outright stunning harmonies, impressed Bob enough that he immediately envisioned whatever the Beatles were up to was surely the direction music was traveling.

In addition, the roots of this, the fourth, and final pure folk Bob Dylan album can also be traced to his embrace of Arthur Rimbaud's 19th century French poetry and the muse of traveling to uncover his poetic writings. The moment the Beatles appeared on Ed Sullivan on

February 9, 1964, Bob was cruising across the United States in the back of a station wagon with three New York friends, searching for avenues to escape the folk song structures that he felt the Beatles had already rendered passe, archaic, and irrelevant.

This cross county pilgrimage across Americana, notably, included a stop in North Carolina to spend time with the aging Illinoisan Carl Sandburg, who annoyed the hell out of Bob when it became clear that Carl had never heard of him and wasn't interested in getting to know him. Nevertheless, while tripping around the U.S. Kerouac style, by talking to people, mostly in bars, and through self-introspection, which Rimbaud claimed was the manner to transcend the senses of human perception, Bob wrote the initial songs that signaled his invention of the folk rock genre, catapulting literary, poetic, and intellectual elements into the limelight of popular music.

At one point while driving across Colorado, the Beatles had 8 of the top ten songs on American radio! This planted the mustard seeds of folk rock, or what came to be referred to as folk rock, as Dylan could not get over what the Beatles were up to. George, Ringo, Paul, and John had changed the entire popular music equation, despite Jack Parr's now laughable editorial comment that they constituted the downfall of British civilization after their actual first appearance, albeit in a brief piece of news footage, on American television on his show in early January 1964. Incidentally, guys like Parr and Steve Allen were quickly becoming passé, relics of a bygone generation, although Allen ventured in vain to apparently somehow appear hip to beatniks when he landed a painfully shy, awkward, and uncomfortable Dylan as a guest performer on his television variety show in February 1964. Unlike the photogenic, always on Beatles, Bob has never been a primetime kind of guy.

The first consequences of Beatle influence on Dylan can be heard on *Another Side Of Bob Dylan* on **Chimes of Freedom** and **My Back Pages** and the outtake of **Mr. Tambourine Man**. Even though Bob's first recording of **Tambourine Man**, with Ramblin' Jack Elliot's harmonies on the chorus, remained an outtake that would not surface until the *Bootleg Volumes 1-3* release almost 30 years later, it somehow got into the hands of the Byrds, inspiring their 1965 hit, the opening 12-string Rickenbacker gee-tar licks of which clearly constituted the birth of what became to be known as California rock.

Chimes of Freedom, J.F.K., Jr.'s favorite Dylan song, and the particularly paradoxical **My Back Pages** will be two of the first citations to support a Nobel Prize for literature, if Dylan ever gets one. When Bob first performed **Chimes Of Freedom** on the west coast toward the end of his '64 search for Americana, it was not only hot off the press, but it swirled the audience into such as frenzy that afterwards Bob's vehicle, for one of the first but not last times in the mid 60s, was nearly crushed by waves of fans, male and female. Thus, it is now apparent that even before Dylan rented an electric guitar when he got back to New York, the tail end of his solo acoustic days had obviously struck a chord, and it was not only Bob's raw nerves that were jangling.

Following Bob's winter 1964 continental U.S. sojourn was a spring trip to Europe. Here, he performed a handful of concerts in England as a prelude to meeting the German model, Christa Paffgen, Nico, in Paris, who served Bob a meal in her flat and then accompanied him to Germany, Austria, and Greece. Although Nico was not yet a recording artist, Bob gifted her with **If You Gotta Go, Go Now**, which she eventually recorded in 1967, two years after Judy Collins recorded it in '65, the same year Dylan finally recorded his rendition that got dumped during the studio sessions for *Bringing It All Back Home*. Meanwhile, while still ostensibly spring vacationing in Europe Bob penned a few more songs for his upcoming album as well as the beginnings of the so-called novel the public could not wait to read, *Tarantula*, which would frustratingly not hit the presses for several years to come.

Back home, he immediately recorded the entirety of *Another Side of Bob Dylan* on June 9, 1964 in studio B at Columbia in a 14 hour marathon ending at 1:30 the following morning after wrapping up with a master take of **My Back Pages**. Now who does that?

A complete take of **Mama You Been On My Mind** was ultimately rejected, but this brilliant lyrical piece was made a hit by both Judy Collins and Joan Baez. As to why this jewel was not on Bob's "A" list, go figure. This could also be said about **Mr. Tambourine Man**, but at least Bob had the sense to include it on the forthcoming *Bringing It All Back Home*.

In Bob's personal life in early 1964 his on-again off-again romance with Joan Baez finally destroyed what was left of his affair with Suze Rotolo, who had had enough. **Ballad In Plain D** pathetically narrates the screaming battleground on which Suze's "parasite" sister Carla completed the demented triad which could no longer withstand the celebrated icon that Bob simply now was. The Rotolos were essentially communist debutants, and Bob refused to be boxed into the corner of any political straight jacket, whether it be the civil rights movement, communism, or anti-military establishmentarianism.

Nevertheless, Bob's human nature was clearly and deeply submerged in subterranean grief over losing what he had with Suze. She had been his muse for a time, and the footprints of her boots of Spanish leather were so imprinted on Bob's psyche that on **Ballad In Plain D** he revealed his inner shadow in a song he later would regret ever penning, let alone releasing. However comma, listening to this song every 5 or ten years over the past 44 years has been one of the prominent pleasures of my life, despite the fact that some place it on Dylan's top ten worst songs list.

It Ain't Me Babe, which charted as a single, and I **Don't Believe You** can also clearly be attributed to the end of the end with Suze. Both found their mass appeal in later live Dylan interpretations and/or covers by other artists. The former is a classic instance of how Dylan's songs can sometimes be so intelligible so as to fall in the wheelhouses of musicians that one would not normally mention in the same sentence. Yet, **It Ain't Me Babe**, for starters but not exclusively, has been recorded by the following diverse list of household names: Jan and Dean, the Byrds, the Turtles, Johnny Cash, Earl Scruggs, Nancy Sinatra, and Boy

George. The signature rendition of **I Don't Believe You**, of course, got transformed into a marvelous psychedelic mirage on the spring '66 tour with the Hawks.

Motorpsycho Nitemare and **I Shall Be Free – No. 10** are hysterical returns to the absurdist form so prevalent on *Freewheelin'* and satirical pokes at American right wing conservatism and anarchy. I can still recall regaling fellow campers literally around the campfire in 1985 in the north woods of Wisconsin with a spontaneous **Motorpsycho Nightmare**. By the punch line at the end of verse 1, they were already all in stitches, and of course, this went on deliriously for the 8 seemingly endless remaining ludicrous, humorous, and last but not least, ridiculous stanzas.

To Ramona, which would go on to shape shift into 89 musical variations in live performances, is a lovely, gripping romantic waltz illustrating Bob at his poetic best. **Spanish Harlem Incident**, virtually ignored in live concerts ever since, is one of those catchy Dylan treasures that sneaks under the radar and won't get out of your head. **All I Really Want To Do** resurrects Bob's best and only yodeling on record since **Highway 51** on his first album. **Black Crow Blues**, the most forgettable 3 minutes and 12 seconds on Dylan's first four albums, is nonetheless a fine 12 bar blues take on the 88s.

When *Another Side Of Bob Dylan* was released August 8, 1964, its whacked-out liner notes were and still are more than enough evidence to suggest Dylan had already begun to write what would evolve into *Tarantula*, his rambling poetic piece of prose he stubbornly claimed was a novel. He spent much of the rest of '64 touring around the U.S. and performing live, writing *Tarantula*, and putting some of the whacked out poetry he was coming up with to music, some of which would eventually find its way onto *Bringing It All Back Home*.

He knew full well what the Beatles were up to, as he met them on a few occasions and attended one of their concerts in New York in late August. They had just filmed *A Hard Day's Night*, which would directly lead to D.A. Pennebaker's filming of *Don't Look Back* on Bob's spring 1965 tour of England. A year to the day after the March on Washington, Bob was turning the Beatles on to marijuana at the Delmonico Hotel in Manhattan. It may well be said that the Beatles brought Dylan to the end of the line of his folk music train. Who the "f" can really say?

After Dylan's appearance at the Newport Folk Festival in July '64, he never did look back nostalgically on the musician he had been prior to being seduced vocally, harmoniously, rhythmically, lyrically, and melodiously by marvelous mop-tops monopolizing AM radio waves. The question of which direction he would be headed was another matter. Dylan was about to bring it all back home, but there simply was no direction home anymore on his folk music compass, whose needle was pointed nowhere his muse was inclined to travel.

Bob Dylan was about to, say it ain't so, go electric. Why, I've never been facetious before in my life. Not!

#5

Bringing It All Back Home

First and foremost, a contextual fork in the road was reached after Dylan finished recording *Another Side of Bob Dylan*. His era of solo acoustic albums had ended, and Bob immediately ventured into the unchartered waters of his electric earthquake albums, *Bringing It All Back Home, Highway 61 Revisited*, and *Blonde On Blonde*. Dylan was willing to try just about anything, like when in December 1964 producer Tom Wilson overdubbed an old Fats Domino piano track over a new take on **House Of The Rising Sun**. It didn't work in the sense that it was scrapped, but the point is that Dylan was prepared and willing to throw out all conventions, and Wilson is to be hailed for aptly assisting in this process.

In retrospect, if our friend Bob Dylan had merely recorded albums 5 through 7, which can, if I may be so bold, be referred to as electric earthquakes, his mark on the course of music history would have been eternally indelible. For, dwarfing the massive commercial profitability of *Bringing It All Back Home, Highway 61 Revisited*, and *Blonde On Blonde* were then and still now are their pervasive influence on musicians, musicianship, music arrangement, music hybridization, songwriting, the relationship between the media and the music industry, the boom in the music recording industry in Nashville in particular, their insidious impact on youth/elder generational relations, and 1960s-to-the-present avant-garde artistic sensibilities spanning fashion design, film making, and intellectual and beat literary conventions.

Whew, dude, that's a whole lotta stuff.

Bob Dylan went electric in the studio with the release of *Bringing It All Back Home* in March 1965, four months *before* he shocked the audience at the Newport Folk Festival by refusing to cow tow to its desire that Bob play exclusively solo acoustic. Therefore, technically nobody except casual listeners had any right to be shocked by what happened at Newport. However, in actuality, booing fans at Newport and/or anywhere else in 1965-66 can be cut some slack for sure. Who on God's green earth could have been expected to keep up with Dylan's mid-60s speed-of-light revisions, ruthless reformations, ridiculous rearrangements, roaring rock, rolling racket, radical reconstructions, reconfigurations, renovations, reconstructions, reckless renditions, remodeling, revolutionary reasoning, remorseless reorganizations, and rampant reprogramming?

Decades of hyperbolic storytelling has gone down regarding what went down at Newport in '65. Let's face it, the larger-than-life myth of the Newport audience's presumed reaction of horror when Dylan supposedly blindsided them with an electric blues version of **Maggie's Farm** makes for fantastic, dramatic, and incredible satire. On the other hand, the very few, certainly the minority, who booed, regardless of their now-un-certifiable motives and actual reasons for doing so, must have only listened to the acoustic side two of *Bringing It All Back Home* and stuck their proverbial heads in the sand while listening the subtly electric side one. Either that, or else in the previous month or so they hadn't gotten around to stopping into their local record store to buy it yet.

Subterranean Homesick Blues, the first stab at hip hop forty years before its time, opens what rightly ought to be termed the trilogy of albums that changed American music forever. *Bringing It All Back Home*, right from the get go with **Subterranean Homesick Blues**, saw Dylan's first foray into increasingly surreal lyrics capturing the intellectually cunning as well as the absurd. Dylan once stated that the inspiration for the title of **Subterranean Homesick Blues** came from Kerouac's novel *The Subterranean* and that its music was stimulated by a hunch that fused 1940s jazz scat singing with Chuck Berry's **Too Much Monkey Business**. It was his first single to break into the top

40 hit parade, and John Lennon was overheard saying that he did not feel capable of writing a better song. Extraordinarily telling.

"Don't look back!", he croons on **She Belongs To Me,** with its lilting electric gee-tar (accent on the first syllable, undoubtedly) refrain, inspiring countless baby boomers to shed the drudgery of their upbringings and take arms in Bohemian virtues in what was quickly becoming the generation war(s) of the 1960s. If **Subterranean Homesick Blues** heralded intellectually cunning absurdity, **She Belongs To Me** ushered in a new-fangled fad of avant-garde romanticism on steroids.

Maggie's Farm, an incredible one take wonder, extols the refusal to be treated like a sub-human in the musical or any other industry, maintaining the theme of standing for or against something, anything, while simultaneously initiating a trifecta of folk, country, and rock and roll. **Love Minus Zero/No Limit**, romantic poetry at its best, features a Bruce Langhorne electric guitar line in Bob's studio entourage and a male protagonist smitten with defenseless infatuation. The zen-like, calming effect of Dylan's soon-to-be wife, Sara Lounds, inspired what is one of Bob's best love ballads ever, quite the mouthful, indeed. Meanwhile, he manages to sneak in some cool, universal philosophy by chanting to Bobby Gregg's restrained backbeat, "There's no success like failure, and failure's no success at all."

Outlaw Blues and **On The Road Again** both indicate Bob's dip into the John Hammond, Sr. intrigue with the Chicago blues sound. **Outlaw Blues**, an easy-to-miss conceptual precursor to the whole album *John Wesley Harding*, reveals Dylan's never-to-be-overlooked self identification as an outlaw who looks like Robert Ford but feels like Jesse James (Ford was the fellow-outlaw who killed James in 1882).

Bob Dylan's 115th Dream serves up a catchy rhythm, indeed a fine melodic line away from that of **Motorpsycho Nightmare** due mostly to its progressive folk rock utilization of a prominent bass guitar and drum kit. Its brilliant wording and satirical poke at American anarchy through the medium of insane narrative completes what is side one of a 180 degree detour from Bob's first four acoustic albums.

Side two marks a fundamental turning point in Dylan's music and literally gives birth to his fascination with the intellectual poetry of the 18th century Frenchman Arthur Rimbaud, amongst countless others. It also reflects Dylan's boredom, annoyance, and impatience with the folk music prison he decided he was in after he heard the Beatles. Furthermore, the all-encompassing template behind everything Bob wrote in the mid-60s, especially, was the mid-19th century cross on which America died and later was resurrected from in the era before, during, and after the Civil War. Bob was fascinated by old newspaper accounts of this period he found in the public library in New York. He particularly noted how chivalry and honor were virtues that got attached to this tumultuous dark turning point in American history after the fact. He found much that the 1960s had in common with the wild and feverish political, religious, and moral rhetoric of America's Victorian age. Generally speaking (and there are certainly exceptions), references, sentiments, and threads to America's 1850s and 1860s are most apparent in Dylan's early/mid-1960's and late era songwriting (think *Love and Theft*, *Modern Times*, and *Tempest*).

Things kick off on side 2 with **Mr. Tambourine Man**, setting a more serious tone than the somewhat frivolous last three songs on side one, and Bob clearly vocalizes the mystical lyrics with more focus, intention, and depth. As for where in the world **Mr. Tambourine Man** came from, studio session sideman Bruce Langhorne's relatively massive Turkish tambourine somehow never is given its due for having inspired one of Dylan's greatest hallucinatory flights into whimsical horseplay with words.

Gates Of Eden and the paranoid **It's All Right, Ma (I'm Only Bleeding)** take the listener into some rather dark chasms cultivated with intellectual curiosity and descents into scorpion spiritual adventures into the below, or underworld, if you will. To say these two songs have influenced American songwriting would be quite the understatement. Whether secular or biblical, and **Gates Of Eden** was both, Dylan's rhetoric here had no fear, no envy, and no meanness, as Liam Clancy once counseled him after 20 some odd pints of Guinness.

It was cutting into a whole generation of baby boomers who were gladly willing to follow, anywhere, anytime. Fittingly, therefore, a cover of **It's Alright Ma** played over closing credits in 1969's *Easy Rider*, perhaps Hollywood's penultimate counterculture bull's eye. Anyone who has ever tried to write songs can only wonder how and marvel at the way Dylan, for a time there from 1962 to 1966, tapped into some other-worldly source to come up with stuff like this. And rather than criticizing him for not still being able to do this nowadays, better to realize that in the 60s he would not have been able to do what he is doing in his 70s.

Bob's final collaboration with producer Tom Wilson, except for **Like A Rolling Stone**, is punctuated with the closing **It's All Over Now, Baby Blue**. Breaking up never seemed this sublime, man. A most-fitting exclamation point for side two, I must say. Of course, when Van Morrison and Them interjected a mellotron in their 1966 **Baby Blue** cover, the rest is rock and roll history. However, if you ever want to hear what drugs can do for a songwriter holding an acoustic guitar, look no further than the entire brushstroke of side two of *Bringing It All Back Home*.

As for liner notes, again we are treated to, or burdened by, schizophrenia in the *Tarantula* tradition, and credit is granted to only Wilson, whose sound work for Dylan just got better and better in the years 1962 to 1965. And this, from a self-admitted highbrow whose career commenced by cutting Coltrane and looking down his nose at dumb-downed folkies. Can we hear it for the late and great Tom Wilson? Give it up! While we're at it, how 'bout a hand for Bobbie Gregg on drums as well as Paul Griffin and Frank Owens on piano, all three of whom went on to contribute to *Highway 61 Revisited* as well. And finally, there is Bruce Langhorne on guitar and to thank for the inspiration for **Mr. Tambourine Man**.

Two sensational *Bringing It All Back Home* outtakes, amongst more than a handful, that cannot go unmentioned are **Farewell Angelina** and **I'll Keep It With Mine**. Both, worth noting, have since made

Dylan lots and lots of mullah via numerous cover versions in foreign languages as well as in English. For starters, Judy Collins had a popular single in '65 with **I'll Keep It With Mine**, and the New Riders of the Purple Sage and John Mellencamp have famously covered **Farewell, Angelina**. Suffice it to say that not only have multiple artists covered copyrighted Dylan songs, but multiple artists have also covered multiple copyrighted Dylan songs. It starts to get exponentially and mathematically mind-blowing.

With *Bringing It All Back Home*, Bob Dylan had irreversibly gone hip, if there had ever been any doubt. He had somehow managed to lump together the absurd, romantic, cunning, and surreal into a mishmash of mindfully marinated melodies mirroring miscellaneous mercurial musical mutations at muses heretofore muffled by mainstream American morality. Perhaps the liner note rhetorical quandary of whether Norman Mailer is more important than Hank Williams ought to be left alone.

Some questions are far more important than their answers.

#6

Highway 61 Revisited

Now this is what an electric Bob Dylan album sounds like, dude. Perhaps *Highway 61 Revisited*, released August 30, 1965, is best portrayed as a, if not the, pinnacle of popular music serendipity. Abandoning the instrumental arrangements, musicality, and lyrical tone of the folk movement, Bob Dylan's sound was busy being born out of an electric fertilization with the Beatles. Moreover, in the nursery room of the maternity ward of popular music was a sound never heard previously or duplicated since.

Immersed in writing *Tarantula*, once again Bob treats us to preposterous prose in the liner notes, but he does manage to make one good point. He states that the songs on *Highway 61 Revisited* are not so much songs, but exercises in tonal breath control. I will actually buy that. These songs, like so many of Dylan's compositions, seem to have written themselves, or else were written by some other dimension. The lyrics. The voice. The sequencing. The instruments. An unblemished blend of manmade sound and human thought.

Is there a better rock and roll LP? Well, Rolling Stone went with *Sgt. Pepper's Lonely Hearts Club Band* in its all-time standings. But wait a minute. Compared to *Highway 61 Revisited*, the presumed crowning achievement of the Beatles was largely comprised of abstract fabrications of studio recording gimmicks. No one in their right mind would ever argue with the results, yet on *Highway 61 Revisited* Bob Dylan and his hand-selected back up cats are actually playing outright rock and roll in real time. First of all, why bother with comparing and contrasting apples and oranges, which, as my father used to say, for some senseless reason, is odious. Furthermore, in 1965, getting back to the album at hand, there simply was no comparing the average two-minute plus Beatle verse chorus middle eight template with the typical 5.5 minute plus Dylan foreign object landing from unexplored territory.

To take this vein a little further (if you'll pardon me for a moment), interestingly, it is difficult, if not impossible, to point to a single Dylan song that is obviously influenced by the Beatles (other than **Fourth Time Around** as a blatant, tongue-in-cheek response to Lennon's Dylan-influenced **Norwegian Wood**). Yet, Beatle songs that without question never would have been written without Bob's effect on John Lennon include **In My Life**, **I'm A Loser**, **Help**, **You've Got To Hide Your Love Away**, and **Nowhere Man**. Any discussion on the Beatles/Dylan mid-60s mutual influence societies might do well to start and end by noting the indisputable matter of fact (in my humble opinion, which, granted, makes no sense), that the best the Beatles ever played together, as a four man band in real time, was on *Rubber Soul*. Here, on the front cover we find four mop tops dressed in *Freewheelin'* brown suede. Putting needle to vinyl, we hear the closest the loveable Liverpool lads ever got to Dylan's game-changing invention of folk rock, music they wrote, recorded, and released in direct response to *Highway 61 Revisited*. Need more be said?

Hence, one might say Dylan was not so much influenced by the Beatles as he was just influenced by himself. An American original. A one-man agitator of popular music songwriting a half step ahead of pretenders, impersonators, and venerating adulators. Nonetheless, the mutual admiration in London and upper New York state, where Dylan now resided, as if he possessed anything resembling domestic roots in 1965, was absolutely a two way street.

Was it the Beatles on Ed Sullivan or did the 1960s emanate with the snare drum snap triggering **Like A Rolling Stone**? What we do know is that after said snare pop came a relentless mockery of American classism couched in the adulation of the almost endless list of blues characters born on or near the highway connecting Bob's hometown of Duluth with New Orleans. Men with last names such as Waters, Presley, House, Johnson, and Patton.

In any case, the long piece of vomit (Dylan's words) that evolved into **Like A Rolling Stone** launched *Highway 61 Revisited*, a title fought tooth and nail by Columbia due to Bob's insistence that corporate correctness not dictate yet another lamentable album title in the wake of *Another Side of Bob Dylan*, a title which Bob held in disdain. It also rejuvenated Dylan's willingness and passion to forge ahead with his recording career, which had begun to bore him to the point of considering retirement after *Another Side Of Bob Dylan*, which, lest we forget, took him all of about 9 hours to record and put a wrap on. Think about that. I reckon the Beatles had put an end to whoever that character was in Manhattan from January 1961 until the impeccable harmonies and tight arrangements of songs like **All My Loving** and **Please, Please Me** hit American airwaves. Truth be told, I think Dylan was inwardly intimidated (he was hardly alone) by such vocal, rhythmical, melodic, and instrumental precision, which he realized he was incapable of and despite having little or no intention, calling, hope, or desire to replicate anything resembling it.

Notwithstanding all this, uncharacteristic hours and hours of nose-to-the-grindstone writing and recording went into **Like A Rolling Stone**, the only Tom Wilson contribution to the album, possibly due to Wilson having a problem with Bob's desire to let a guy named Al Kooper provide the most famous organ licks in rock and roll history. *Rolling Stone's* number one rock song in history did not just happen, but it did help ignite a fresh vision for a direction Dylan wanted to go.

Bob's all-time favorite lead guitarist, Mike Bloomfield, had a lot to do with it. Harvey Goldstein on bass and Bobby Gregg on drums. Bravo, dudes. And somewhere along the lines Kooper came up with that killer organ riff, Bob instantly knew his epic masterpiece had popped, the organ track was turned up, and the next thing we knew AM radio stations were playing the longest and best song in pop music history up to that point.

The epic stir in the wake of his July 25, 1965 unveiling of **Like A Rolling Stone** at Newport, both exaggerated and muddied in lore for 59 years and counting now, occurred only days before the arduous completion of *Highway 61 Revisited*. The whole LP is laced with parades of historical as well as colorful fictitious figures embedded in lyrics subtly skirting the edge of reason and an energetic panache leaving the entire field of Bob's contemporaries ridiculously in the dust.

Penned with lyrics light years ahead of their time in the Byrdcliffe artist colony near Woodstock in the late spring and early summer of '65, all *Highway 61 Revisited* songs, except **From A Buick 6,** have remained staples in live Dylan set lists over the years. Isn't it a pity? I'm mean, I have always yearned for a **Buick 6** steam shovel mama and/or a dump trunk baby to put a blanket on my bed in case I go down dying. Come on man, don't we all have this in common? What, just for instance, Dylan's 2015 touring band could do with this blues shuffle, especially Charlie Sexton on his hollow body Gibson. I guess one must admit being a Dylan head when daydreams such as this make your day.

During a lunch break one day, Bob turned **It Takes A Lot To Laugh, A Train To Cry** into a tender ¾ time sensual blues anthem. Earlier grinding two-step grooves would have sufficed, but alas, they were destined to outtake re-runs on obscure channels at 3 in the morning. Eric Burton and the Animals never came up with anything resembling Al Kooper's spooky organ riffs on **Ballad Of A Thin Man**, which only accentuated the hip exclusivity of a burgeoning 1960s counterculture while giving birth to the Philistine Mr. Jones, a superficial, well-bred yet walking dead man ignoramus practically unrivaled in the pretty much endless index of Dylan archetypes. **Ballad of A Thin Man** is the early Dylan composition that really hooked me when I got to high school in the early 70s.

Queen Jane Approximately, an example of Bob's playful tendency to place adverbs of degree in song titles, appropriately mirrors the stifling nature of an upper class existence, one of if not the only discernible themes of the album. In the 1970s and 80s Dead Heads eventually became more acquainted with **Queen Jane** than Dylan heads, despite the fact that for decades both the Grateful Dead and Dylan have re-interpreted it with sheer elegance and to the delight of many an air-dancing hippy.

The title track **Highway 61 Revisited** casts dubious characters careen-ing haphazardly on the highway central to the history of the blues, winding from Dylan's birthplace in Duluth all the way to New Orleans. No wonder he feels such a kinship with it. Although Bob has played this one live thousands of times thousands of ways, I reckon about 1 in 3 or 4 renditions have worked more effectively than just filling venues with lots of low end rhythm section dance grease.

Just Like Tom Thumb's Blues narrates a trance-inducing epic mind-altering voyage south of the Rio Grande, the boudoir of the limited-English speaking junkie whore Sweet Melinda, and ending up alone and abandoned by everybody and everything but booze. From this jolly note, **Desolation Row**, featuring Charlie McCoy's fine classi-cal guitar doodling, was just around the corner and down the alley. Rather than falling into the lap of Dylan's folly of venturing to unravel any sense from **Desolation Row**, common or otherwise, can we just leave it that Bob implies a mere suggestion of the idiotic idiosyncrasies of it all. You gotta reckon that outrageous in an outstanding way songs like **Desolation Row** were the sort of demoralizing stuff that caused the Dylan alter-ego worshipping Phil Ochs, down the line in the 70s, to take his life. I mean, who's gonna top the closing track to *Highway 61 Revisited*? Add in Ochs' sad, pathetic, and deep-seated inferiority complex, and you come up with a tragic suicide (and stinging loss in folk circles).

Tombstone Blues reverts back to Dylan's penchant for absurd lyr-ics, but is marked mostly by Bloomfield's cutting edge licks, which he sharpened in the Paul Butterfield Blues Band, on what sure sounds like a Fender Telecaster to me. I'm still trying to wrap my head around a tuba rehearsal at the same location where Beethoven and Gertrude (Ma) Rainey unwrapped their bed rolls.

As for outtakes from *Highway 61 Revisited*, **Positively Fourth Street** rightly viewed as one of Dylan's top ten recordings ever, finds Bob spewing bitter venom while concealing his fury in a happy-go-angry melodic groove that is a throwback to the covert pain in **Don't Think Twice, It's Alright**. **Can You Please Crawl Out Your Window** enjoyed popular exposure as a single, albeit briefly due to a mix up at Columbia which led to its inadvertent release. **Sitting On A Barbed Wire Fence** features Bloomfield at his wild best, but the decision to hold off on this one until *Bootleg Series 1-3* in 1991 was the right choice. Remaining unreleased from *Highway 61 Revisited* are **Why Do You Have To Be So Frantic** and several alternate versions of songs that made the cut.

As for what else was going on in the personal galaxy of Bob Dylan in the summer of 1965, given that Bob's first son, Jesse, was born in January '66, and that Bob married Sara Lownds in November '65, it is presumable that in the midst of the red wine, amphetamines, and head-spinning lifestyle surrounding the making of *Highway 61 Revisited*, Bob was already on a search for how to unplug from the stardom infecting his personal life. No songs on *Highway 61 Revisited* can directly point to Sara as their muse, but that would not be the case on *Blonde On Blonde*, which resulted immediately in the aftermath of *Highway 61 Revisited* and Bob's new bride and baby boy.

On the other hand, however (how dramatically redundant), previous to *Highway 61 Revisited*, **She Belongs To Me** and **Love Minus Zero/No Limit** were very likely inspired by Bob's late 1964 first impressions of Sara. Former Playboy bunny Sara Lownds, whom Bob met through his manager Albert Grossman's wife Sally Buchler, who adorns the background of the cover of *Bringing It All Back Home*, can rightly be credited for introducing Bob to D.A. Pennebaker, the director who piggybacked on Richard Lester's black and white fly-on-the-wall documentary on the

Beatles, *A Hard Day's Night*, in the spring 1965 filming of the now classic *Don't Look Back*. The *Highway 61 Revisited* era was the genesis of the Bob and Sara act which brought offspring Jesse, Anna, Samuel, and Jacob into this world, not to mention the adoption of Sara's daughter Maria from a prior marriage that ended when she fell in love with Bob.

Making logical sense of Bob Dylan's art, especially by talking to him about it, has been a futile endeavor throughout his lifetime, particularly in the era of the trilogy of his electric albums in the mid '60s. A Chaplin-like maestro at deliberately, deftly, and surreptitiously changing the subject and slippery self-effacement when put on a pedestal, Bob has consistently, to practically no avail, urged his listeners to look to his song lexicon for meaning. His refusal to place coherent significance on any of his music has forever confounded critics and fans alike. The fleeting, whirlwind *Highway 61 Revisited* era marked a zenith in curiosity with what Bob was up to and trying to say.

Hence, when *Playboy* invested 3 hours plus of writer Nat Hentoff's time in what is widely acknowledged as Bob's all-time most incomprehensible interview, a titanic mouthful that utters volumes, right on the heels of the release of *Highway 61 Revisited*, the reader/listener is wont to query, "Did he just actually make a point?" And, "Did he then, slimily revoke what I am not quite sure he said in the first place?" Choice Dylan at its best. Bob was then and remains now unrivaled in the age-old knack of pretending to be a non-recluse in the face of petty, annoying critics and then proceeding to revengefully, with a charming smirk, hand out fascinating bread crumbs which are impervious to inevitable hapless follow-up questions, all the while steering aimless streams of consciousness into opaque black holes of highbrow balderdash.

Then, out came *Blonde On Blonde*.

Photo by author of a digital printout of an oil painting portrait of Bob Dylan by Michael
Birnbaum…michael@transformedbycolor.com…www.transformedbycolor.com

#7

Blonde On Blonde

Recorded in Nashville after unsatisfactory results in New York, *Blonde On Blonde*, widely regarded as the most prolific, auspicious, and legendarily epic album Dylan has ever made, both preceded and coincided with Bob's now famous spring '66 world tour on which booing was common. The album was quite the feverish, whirling dervish recording process that commenced just prior to as well as during the fall '65 *Highway 61 Revisited* live tour and culminated upon its release May 16 of '66, just as Dylan and the Hawks were about to wind up their mythical tour in legendary (thanks largely to Bob Dylan) British arenas such as Manchester Trade Hall and Royal Albert Hall in the South Kensington neighborhood of London. Like *Highway 61 Revisited*, the entire album was electric, or better yet, on fire, unlike *Bringing It All Back Home*, which only peeked its creative head into the realm of Gretsch, Fender, and Rickenbacker guitars that the Beatles were splashing onto the planet.

With a seemingly endless supply of lyrics and melodies, Bob's first double album quickly became the standard for "folk rock", a box/label Dylan rejected. This did not stop the likes of the Byrds, the Mamas and the Papas, Donovan, the Youngbloods, and, at first, the Jefferson Airplane from emulating and eventually spawning an entire musical genre that Dylan concocted and Roger (Jimmy) McGuinn gave birth to with his June 1965 opening licks on a 12-string Rickenbacker guitar on **Mr. Tambourine Man**. Furthermore, *Blonde On Blonde* signaled Dylan's switch from New York to Nashville as his preferred recording venue for four consecutive albums, a move that is widely credited with causing an eruption in not only the recording business in Nashville, but a widespread burst in the commercial popularity of country music overall.

Strangely enough, *Blonde On Blonde's* emphasis on blues structures might have been more at home at Stax records in Memphis, but that is neither here nor there. Eventually, after two light years of personal and professional costume changes, in 1968 and 1969 Dylan would return to Nashville and point-blank salute the then-lowly country music crowd on *John Wesley Harding* and *Nashville Skyline*.

Bob kicks off *Blonde On Blonde* with **Rainy Day Woman #12 and 35** (i.e. "Everybody must get stoned") and the comical, playful riff, chords, and chorus line anchoring the song's hook. In the wee hours Bob told the band he wanted a Salvation Army band sound, and Charlie McCoy playfully replied, "Then, you don't need a really good trombone player, right?" The rest is history. Bob's first double album intrigued the listener from its opening blasts of Wayne Butler's brass trombone, Kenny Buttrey's bass drumming with a timpani mallet, Al Kooper's tambourine, McCoy's trumpet, and Dylan's slurred, almost drunken-sounding vocals all the way to the lengthy organ notes and Sara Lownds-romantic-infatuation driving of the album's practically transcendental closer, **Sad Eyed Lady Of The Lowlands**.

However, that "thin wild mercurial" sound more plainly and demonstrably came to life in the second track of side one, the 8-bar blues **Pledging My Time**, introducing the then world's record for longest harmonica notes known to man. Good stuff on a barroom jukebox.

Next, creepy organ lines, crackling snare drums, snarled vocals, and humming harmonica underscore a 1960s song that has inspired more would-be songwriters than one can shake a stick at, the one and only **Visions of Johanna**. Now here is one of those Dylan songs which can be enjoyed in either of two ways over the course of repeated listenings in the triple digits. First, by intellectually analyzing every syllable and word ad nauseam, or else by throwing up your hands and surrendering to not having a clue what it's about and letting the flawless arrangement of instruments, rhythm, syncopated poetry, and intellectual stimulation wash over you. One works just as well as the other, depending on what kind of mood you, Louise, Madonna, and/ or Johanna are in.

One Of Us Must Know introduces a carnival-like swirling organ punctuated by Bob's bouncy banging on the 88s, returning to that relaxed wild mercurial thing nobody has seemed to be able to replicate, let alone capture, ever since. Side one of **Blonde On Blonde** grabbed then and still grabs the listener by the throat, and things were just warming up. Strap yourself in now, while you can!

An AM radio hit in the summer of '66, just as I embarked on my sojourn into puberty, **I Want You**, starts off side two and, more importantly, had neighbors in my childhood twisting by the pool at the cement pond in the back yard of the Spanish mansion Dr. Bill Requarth (thanks for that right inguinal hernia job back in '82) owned down by the Sangamon River in Decatur, Illinois. **I Want You** is one of my fondest, most vivid, and earliest conscious memories of the mid-60s mojo of Bob Dylan. Perhaps this has more to do with the magical Requarth pool than Dylan's music, for it also feels like yesterday at this legendary skinny dippin' hole that I heard Roberta Flack's **The First Time Ever I Saw Your Face** in the summer of '69 and countless other 60s summer hits on WLS AM. Think Tommie James and the Shondells, the Temptations, Johnny Rivers, the Hollies, Creedence, and the Lovin' Spoonful.

Side one carries on with **Memphis Blues Again**, on which Bob is repeatedly unable to extract himself from Mobile, Alabama. Meanwhile, a parade of literary protagonists suffer the slings and arrows of outrageous fortune compliments of random happenstances, disconnected fragments, and a complete symphony of discordant worldly collisions. It has never been exactly clear to me the origin of the descriptive phrase wild, thin, mercurial sound, but on songs like **Memphis Blues Again**, Texas medicine (uppers) can probably be credited for helping Bob to visualize his music in terms of this intentionally imperfect sound, not songs.

Leopard Skin Pill Box Hat, passively aggressively introduced as a folk song to the spring '66 Manchester Trade Hall audience in order to quell their angst over Bob playing a Fender Stratocaster, pokes fun at the Jackie Kennedy headdress which became so chic in the 60s with a sarcastic satire on materialism, fashion, and faddism.

Edie Sedgwick, or some similar type of debutante, is the inspiration of the misogynistic **Just Like A Woman**, which started out in early takes as disconnected indecipherable fragments and semi-gibberish and ended up as a sordid sketch of female wiles and vulnerability and one of Bob's most venerated compositions ever. At this point, compliments of side two, we are now formally in the throws of a rock and roll mirage of musical and poetic fantasy the likes of which didn't know existed.

On the heels of *Highway 61 Revisited*, fall '65 trysts with Andy Warhol, Ms. Edie, Bob's new romance with Sara, and taking up residence in Manhattan's famed Hotel Chelsea (where Dylan Thomas was staying when he died of pneumonia in 1953 and about which Arthur Miller had written an early 60s short prose piece entitled *The Chelsea Affect*) instead of his rural Woodstock home all somehow made for just the right recipe and/or concoction of chemistry to yield an album for the ages. A lack of verbosity evidently is both unimaginably and inappropriately insufficient as well as outright impossible when expounding on the dynamic lyrical delights of *Blonde On Blonde*.

All humor or attempts at it aside, side three takes on a decidedly blues bent as **Most Likely You'll Go Your Way and I'll Go Mine** reverts to a twelve bar stomper about lovers parting. **Temporary Like Achilles** is a slow-moving blues with a dusky barrelhouse piano, harmonica wheeze, and double entendre in the chorus line, "Honey why are you so hard?", a line that Dylan had been wanting to fit into a song. **Absolutely Sweet Marie** accelerates into an up-tempo blues shuffle with obvious pop sensibility and sexual metaphors like "beating on my trumpet" and the oft-repeated in Bohemian circles, "To live outside the law you must be honest."

4th Time Around sounds like Bob Dylan impersonating John Lennon impersonating Bob Dylan. Written in response to the circular structure of **Norwegian Wood**, Dylan takes his take in a far darker direction than Lennon's tale of a northern mistress. **Obviously Five Believers**, the best rhythm and blues on *Blonde On Blonde*, was recorded in four simple takes after Bob told the band, "It's very easy, man!"

Sad Eyed Lady of the Lowlands, a wedding song for Sara, whom Bob had married three months before, has questions but no answers, with Bob at his most elusive and romantic, penning what he himself depicted as old time religious carnival music. Whatever, Bob. The soothing chord progressions, stretching out to the then-unthinkable length of 11 minutes and 23 seconds, manage to take up the entirety of side four of this double album vinyl climactic crescendo to Dylan's electric trilogy, which permanently altered the course of popular music in the 20th century.

Meanwhile, the infamous spring '66 world tour that was intended to market *Blonde On Blonde* found audiences at the pinnacle of 1960s Dylan fascination, curiosity, worship, and confoundedness. With the unheralded and under-praised Mickey Jones more than adequately filling in for Levon Helm on drums for the Hawks (later to become the Band), Bob played to sold out audiences across the Pacific rim, Europe, and the U.S., reworking a couple dozen of his culturally revolutionizing compositions into two sets of utterly theatrically juxtaposed performances of electric and solo acoustic material.

Martin Scorsese's epic 2005 documentary *No Direction Home* captures a sliver of the mania of the spring '66 world tour. One had best refer to the *Bootleg Series Volume 4 Live 1966* for an audio glimpse into the mystical essence of Dylan's mid-60s influence on an array of cultural mediums including, but not limited to music, art, film, literature, beat intellectualism, dress, hairstyle, and avant-garde philosophy. However, the paramount video glance into Dylan's mid-60s mystique would be D. A. Pennebaker's black and white *Don't Look Back*, a groundbreaking documentary recorded a year earlier on Dylan's British tour sandwiched between *Bringing It All Back Home* and *Highway 61 Revisited.* Richard Lester and the Beatles' *A Hard Day's Night* are rightly credited for having partially inspired Pennebaker's masterpiece in film making.

By the spring of '66, though, after four consecutive years of amphetamines, red wine, and virtual 24-7 artistic output, Dylan was simply fortunate to still be among the living, on the one hand, plus humanity was reaping the opportunity to witness the crescendo of perhaps the greatest run of over-the-top game-changing music of the 20th century. Little did Bob or could the public have foreseen the radical, enduring transformation that was just over the horizon in his daily life. Revolted by the pedestal he had been placed on and privately exhausted, Bob's new marriage to Sara was about to beacon a fresh artistic vision that had less to do with making music than with making babies.

Meanwhile, being rejected by some and exalted by far more others was simply blowing Bob's mind, and he consciously chose not to deal with it all. It was at some point in 1966 that some of Dylan's folk faithful, having had enough after three-straight-electric-album-strikes-and-you're-out unforgivable misdeeds by their former commander in chief, abandoned him and never looked back. Bob's folk/electric reinvention of himself, the first major of pretty much countless mask changes in his public persona and musical meanderings (not counting all the masquerading he pulled off when he left Hibbing in 1959), became a pigeon hole Bob would never escape in the rigid minds of lightweight fans doing good to get their minds wrapped around even one layer of skin shedding. Dozens would be simply out of the question. Ever the artistic visionary, Bob Dylan could already smell the stench of labels like king of folk rock, voice of a generation, countercultural icon, and social justice troubadour. Alas, not to worry, for Dylan's out has always been another masquerade party, costumes mandatory. Bob's not about to get boxed in by anybody, anywhere, anytime.

Only this time, precisely when he could not get any bigger or more fried, just as the record industry he helped launch was rocketing to galaxies hitherto unexplored, instead of a costume change, in 1966 Bob had a disappearing act in mind.

#8

Bob Dylan's Greatest Hits Volume 1

Bob Dylan has released three predictably outstanding volumes of greatest hits compilations over the years. A bizarre peculiarity, in true vintage Dylan style, which characterizes all 3 of these offerings is that they each include songs which were previously unreleased. Now, why would such songs be commercially unveiled on volumes of greatest hits? Well, ya gotta figure Bob thinks highly enough of them that he himself deemed them worthy of greatest hits status. Another, ho hum, yawn, what the hell in the go-figure Bob Dylan department, to be sure.

Bob Dylan's Greatest Hits Volume 1 came out on March 27, 1967 right in the midst of Bob's disappearance from public view, after his July 29, 1966 motorcycle accident, and just prior to getting started on the homespun musical endeavors that turned into *The Basement Tapes*. The original vinyl release contained a famous psychedelic poster of Dylan, which upped the purchase price to the then-unheard of $5.98. The eminently memorable album cover photo, taken by Rowland Scherman in Washington D.C. on November 28, 1965, was awarded the 1967 Grammy for best album photo cover, and although initially the album only reached #10 in the U.S. (imagine the stiff completion facing ANY March '67 release of commercial music!), it has since sold more copies domestically than any other Dylan album.

Columbia executives, who could see that Dylan was not about to put out any new material any time soon, not only came up with the concept of a greatest hits record, but also selected the song list and sequence.

The compilation of songs on *Volume 1* is a de facto singles collection of every top 40 Dylan single through 1967. Inexplicably included was the previously unreleased (?!) *Highway 61 Revisited* outtake and hit single **Positively Fourth Street**, a longer version of which later appeared on a 1997 re-mastered CD version of *Greatest Hits Volume 1.*

In addition, *Volume 1* reminded the general public that some of Bob's songs made famous and cashed in on by other artists were in fact his original creations. Examples of this were **Blowin' In The Wind**, which Peter, Paul, and Mary most notoriously profited from in '63, **It Ain't Me Babe**, a huge hit for the Turtles in '65, and another smashing success for the Byrds, a truncated electric take on **Mr. Tambourine Man**, which not-so-incidentally can be pointed to as the genesis of what later was coined California rock (as opposed to New York, I guess). Rounding out the lineup on *Volume 1* were **Rainy Day Woman #12 and 35, The Times They Are A-Changing, Like A Rolling Stone, Subterranean Homesick Blues, I Want You**, and **Just Like A Woman**.

Unbeknownst to Bob, who could not have cared less and was fully out of the picture, the European version of *Volume 1* had a vastly different song list. He was too busy evolving into the role of country gentleman and man of sloth/leisure, a role that didn't last long, but even if it had continued into perpetuity, just off of albums 1 to 7 and *Greatest Hits Volume 1*, Bob Dylan would no doubt be a millionaire today, not to mention a permanent influence on 20th century American music. In fact, the indisputable naked truth is that he would have, just from what he accomplished before his 25th birthday, have forever changed not only the course of rock and roll, but actually popular music overall.

With this, our good friend simply could not be bothered. He had a life to save and a family to raise.

#9

The (Complete) Basement Tapes

Not released by Columbia until June 26, 1975, halfway between *Blood On The Tracks* and *Desire*, *The Basement Tapes* was a homespun fabrication conceived, composed, and created amidst a cannabis cloud collaboration from roughly May to November 1967.

This followed a six to nine month sobriety clean up (at least relatively speaking) during which Bob was medically treated for spinal cord injuries suffered from his nasty motorcycle crash in the summer of '66, which nixed Albert Grossman's hectic live tour date schedule, not to mention any studio recording desired by Columbia executives. Outside the day-to-day secluded solitude in which Bob Dylan and the Band were operating, to say much was happening in the world would be a gross understatement.

First, the so-called Summer of Love was in full flowering mode, giving birth to *Sgt. Pepper's Lonely Hearts Club Band*, the Rolling Stones' *Their Satanic Majesties Request* (with highly produced works with heady titles like **2000 Light Years From Home**), and the rise of a San Francisco Bay area tourist industry centered around hippie gawking and a burgeoning drug culture. Moreover, there were the October 3 death of Woody Guthrie and the birth of Sara and Bob's second child, Anna. Furthermore, Bob's personal life was punctuated in August by his final face-to-face interaction with his father, Abraham, when Abe and Beatrice paid a visit to Woodstock. This is not to mention the geopolitical earthquakes of America's unpopular war in Southeast Asia and the on-going civil rights uproar occurring in the streets, newspapers, and evening news of the U.S. on a daily basis.

Somewhere along the lines in 1966, around the time of a major Bob Dylan *Look* magazine expose right after the whole debacle at Royal Albert Hall and *Blonde On Blonde*, Dylan, whether he liked it or not, justifiably or not was/had been crowned king of the avant-garde wave in popular culture, a thorny insignia that, if one looks back at historical signposts with 20/20 hindsight, he never was comfortable with going back to the Newport Folk Festival of 1963. Yet, here, in the most pro-lific year of his life as a songwriter, in 1967 Bob was leisurely spending his days rethinking the direction of his life and music, recovering from a sense of having been exploited by the press, his manager, and his fans, and ultimately searching for and/or inventing a way for a rock star to be in control. By turning his back on his reputation, Dylan figurative-ly was grabbing his life by the throat and consciously choosing, once again, to reinvent himself as a man and an artist, to shed one more layer of skin, a lifelong, chronic chameleon pattern that first manifested the instant he left Hibbing in 1959. All this remained unbeknownst to the general public, which mistakenly, to this day in many cases, has generally assumed he was artistically unproductive in, again, the most productive songwriting phase of his life (the 1967 calendar year).

The Great White Wonder, the planet's virgin and quite profitable boot-leg album from 1969 to 1975, contained samples of what evolved into *The Basement Tapes*. It started a virtual industry all by itself, and mil-lions were made off it and its spinoffs capitalizing on numerous unre-leased recordings of other artists in the music enterprise, particularly in the rock genre. Once again we find our friend Bob leading the way of the future, whether he liked it or not.

In 1975, however, after *Blood On The Tracks* sort of proved that *The Great White Wonder* was no longer the final reminder of Dylan's lost status as a genius, not to mention the resolution of the Albert Grossman dispute over the Dwarf Music copyrights on Dylan's songs, Dylan fi-nally consented to Columbia the release of a mere 16 of the original recordings from 1967 (plus 8 more songs done later by the Band exclusively which excluded Bob). Hence, Robbie Robertson teamed with Rob Fraboni to compile the long-awaited 1975 release of what turned out to be a mere smattering of what Bob and the Band were up to in 1967. Commercially quite the smash and critically hailed as a Dylan return to ingenious form, it was given fresh overdubs of keyboards, guitar, and drum parts, although Dylan's virile vocals were maintained as the audio centerpiece. The double album reached #7 on the billboards in the U.S. and #8 in the U.K. and served as the gist at the time of what the general public realized Dylan and the Band had achieved in 1967.

That is, until 39 years later when the November 2014 *Complete Basements Tapes* clued humanity into a staggering 122 additional tracks featuring Dylan as either writer, co-writer, or lead singer. That album (long awaited does not begin to describe it), worthy of yet another whole book in its own right, provides a number of answers to 40-year-old riddles, secrets, and misunderstandings swirling around the original 1975 release of *The Basement Tapes*.

Even though Fraboni and Robertson were rightly praised for the talent and diligence displayed in their 1975 undertaking, in retrospect their work can be questioned on two key fronts. First, the eight Band songs sound like not much more than demos. More to the point, they ruin Dylan's continuity on the rest of the album and wrongly imply a more equal alliance than what took place. Their other glaring mistake was the omission of virtual master works such as **Sign On The Cross, I'm Not There**, **The Mighty Quinn**, and **I Shall Be Released**. This also goes for **Crash On The Levee**, or **Down In The Flood** as it was entitled on Bob's greatest hits volume 2 double album in 1971. Robertson's alibi for what appears to be this maniacally egotistic maneuver, which I reckon can be taken at face value, is that he saw *The Basement Tapes* as a process with a homemade feel, so he could include recordings from a wide variety of sources. Whatever, dude.

That the Band on its own achieved greatness and a permanent place in the annals of American music aside, their ride on Dylan's coattails is perhaps no better exemplified than by what now is regarded as an historical overemphasis on them on *The Basement Tapes*. This little secret became all the more painfully obvious when *The Complete Basement Tapes* revealed not only that Dylan was in full-charge at all sessions back in '67, but the existence of copious quantities of scraps of paper and once thought to be misplaced and long gone Dylan notebooks filled with seemingly limitless handwritten lyrics which were never put to music. In 2014, in conjunction with *The Complete Basement Tapes* release, Dylan allowed T. Bone Burnett and a cadre of rock stars led by Elvis Costello to put music to some of these lyrics, which resulted in a 2 disc CD and documentary film, *Lost On The River: The New Basement Tapes*. One can only hope that the financial milking of the '67 adventures in the outskirts of Woodstock, New York in the Byrdcliffe area has reached completion.

What inconspicuously started in the red room of Dylan's country estate, Hi Lo Ha, once Bob had metaphysically come to and sufficiently recovered from his July 29, 1966 motorcycle accident, eventually migrated to Big Pink merely because all the people, instruments, and noise were disrupting the two infants residing in the Dylan family household. The red room still remained the venue for Bob's new-found preference of typewriter pecking to handwriting of poetry. Garth Hudson was deemed chief recording engineer sort of by default after two stereo mixers and a tape recorder were borrowed from Albert Grossman and some mikes were lent by Peter, Paul, and Mary. The casual sequestered setting and road-tested, disciplined musicianship of the Hawks proved the perfect backdrop for Dylan to musically experiment with self reinvention by trial and error.

The strategy basically involved playing in a little huddle, and if one could not hear the singing, one was playing too loud. Open screen doors and windows, laid back dogs, and summer breezes provided the needed tonic after the globe-trotting psychosis of the 1965-66 world tour. Levon Helm's practically two-year absence from the scene due to his discouragement over the booing and whatnot that was part and parcel of electrically backing Dylan did not hold back the remaining band of Canadian brothers. Dylan and the boys were more than content laying down simple, down-to-earth sounds and narratives that were a cross between the songbook of Hank Williams and *The Holy Bible.*

Though either stoned on marijuana and/or inebriated on alcohol on most but not all occasions, as many as 8 to 15 songs a day were laid down, some made up on the spot as Dylan went along. Many pointed toward the search for salvation and moral dilemmas portrayed by outlaw after outlaw that would appear on *John Wesley Harding.*

Given the standards for record lengths in the late 60s, we now realize, thanks largely to the *Complete Basement Tapes,* that what emerged as *John Wesley Harding* the last week of December in '67 could easily have been expanded into no less than five or six albums of commercially viable original material, especially on the heels of *Blonde On Blonde.* Approximately two or three of these records would have been comprised of material that Bob never bothered to re-evaluate, re-record, re-address, or reconsider on any subsequent albums in the past 45 years. It is noteworthy that well up to half or more of these songs represent products that most professional songwriters, let alone pretty good hacks like yours truly, would donate their right testicle to charity to have written. But to Bob, they were mere throwaways. Of all the countless mind-boggling historical facts coming out of the 1960s, the one that stands out for me is that Dylan's 9 albums of original material in the 60s could, conservatively speaking, have numbered in the neighborhood of 17 LPs had he chosen to actually release all the commercially viable songs he wrote and recorded. Holy crap.

Two of Dylan's strongest compositions from 1967, if not ever, ought to musically be partially credited to members of the Band. Richard Manuel wrote the tune for **Tears of Rage**, and Rich Danko came up with the melody line for **This Wheel's On Fire**. Without nauseatingly listing the entire slate of original tracks and titles on *The Complete Basement Tapes,* Dylan composition standouts not already singled out include, but are not limited to: **Goin' To Acapulco, Apple Suckling**

Tree, You Ain't Goin' Nowhere, Nothing Was Delivered, Crash On The Levee (Down In The Flood), Tiny Montgomery, and **Santa Fe**.

Is the legacy of *The Basement Tapes*: A) a slice of musical Americana roots in an evolving tradition of Stephen Foster, Porgy and Bess, the roaring 20s jazz age, Harry Smith's *Anthology of American Music*, the show tunes of Rogers and Hammerstein, rock and roll roots of Little Richard, Chuck Berry, and the million dollar quartet?, or: B) just a guy searching for a country croon for his next album?, or: C) both of the above?, or: D) none of the above? I lean toward B, but I wouldn't argue with C, either. Who could? Only somebody wanting to be right and/or (perhaps more importantly) make you wrong. Nobody knows, and what difference would it make anyway?

Why so much confusion, hyperbole, and mystique have swirled around *The Basement Tapes*, complete or otherwise, all these years is easily explained. You see, even though the answer to the multiple choice question just posed is B and/or C, Dylan just so happened to, in chorus, compose more than a handful of some of the best songs of the 20th century in the red room of his rural New York domicile and the cellar of Big Pink. Be that as it may, this was never his mission during that fateful summer of love. Truth be known, he was also toiling away in an attempt to at least appear to be satisfying contractual demands from Colombia, not to mention possible (who knows) self-imposed sub-conscious ethical ones (for lack of a better term) from his enormous global fan base. Because he happened to unintentionally change the course of popular music in a retrospective direction, not only have his 1967 motives been intensely hyper-analyzed, but such well-intended, zealous scrutiny has evolved into a mystique bordering on occult fanaticism. I mean, basically it gets down to this. How could a guy leisurely do what Bob Dylan did in 1967? Ever since, musicians of all walks have set out to replicate laid back environments free from everyday cares and stress from which pure artistic gold might be struck.

With all due respect to Dylanite idolizers, which I would never deny that I am, my respect and love for Bob the man will always trump my urge to over-speculate and investigate and thereby canonize him hero. Bob has earned the right to be trusted at his word and deserves an exemption from being commissioned cultural paragon. KISS – keep it simple stupid. His word has never, even once, wavered. Look to the songs. The lexicon. The songs mean whatever thoughts and/or emotions evoked while, and only while listening to them. Do not make him out to be anything other than what he is. An artist. Unwavering to the vision, the call to charm, cavort, and carouse with the soul. Devoted to the creative wellspring within. Be reverent to your own intuitive fancy. Venerate the wizard within. Drop it. Next question. No wait – stop with ALL the questions.

Next album.

#10

John Wesley Harding

Oh, where have you been, my blue-eyed son? Little did the public know that 1967 had been and still stands as the most prolific song-writing and recording period in Bob Dylan's entire life.

Regardless, when it hit record stores two days after Christmas 1967, "What is this sh*t?", now ironically, was one of the many and varied typical initial responses to *John Wesley Harding's* pared-down acoustic guitar, soft bass, and brush-stroke drumming. Coming off of *Blonde On Blonde*, and really Bob's first greatest hits album, what could possibly account for Bob simplifying his arrangements and forcing his fans to scratch their heads in amazement at his bullheadedness? Well, we now realize that *John Wesley Harding* was just Bob Dylan's latest masquerade party. To get there, Bob drove deep into the Bible belt. Dumbfounded devotees, disappointed due to diametrically different desires of Dylan, ditched the disturbing *John Wesley Harding*, which dicked with and disgusted them and disregarded their delusional demands.

Therefore, Griel Marcus' famous what-is-this-shit opening to his Rolling Stone review of *Self Portrait* was a question that had been swirling in many a sub-conscious mind ever since we first heard songs like **Dear Landlord** and **Down Along Cove** two years before he coined this notorious question that so well illustrates Bob's relationship with his listeners. Keep in mind Hendrix had just put out *Are You Experienced?*, the Stones were writing songs like *She's A Rainbow*, the Beatles were releasing *Magical Mystery Tour*, and Jim Morrison had recently been arrested for the trifecta of simultaneously inciting a riot, indecency, and public obscenity on a New Haven, Connecticut stage. While the Rolling Stones had put out three LPs in 1967 alone, music stores had not heard a peep from Dylan for 19 months.

What is so easy to forget is that today nobody would ask about the nature of the manure on *John Wesley Harding*, for it is universally (if I may be so boldly presumptuous) cherished as a one-of-kind Dylan sound never heard before or since, rising out of the ashes of his public disappearance in the wake of his July 30, 1966 low-speed motorcycle accident on his Triumph near Woodstock, New York. It was here that Bob had begun to father, not just biologically, his soon-to-be family of four, and pen and record a treasure chest of upwards of 150 songs, mostly shared with the Band in what came to be *The Complete Basement Tapes*, but twelve of which ended up on *John Wesley Harding*.

Musically, a variety of stylistic threads fabricate *John Wesley Harding* into a feverish, pithy, austere record that hit retail stores in the quick turnaround time of three weeks after its wrap in Nashville. Under the expert production magic of Bob Johnston, who spent a whole career excelling at the art of putting musicians at ease, Bob employed pedal steel studio session man Pete Drake on only the last two songs, **Down Along Cove** and **I'll Be You Baby Tonight** (was this a taste of what to expect on *Nashville Skyline*?), and bassist Charlie McCoy and drummer Kenny Buttrey on all the tracks. The Johnston, McCoy, and Buttrey recipe in Nashville (now there's another book waiting to be written) stretched its enchanting artistic arms around three consecutive Dylan masterpiece LPs, *Blonde On Blonde*, *John Wesley Harding*, and *Nashville Skyline*, which culminated an unprecedented, unrivaled, and unparalleled eight album run going back to *Freewheelin'*. Not to minimize what this trio accomplished, truth be known, they all helped out on *Self Portrait* as well, but roughly 46, yes 46, others can also lay claim, or refuse to admit, to backing up that disastrous conglomeration of disappointing confusion (Bob would famously come up with three more of these in the 80s) which will forever beg the question, "Who the heck is in charge here?"

John Wesley Harding represents the mirror opposite of such distorted artistic vision. Paired down lyrics featuring not a single superfluous word, bold imagery of no less than 60 biblical allusions in 38 minutes, nylon string classical guitar, wildly intoxicating surrealistic poetic narratives, and earthly, crisp streams of consciousness characterize the novel which *John Wesley Harding* transcribes. Bob's increased interest in painting in 1967 is likely reflected in the colorful outlaw characters and Old Testament morality meandering throughout pretty much each song. Most auspiciously, in the end Johnston came up with an utterly flawless audio masterpiece firmly grounded in sonic subtlety.

John Wesley Harding was a product of a new-found voice Bob discovered in the 1967 spring, summer, and fall time frame(s), during which he wrote both lyrics and melodies at a feverish pace and laid down hundreds of tracks with the Band. As previously chronicled in this here book, these laid back sessions almost immediately got bootlegged in the form of the vinyl record known as *The Great White Wonder* that led to quite the coup d'etat in rock, country, and folk circles. More importantly, it served to let Dylan explore the direction changes he wanted his music to take after his electric earthquake in '65-66.

In fact, a few of *The Basement Tape* recordings occurred just after the first *John Wesley Harding* recordings in Nashville on October 18, 1967 and the final ones on November 21. On these, at Rich Danko's house, not the famed Big Pink, Dylan's voice in the very last *Basement Tapes* stuff starts to take on a sort of *Nashville Skyline* sort of vocal quality. Furthermore, Robbie Robertson was actually invited by Dylan to add some musical embellishments to *John Wesley Harding* but told Bob that the songs sounded fine as they were, so they remained unchanged. Why are any of these details pertinent? Point being that the shocking alteration in Dylan's music that took place between *Blonde On Blonde* and *John Wesley Harding*, from a musical perspective, resulted entirely from Bob's intimate, extemporaneous collaboration with Robertson, Danko, Hudson, Manuel, and (at the very end) Helm. Parenthetically, *Music From Big Pink*, which transformed American popular music sensibilities in its own right, likewise can be largely chalked up to Dylan's influence on the Band. Why on earth did NOT the Band (who were young, talented, and ambitious) resent Dylan for, without them, recording and releasing music they not only widely influenced, but that Bob would point blank never have been able to generate without their help? Well, they were all too glad to distance themselves from Bob publicly as they had been toying with hitting it big ever since they broke from Ronnie Hawkins in 1964 and were more than overdue to release their own album and chart their own course.

John Wesley Harding became the title track on *John Wesley Harding* only because Dylan deemed that it otherwise would be labeled a throwaway tune. This lovely, catchy melody sets the tone, giving us our first, but certainly not last, exposure on *John Wesley Harding* to a heroic outlaw shrouded in moral dilemma. **As I Went Out One Morning**, driven primarily by McCoy's bouncy bass backed by Bob's understated acoustic guitar strumming and ending on a discordant minor harmonica note, stars none other than the revolutionary Thomas Paine protecting freedom threatened by a fair damsel seeking refuge in the heart of the American South.

The next four songs find Bob playing tour guide to a holy march meandering into a myriad of foreboding biblically-laced parables, images, flashes, and subtle references couched in captivating storytelling flat-out unmatched by his contemporary (at the time but really going back to 1963 and ever since) pop music composers. **I Dreamed I Saw St. Augustine**, a much more contemplative narrative haunted by a vision of the 5th century Augustine of Hippo coming to life, puts the brakes on the tempo of the opening two songs, and this time a mystical protagonist is the target of mob psychology, comforted by a vague reference to a spiritual power out there running the show. **All Along The Watchtower**, with its much-since copied vi-V-IV chord progression, harkens back to the fall of Babylon before abruptly shifting to a thief foretelling the second coming of Jesus in the Book of Revelations, without any resolution to the plot. The Jimi Hendrix version, recorded merely a couple months after Bob recorded his own, has obviously rendered Bob's original rendition practically so long-forgotten that untold numbers have wrongly assumed it was written by the acid blues rock guitar God who met his maker in an untimely fashion just as he seemed to be peaking in 1970.

The Ballad of Frankie Lee and Judas Priest narrates an epic drama, a sort of facetious tongue-in-cheek morality play laced with no fewer than 15 blatant biblical references. Closing side one, **Drifter's Escape** features another lovable reject, this one escaping the wrath of an unjust jury in the nick of time during a lightning storm with the aid of merciful divine intervention. Thus ends an entire side of an album laced with ethical, spiritual, and metaphysical riddles wrapped inside deft dialogue and sensational storytelling.

Dear Landlord paints another sympathetic portrait, this one of a humble tenant pleading for mercy at the hands of a ruthless landlord, leaving room for the listener to cast the laconic landlord eccentric as either Dylan's manager Albert Grossman or any of those bad bosses you have ever had. **I Am A Lonesome Hobo** warns the rich that persecuting the enlightened poor is a fool's game. Possibly the most endlessly curious and entertaining all-time Dylan song to play the what-is-this-song-about game with, **I Pity The Poor Immigrant,** laments travelers who search for greener pastures only to lose their soul in what just might be the most enchanting melody of the bunch. Try imagining almighty God as the antecedent of the title's subject pronoun, I. Or not.

The Wicked Messenger is another ballad shrouded in apocalyptic metaphors that brings to a close no less than ten consecutive songs that mythologize, in some way or another, individuals who somehow stand out from or against social conventions. Finishing off the album are two warm, rather cheerful romantic interludes lightening the air highlighted by Drake's pedal steel guitar, namely the playful **Down Along Cove** and the lusty country croon, **I'll Be Your Baby Tonight**.

Of all the album masterpieces in the Dylan catalogue, *John Wesley Harding* can credibly be argued to represent Bob's captivating storytelling at its zenith, succinctly achieving his most distinguishable novel, as it were, of terse short stories. Woven into a rational thread of well-worded plots and ironic dialogues which make heroes out of seeming losers, it mythologizes the downhearted, lost, unsung, battle-torn, hopeless, helpless, condemned, and worse. In the process, be careful, for this medicinal record just might cure what ails ya.

In January 1968 times were changing, or even had changed, granted, but, WTF, the hermit formerly known as Bob Dylan was putting out music that was beyond time, as in timeless. *John Wesley Harding* unmistakably and vividly constructed a long and winding bridge between *Blonde On Blonde* and *Nashville Skyline* reinforced with a foundation of Big Pink and *The Holy Bible*.

#11

Nashville Skyline

On April 9, 1969, when *Nashville Skyline* was released, the polariza-tion of the American political climate had reached a, if not its, pin-nacle. Social turmoil such as the assassinations of Robert Kennedy and Martin Luther King, the Democratic National Convention vio-lence in Chicago, the inauguration of Richard Nixon as president, the on-going lack of support for escalating U.S. military engagements in southeast Asia, and protests over wide-ranging political hot potatoes such as women's rights, gay rights, environmental destruction, and capitalism were constantly in the headlines. Bob Dylan, on the other hand, seemed oblivious to it all, busy writing bucolic melodies with simple structures and charming lyrics sung with a radically new coun-try crooner vocal style. Where was the trumpet of the counterculture just as the 60s were taking their nastiest turn?

The answer was quite simple, with 20/20 hindsight. Dylan had become a satisfied man, and the soft affect of his voice on *Nashville Skyline* was proof positive. It is inaccurate to say Bob ever abdicated his hold on the rock and roll constituency. The truth is that he had never felt a part of the baby boom generation that had unceremoniously, rudely, ignorantly, and misguidedly crowned him king in the first place; nor did he even understand it.

Bob was, after all, born before World War II started, not afterwards, a fact that, oddly, speaks volumes about the Dylan mystique. He was, is, and will always be a beat artist, much in the Kerouac and Ginsburg veins, men who may have highly influenced the children of the 60s, but who really were born of a previous era.

More importantly, the non-rational, as opposed to irrational, drummer whose beat Bob has forever shadowed and will always march to is that of the creative wellspring of the artist within. Perhaps the prevailing legacy of Bob Dylan, to which *Nashville Skyline* stands testimony, will be his insistent devotion to giving birth to beauty, not only through his heralded poetic music, but his little-known painting and three dimensional artwork.

Nashville Skyline is, first and foremost, an album that many a Dylan fan claims as their favorite, and not without reason. This record achieved the artistically impossible by shattering the prevailing counterculture hipster hippy archetype by successfully showcasing the despised, hick music known as country, thereby kicking open a looming Americana roots music movement that survives to this day. It established country rock as a commercially viable genre while simultaneously, particularly in the closing number, **Tonight I'll Be Staying Here With You**, exploding genre limitations in an unquestionable glorious flow of country, folk, rock, and standard pop. This pearl of a tune and recording is a fitting closing to an album that paradoxically offers fewer mysteries than any of Bob's preceding albums, yet more comforting rewards.

By the end of the 1960s Bob Dylan had evacuated the pedestal of his pop cultural status, one he had simultaneously and counter-intuitively neither sought nor ever lost. *Nashville Skyline* contains absolutely no social or political commentary. What it does have is a collection of songs that can be described as rustic, romantic, happy, uncomplicated, domestic, and completely disconnected from world events. Bob appears to be immersed in a rural landscape in which he speaks in clichés, blushes as if every day were Valentine's Day, and floats around on a pink cloud in a world too good to be true.

Unlike *John Wesley Harding*, on which Bob superimposes intellectual complexity onto the warm inherent mysticism of Southern music, *Nashville Skyline* reveals three entirely lightweight numbers, **Peggy**

Day, One More Night, and **Tell Me That It Isn't True**, all of which toy with the my-baby-left-me concept, but without a speck of resentment. Even on his re-work of **Girl From The North Country**, the most dark and/or painful verse is omitted (the one that admits many times I've often prayed in the darkness of my night and in the brightness of my day).

Perhaps the clearest evidence of Bob's carefree bliss is the photo of him on the album's cover in which he appears to be delightfully glad without a care in the world. Can you say inner joy for no reason? Or was it the power, sensation, and security of domestic ecstasy? Here is a man at peace, not only with the world around him, but with himself. Contrast this with the brooding, sardonic, dark scowls that mark the covers of *Bringing It All Back Home* and *Highway 61 Revisited*. On *Nashville Skyline*, Dylan rediscovers his heartfelt, passionate romance with rural music, conjuring up images of hillbillies sitting on the back porch pickin' and grinnin'.

Musically, *Nashville Skyline* was an ambitious effort to conclusively cross over into country music and out of folk rock. Retaining drummer Kenny Buttrey, guitarist Charlie McCoy, and pedal steel guitarist Pete Drake from *John Wesley Harding*, Bob returned to Nashville, where *Blonde On Blonde* had been recorded, and added session players Charlie Daniels on bass and Norman Blake on flat-picking guitar. His then-trusted producer Bob Johnston handily held down mixing duties, and Johnny Cash contributed liner notes that generously provided a salute from one of country music's royalty.

Bob and Johnny's mutual appreciation society goes back to Johnny's steadfast public support of Bob's early folk achievements as well as his initial forays into electric rock. Johnny had always felt grateful to Bob for standing up for him during his numerous personal and professional down times, and Bob, in turn, has never forgotten what Johnny's support for *Nashville Skyline* meant not only for his overall career, but for the country audience's embrace of Dylan as a bona fide country music artist. Amazingly, the debt country music will eternally owe to Bob Dylan for turning on an entire generation of baby boomers to the once-exiled trash genre of country can and never will be repaid. The country artists that have been influenced by Dylan since *Nashville Skyline* are countless, and all you have to do is ask songwriters like the deceased (okay, that doesn't make sense) Townes Van Zandt, Willie Nelson, Merle Haggard, Dolly Parton, Alan Jackson, Steve Earle, Garth Brooks, and/or Hank Williams, Jr., just to name a few.

The album begins with a duet of **Girl From The North Country** with none other than the Man In Black himself, on which the vibration and playful harmonizing sounds at times like the two are drunk at 3 in the morning. Two months after the release of *Nashville Skyline*, Bob appeared live on The Johnny Cash Show to market the record, which was commercially extremely profitable, especially in the U.K., where a Dylan LP reached #1 for the fourth time. Come to think of it, the Dylan/Cash story is another book waiting to be written.

The song sequence then veers into a tremendous take on a straight country ditty with Blake and Bob trading some perty (twang the pronunciation of that "r", dude) fancy licks on **Nashville Skyline Rag**. The album seems to really get rolling on the third tune, **To Be Alone With You**, which starts off with Dylan asking his producer, Johnston, "Is it rolling, Bob?" before launching into a whimsical vocal delivery that cannot be characterized as anything less than spot on. Bob is undoubtedly having fun, showing a quite soft and personal side of his human nature that he had hitherto never publicly divulged, perhaps a prelude to his next and tripped-out-in-a-bad-way album, aptly but bewilderingly titled *Self Portrait*.

Next comes the closest thing to a lover's lament on *Nashville Skyline*, **I Threw It All Away**, a single that Bob blatantly marketed by performing it on national television on Johnny's variety show. Rounding out side one is the frolicking **Peggy Day**, featuring some nice pedal steel and Norman Blake fillings, not to mention an Elvis Presley rave-up finale highlighted by Mr. Happy-go-lucky banging out some killer piano major chords with his left hand.

Now a Dylan classic, **Lay Lady Lay** kicks off side two with its lovely percussion, timely pedal steel riffs, and a vocal quality never heard from Bob in 1969 or since. Bob's clothes are dirty, but his hands are clean as he swoons and croons in and out of bed with his lady lover on a song that was briefly number 1 on AM radio in the summer of '69. I cannot ever hear this song without recalling the summer trip that August my family took to Beulah, Michigan and the shores of Crystal Lake. Larry Lujack on Chicago's WLS AM radio dial came in semi-crystal clear 500 miles away up there in the north country. Had it been recorded in a timely fashion, it may have made its way into the soundtrack for *Midnight Cowboy* in 1969, which was the original intention.

Buttrey's bongos on **Lay Lady Lay** are, according to Kenny himself, the best work of his storied career. Interestingly, neither Dylan nor Johnston was able to answer Kenny's question when he asked what kind of drumming was needed for the song. As a result, all Buttrey knew was that he was supposed to play bongos as opposed to a drum kit. Nonetheless, he was able to find the iconic drum groove on **Lay Lady Lay** that we all know and love. Also standing out on bass guitar on Nashville Skyline was Charlie McCoy, who for the fourth Dylan album in a row provided Bob with great country soul in the recording studio. Talk about a low key, under-the-radar music legend. Charlie contributed no less than six different instruments (even vibraphone on *Self Portrait*) on five straight Nashville Dylan albums. Charlie McCoy. His 2009 induction into the Country Music Hall of Fame was well deserved.

One More Night is a throwback to **Don't Think Twice, It's Alright** in that the music is happy-go-lucky, but the lyrics ring out a sad lover's refrain. Where is Bob's dark side? Good lord, he's getting dumped left and right, but he remains blanketed in a cocoon of peaceful gladness. He takes another left jab to the heart in **Tell Me It Isn't True** as he marinates himself in a state void of even a trace rueful remorse.

The just plain silly **Country Pie** follows, an unabashed tribute to country music sustaining the wonderful backwoods ensemble and fun-fun-fun, carefree theme characterizing the entire record. Saving the best for last, as the Beatles had done on *Sgt. Pepper's* with **A Day In The Life**, **Tonight I'll Be Staying Here With You** closes out the album on one last romantic note. This song is perhaps the least elementary composition on *Nashville Skyline*, and Bob's Jerry Lee Lewis piano playing is a delight not to be missed, which emphatically ensures that not a single depressing note can be found on Bob Dylan's last record of the 1960s.

Nashville Skyline stands as a testimony to the deep, humane, universal, and compelling proposition that being happy is a conscious choice. The question posed in **Lay Lady Lay**, "Why wait any longer for the world to begin?" seems to suggest the possibility of creating one's own beautiful inner world while still anticipating the better one out there in the world at large. In the spring of 1969 certainly society offered no tangible hope for anything resembling peace or joy. Nonetheless, Bob was not about to let that stop him as his marital and domestic bliss phase in upper New York state approached its zenith. Amidst all this, he came up with, of all his one-of-a-kind LP "sounds", the one that pretty much takes the cake.

Nashville Skyline reflected Bob's psychic harmony while clashing with the never-ending tumultuous turmoil that surrounded him and all women and all men of all nations at the conclusion of the 1960s. However comma, Bob's little dip into the icy and dicey waters of country music would soon prove to find him lost and searching for a way to manifest his desire to comfort himself with music that seemed to be going backward, not forward, and as if he did not really want anything to do with the 1970s.

Okay, at this juncture a deep breath is well advised, man. Strap yourself in. It's about to get (mind) f-ing weird, to say the least.

#12

Self Portrait/Parody

What follows is going to be painful, but somebody's gotta to do it.

Can you say, "Travesty?" Possibly (on a deep sub-conscious level, who knows?), "Intentional mockery?" If there is such a thing as bad Bob and good Bob, this LP, which came off more like a spoof than what we'd come to expect from a guy who had established a pattern of raising the bar album after album, was our first glimpse of bad Bob, as in naughty boy, cut that out, it's not funny anymore!

"What is this shit?", the infamous, legendary opening query of the Greil Marcus review of *Self Portrait* in Rolling Stone, has long since far outgrown any long term memory of the album itself, which was immediately forgettable from the get go. Released a mere four months before *New Morning* on June 8, 1970, *Self Portrait's* (heretofore to be referred to more befittingly as *Self Parody*) 24 mostly cover versions of well-known pop and rock songs, rowdy *Basement Tapes* leftovers, random Isle of Wight soundboard performances, operatic orchestral pop, a handful of instrumentals, uncharacteristically lousy sound production by Bob Johnston, and its smattering of original compositions suffered from dismal sonics, indifferent performances, overall poor cover choices, and atrocious song sequencing. Forty three years later, proving that the original concept for the album had considerable merit was, albeit with mind-bending irony and confounding tardiness, Columbia's 2013 release of *Bootleg Series #10 Another Self Portrait*, a stunning masterwork which finds Mr. backwoods country gentleman Bob Dylan totally both more relaxed, and more importantly, completely convincing. 43 years late! Once again, go figure!

Wild speculation and great debate over motives have raged about *Self Parody* for over 50 years, not that anyone actually cares enough to have lost any sleep over the matter. Most considered it the end of Dylan's career at the time, much as the 60s had died with the breakup of the Beatles. Dylan himself even omitted **Living The Blues** and **Minstrel Boy** from his 1973 lyric compilation *Writings and Drawings* as if even he acknowledged and refused to further the damage he had done. Twenty years after it came out *Self Parody* managed to still emit a foul enough stench to rank #3 on 1991's *Worst Rock and Roll Records of All Time*. What remains inscrutable to this day is just how, in the wake of a decade of unmitigated brilliance, Bob managed to irritate and/or purposefully attempt to ditch his audience by abandoning the imaginative backing on all his other records in order to accomplish routine quality at times so bad as to resemble the likes of an up-and-coming schoolboy.

Self Parody features a 1 or 2 take strategy that is at best charming and at worst boring. The greatest feather in its cap is its premier status as the first, but certainly not the last, Bob Dylan record that gives rise to cynicism of the bitter variety. It would take another 15 years for *Knocked Out Loaded* to affirmatively conclude the quandary as to whether Dylan could make worse music than what is found on *Self Parody*. Enough king killing…on to the excruciating songs.

An original song, **All The Tired Horses**, rises from an operatic canyon of a girl glee club reiterating a rhetorical question as to how horses tired out by the noon day sun can possibly be ridden? Okay, I guess we are on Bob's Minnesota farm without a care in the world. Is that the deal? Bob seems to be suggesting that the listener slooooowww down, man. Right off the bat, Dylan's intention(s) fail at a depth which was unprecedented at the time, but which would repeatedly be surpassed within minutes and persist in lowering the bar throughout the remainder of a double LP audio marathon of awfulness brought to life.

Next is the traditional **Alberta #1**, commencing with Bob mumbling something indecipherable and ending on a wholly out of tune acoustic guitar strum. Noteworthy is that fact that the album closer **Alberta #2** also falls short of the killer dobro, harmonica, and credibility of **Alberta #3**, which did not surface until Columbia's aforementioned 2013 *Another Self Portrait* bootleg. On to Cecil Null's country classic **I Forgot More Than You'll Ever Know**, on which Bob reverts back to his now familiar country croon on *Nashville Skyline* and sort of inadvertently slips into his best Elvis impersonation.

Days of 49 takes an Alan and John Lomax folk standard and turns it into nothing more than a working demo aching from insufficient effort and what sound like rehearsal collapses over and over. Once again the 2013 release finds Mr. Bob far more relaxed, committed, and, in the end, more convincing. Bob then salutes his Canadian buddy, Gordon Lightfoot, with **Early Morning Rain**, a favor Gordon surely must have sheepishly regretted given the perfunctory treatment brought to this lightweight-to-start-with folkie number.

The traditional **In Search of Little Sadie** finds Bob straining his vocals to reach notes easily within his range and David Bromberg flailing around with his chords and lead fills. The song is repeated at a faster bluegrass rhythm two songs later with more favorable results despite a train wreck ending. Of course, the 2013 re-release is less tentative vocally, and the lead guitar has the aromatic fragrance of Norman Blake, not Bromberg, at his best.

Trudging agonizingly ever onward, we find a too formal rendition the Everly Brothers cover of Gilbert Becaud's **Let It Be Me** that lacks any emotion whatsoever and is smeared with painting-by-numbers execution. The oddest of all ironies on *Self Parody*, which speaks volumes, might well be how Senor spontaneous intuition himself intends to make a casually instinctive album, but due to mistakes already enumerated and too tormenting to reiterate, the affair, on the whole, comes off as a hair too persnickety, and thus, annoying as hell.

Next we encounter an original composition instrumental, **Woogie Boogie**, which is nothing more than a poorly masked version of the theme song for the Batman television show, complete with another disastrous finish line collapse. Nonetheless, Dylan's feel for music is, granted, somewhat apparent on this cut, a characteristic sorely lacking elsewhere on *Self Parody*. Then, a dreadful song sequence, the annoying calling card of *Self Parody*, rears its ugly head with a rendition of the traditional Irish folk ballad **Belle Isle** containing too many overdubs, which were fortunately omitted on the more forthright 2013 re-release bootleg. Whew, how gratifying after four distressing decades in the department of hide, repress, and deny. Can I have an "Amen" for ignoring reality as a life coping strategy? Be honest now.

Living The Blues is a Dylan original that could absolutely have found a proper dwelling place on *Nashville Skyline*. Here we find Bob blatantly slipping into a whimsical Graceland Elvis croon quality that builds into more of the Las Vegas pelvis odor that we all know and love/hate. Give this a ten, but why wasn't it utilized to prolong the fun we had on *Nashville Skyline*? Unfortunately, though, **Living The Blues** is followed by a horrendously embarrassing fake dragging Isle of Wight/the Band take of **Like A Rolling Stone**. Bob's mixing up of lyrics comes off as mere ineptitude, not spontaneous improvisation. Here we find *Self Parody* bottoming out and leaving us with pathetic pity for no less than Bob Dylan for what has become a suicidal bad joke that wore itself out back on the first version of **Alberta**.

Fortunately, if anyone still is clutching to any shreds of credibility, Alfred Frank Beddoe's **Copper Kettle**, a number smack dab in Bob's wheelhouse he first noticed on a 1962 Joan Baez live album, futilely raises the bar by capturing an idyllic backwoods existence equating moonshine with pleasure and tax resistance. Bob's affecting performance and **Copper Kettle's** striking of the right chords momentarily resuscitate a gorgeous, sublime song and a toilet of an album. Again, inexplicably, confusingly, and confoundingly Bob's more effortless and believable vocal on the 2013 re-release bootleg raises the bar even further. The ensuing **Gotta Travel On**, a Paul Clayton cover, comes off as pedestrian and needing just one more all-hands-on-deck take, a refrain we have become all too familiar with at this pathetic point.

A lovely waltz written by Lorenz Hart and Richard Rodgers, **Blue Moon**, is afflicted with the insidious disease known as sounding too much like all the rest of the songs on this album. Pity, because what promise this pearl possesses. Fingernails on the blackboard await the listener on Bob's double track harmony of Paul Simon's **The Boxer**, more pointed parody of Art Garfunkel's partner in crime than artistic salute.

A party-friendly Dylan original popularized by the 1968 Manfred Mann hit of the 1967 *Basement Tape* masterpiece made into an iconic concert favorite by both Phish and the Grateful Dead, **The Mighty Quinn**, is a soundboard recording from the 1969 Isle of Wight musical festival. How's that for date-dropping confusion? More to the point, what is this sort of other galaxy sound quality, worth listening to or not, doing on *Self Parody*? We are then yanked back into a Nashville country ballad written by Boudleaux Bryant, **Take Me As I Am**, which would have also fit well onto *Nashville Skyline* were it not a common-place cover.

Wincing and lurching ever forward, we abruptly and startlingly encounter **Take A Message To Mary**, another Boudleaux Bryant composition which cries out for Bob Johnston to turn down the treble. One gets the distinct impression that, on the entire album of *Self Parody* for that matter, fooling with pan controls to bring the whole mix closer to the middle would have done wonders. The traditional **It Hurts Me Too** ain't too shabby as a result of some fine and dandy doodling contributed by presumably Bromberg that somehow is not ruined by a vocal that is much too rigid and yet another catastrophic ending.

Bob's more-than-decent **Minstrel Boy** contains what is not the most soulful vocal treatment Bob has ever offered us (a shortcoming much improved upon on the 2013 re-release), but the Robbie Robertson-esque electric lead by Bromberg steps to the plate. Next we get another out-of-place Isle of Wight rework of **She Belongs To Me**, reminding us again of the impression that Bob was just mindlessly mudslinging material onto *Self Parody* at this point.

A wonderful cowboy instrumental befitting the soundtrack to *Pat Garret and Billy the Kid*, **Wigwam**, actually glimpses squarely into the clever brilliance that Bob has displayed as a musical interpreter throughout every decade since the 60s. Can you say Montovani strings? The much-preferred version, of course, found its way onto the 2013 re-release. Finally, and I mean thank the Lord finally, **Alberta #2**, as previously mentioned, brings the *Self Parody* train wreck to a monotonous standstill, finally giving us time and room to come up and gasp for air.

Bob Dylan has achieved the unthinkable in too many ways to enumerate such as redefining the role of vocalist in pop music by breaking down the notion that a singer must have a conventionally good voice to perform. The list of credits for which Dylan ought to be hailed is endless. Yet, in 1970, while he remained at the very top of the food chain in terms of universal intrigue, artistic worship, and commercial popularity, his *Self Parody* concept, despite its admittedly potential artistic merit, was justly embraced with widespread critical disdain. I mean, this album sounds like it's coming from an up-and-coming pretty good artistic hack who is, to be brutally honest, going nowhere. Were it created by one of your pals, well, a standing ovation is in order. But, Bob Dylan? I don't think so.

Was Bob sick and tired of being sick and tired of being tagged "spokesman for a generation" and playing a sick joke to get society off his back and out of his private life, which plainly did not exist for him, his wife Sara, or his four young children? Only your hairdresser knows for sure. I'm not going there, dude. A psychoanalyst I am not. A weirdo I am, and for my dear fellow oddballs, I must sometimes cut some proverbial slack and thereby live and let live, if you follow my drift. Yes, I just included Bob Dylan as a fellow oddball. Comin' from me, bro, no better compliment!

The *Self Parody* recording sessions were immediately, simultaneously, and seamlessly blended into what became the *New Morning* recording sessions. Everything sort of turned into a blur. Bob got an honorary degree from Princeton while getting stoned out of his mind with David Crosby, told Columbia to start a rumor he was going back to college, and continued toying with a variety of musicians ranging from George Harrison to Earl Scruggs to Happy Traum to Charlie Daniels to Leon Russell to Alan Ginsburg to Al Kooper to all five members of the Band. Looking back (I know, Bob told us not to do that), it is historically impossible to identify the point at which *Self Parody* left off and *New Morning* began. Having said that, *Self Parody* was simply a brief bump in the road, for Bob was about to return to form with a whimper of a vengeance, but a return to form just the same.

Will you ever come back, my blue-eyed son?

#13

New Morning

Accordingly, *New Morning* was released October 19, 1970. I had, wisely in retrospect, decided to not go out for freshman football at my Catholic high school of 400, so after school let out, my afternoons were often spent meandering around downtown Decatur, Illinois in search for the lost album. Osco Drug, K's Merchandise Mart, Goldblatt's, Sears, and even Woolworth's all had vinyl record collections worth perusing, even though I was almost never buying due to my unemployment and lack of cashola. My bedroom had a cache of sensational 60s albums owned by my older brother, John, who had vacated the scene for college three years before, all of which made me feel connected to hippy baby boomers like my brother born in the late 40s, not the mid-50s like me. Included were *Freewheelin'*, *Bringing It All Back Home*, *Highway 61 Revisited*, and *John Wesley Harding*, more than enough to catch my ear. In addition, I possessed a couple dozen 60s LPs ordered through the Columbia record club, which I had joined with one of my older sisters, Cathy. None of this music made any sense, though.

Then, I scraped up the $3.99 to buy *New Morning*, the first album I had ever purchased in a retail store, and my taste for music instantly coalesced. Suddenly, unbeknownst to any friends or family, I began to memorize lyrics and sing along to Bob Dylan, personifying a guy who could stay in key but really couldn't sing. The first amendment in the Constitution of Bob Dylan grants the vocally challenged human race, not just commercial artists, to heartily belt out their most beloved musical verses without shame, remorse, or hesitation. Memories of singing **Blowin' In The Wind** around campfires at (the Catholic-based) Camp Sheridan at age 9 in East Troy, Wisconsin came flooding back. Thus began my intrigue with my alter ego, Bob Dylan. Innocent enough. Little did I know.

Simultaneously, Bob Dylan (the other Bob) was residing in domestic rapture near Woodstock, New York, regularly called upon by meandering goons, the nomadic homeless, pathetic moochers, psychotic stragglers searching for a party, bums wanting to raid the pantry, and vegetarian hippies seeking advice on organic gardening. Bob had been christened the voice of a generation with which he had little in common and about which he actually knew little. The Beatles had gone to India, Don Juan had become a fictitious messiah, acid had chiseled the right attitude, the press was fanning the flames of hysteria, the Kennedys, Malcolm X, and Dr. King had left their children fatherless, Bob's motorcycle accident had driven him into retreat, the whole country was draped in thick smoke strapping the country down, and all of the sudden, upon returning to Woodstock from his father Abraham's funeral in Minnesota, Bob opened a handwritten letter in which he was invited by poet Archibald MacLeish to write some songs for his theatrical production *Scratch*. Although *Scratch* eventually folded after only two days of performances in 1971, the songs Bob composed for it, which were never utilized, formed the foundation for *New Morning*. Nonetheless, Macleish clearly served in a sort of elder/mentor role by imparting loads of artistic wisdom onto our friend. For example, he pointed out that in the art world, it is not what the art costs that counts, but what it costs the artist. That sentence, when you think about it, could serve as a jumping off point to examine not only all of Dylan's music, but all art. Yet, that's another book, or at least another weekend seminar/retreat.

In 1970, though imprisoned by the occupation of fame about which Tony Curtis had once warned him, Bob may have been surrounded by the chaos permeating society, but he and his music refused to be held prisoner by it. Like *Nashville Skyline*, *New Morning* is actually, according to Dylan standards, a most happy-go-lucky affair. Employing some of his favorite comrades such as Al Kooper and Bob Johnston, and with the help of Charlie Daniels and David Bromberg to name two, Bob created what was then a comeback album, his first but not his greatest. It was his last effort under the management of Albert Grossman, who dissolved their business ties immediately after the release of *New Morning*, and Bob went on in 1971 to replace Big Sky Music with Ram's Horn Music in order to establish complete control over his personal management and music publishing. This was followed by his least active period musically, from mid-1970 to 1973, in his 54 year and counting career.

Hindsight being 20/20, it is certainly plain why Bob Dylan made an album like *New Morning* in 1970 and subsequently produced virtually no commercial music for almost 3 years. We all need a little space between events from time to time. Bob was determined to put himself beyond the whole shebang of free love, the contra communes, government crackdowns, student radicals versus the cops and unions, civil rights and political leaders being gunned down, the mounting of barricades, the streets exploding, the fire of anger boiling, the anti-money system movement, and bald-faced lying by one and all. Hence, upbeat poetry, music, and domesticity were signs marking a road, out of the limelight, Bob was trudging toward a destiny of joy and freedom.

The overall classy musicality on *New Morning*, jazzy, soulful, and light, is most predominantly blessed with the hands-down finest piano accompaniment (some compliments of Al Kooper and some served up by our domestic duke and societal drop out himself) on any Dylan studio album of all time. Having yanked THAT mouthful of or my jaws, as for the songs, the opener **If Not For You** aptly launches things off with a sincere, sentimental love song that made the cut on *All Things Must Pass* for George Harrison and became the title of Olivia Newton John's first album, which went more than gold.

Day Of The Locusts either masks or marks the nightmare of Bob's receipt of an honorary degree at Princeton, where an every-seventeen-year cicada infestation was taking place when he got all stoned up with his obstreperous companion, David Crosby, who convinced Bob (or was it the other way around?) to show up in the first place. This musical treasure is complete with carefree, lighthearted banging on the 88s and

nostalgic visions of locusts lulling Bob into a state of resigned compla-
cency over the completely unthinkable, stiff, and miserably wretched
New Jersey set up, complete with caps, gowns, and false pretenses rul-
ing the day. Reminds me of being in tassel and mortarboard altered
states a couple times myself.

Time Passes Slowly again features some fancy piano slamming by
Mr. Bob on a romp through the valley of good-ole-boy country living.
An imaginary Elvis encounter, **Went To See The Gypsy**, contains a
standout lead guitar by David Bromberg, as well as a rare reference to
Hibbing. Notably, Bob never did meet the King in person, although
he had opportunities and intentionally passed them up, not wanting
to inevitably be let down by what he knew would be an Elvis less
than. **Winterlude** infuses satirical humor into an enchanting winter
night by the fireside. A jazz beat with Al Kooper on outstanding
keyboards and scat singing by Maereth Stewart make **If Dogs Run
Free** pop.

Side two commences with the title track **New Morning** and **Sign On
The Window,** both underscoring the merriment of domestic ecstasy,
somehow not copping out with their acceptance of middle age sensibilities. Even as a 17 year old, I vividly recall listening to this album
with my, trust me, knockout girlfriend, Brenda, and wanting to march
right down to the Macon County, Illinois Building, a mere 6 blocks
from my boyhood home, and ask for a marriage license. On this one,
Dylan makes his committed romance case convincingly.

One More Weekend amps up the vibe with a raucous, carefree 12 bar
blues highlighted once again by the backing provided by Kooper and
Bromberg. **The Man In Me**, which 25 years later was used twice in the
Coen brother film classic, *The Big Lebowski*, shines light on unflinching cues of intimacy between Bob, and presumably his then-adored
and adoring wife, Sara. A gospel-tinged walk through an urban scene,
Three Angels, drops a soft, sweet organ vibe into the depths of the
faceless compassion of man's humanity toward man. This one landed
right smack in my high school wheelhouse, man.

Ending on characteristically classic Bob Dylan piano pounding, **Father of Night** is an interpretation of a Jewish prayer, *Amidah*, initially suggested as a working title by Macleish. This higher conscious ending to *New Morning* is a perfect plot resolution on which to terminate another Dylan musical version of a novel. If and when Dylan ever finally receives a Nobel Prize in Literature, such heralded distinction will be in no small part warranted by albums like *New Morning*, *Blood On The Tracks*, and *John Wesley Harding* that inextricably tie poetry together with music enough to make sense out of a larger narrative and loosely-woven character development(s).

It would turn out to be an interminable 3.5 years before Dylan's next release of new studio material. By the middle of 1970 Dylan seemingly embraced the unchangeable reality that he was not so much personally lost as he was artistically aimless. Perhaps he took the sting of criticism of *Self Parody* too much to heart. Perhaps he did not have anything worthwhile to say or contribute and took the opportunity to reinvent, float, reassess, and reload.

He did manage to release his second greatest hits album (vignette of which forthcoming) in November 1971, a superlative collection that is masterfully sequenced and included wonderful new material such as **Watching The River Flow**, *Freewheelin'* outtake **Tomorrow Is A Long Time**, and **When I Paint My Masterpiece**, not to mention a handful of newer versions of *Basement Tapes* melodies such as **I Shall Be Released** and **You Ain't Goin' Nowhere**. Furthermore, in late 1973 Columbia, not Dylan, finally issued an under-rated cover album entitled *Dylan* (vignette of juicy tidbits also of which forthcoming) that contained some great, some okay, and some not-so-okay versions of **Lily of the West** (okay), **Can't Help Falling In Love** (not so okay), **Sarah Jane** (not so okay), **The Ballad of Ira Hayes** (great), **Mr. Bojangles** (great), **Mary Ann** (not so okay), **Big Yellow Taxi** (not so okay), **A Fool Such As I** (okay), and **Spanish Is The Loving Tongue** (great).

Still, the 3 calendar years of 1971, 1972, and 1973 constitute and remain the most creatively capricious and least prolific period in the life of Senor Bob Dylan ever since he skedaddled out of Hibbing in 1959 and never looked back. The question is begged, naturally, as to what else in God's green earth was Bob up to from '71 to '73. Well, compared to average run-of-the-mill artists, quite a bit, to be sure.

In the summer of '71 he gave an outstanding last-minute supporting performance at George Harrison's Concert For Bangladesh and later helped George edit his blockbuster film. His 52-minute, incomprehensible, mid-60s oddball artsy-fartsy film, *Eat The Document*, premiered in New York to appalling, unmerciful, but wholly merited reviews. He did a stint along with Bromberg as a studio artist for an album by Texan Doug Sahm under the sound production of Jerry Wexler. In late '72 and early '73 he not only acted in but wrote an entire Hollywood film soundtrack, which evolved into a commercially successful album in its own right, for the quite hip spaghetti western *Pat Garret and Billy the Kid*, which included the solo AM radio hit **Knockin' On Heaven's Door**. He bought his Malibu estate and moved his family there. He finally dissolved all business relations with Albert Grossman and briefly signed with David Geffen's Asylum Records when his close associate Clive Davis got fired by Columbia, which had no patience with the lack of quality and quantity of music output Dylan was starting to come up with. He began collaborating with the Band again by recording some new songs that would evolve into his next studio release, *Planet Waves*, which was to be followed by a never-before never-since as anticipated world tour with the Band that opened his first American tour in 8 years at Chicago Stadium, the madhouse on Madison.

All the while, Bob's marriage bliss had moved at this point from New York to Woodstock back to New York to Malibu, and this rocky road was being reflected in a domestic devolvement devoid of hope. Although not officially divorced until 1977, Dylan's songwriting, return to touring, and private shenanigans out of Sara's sight exhibited rumblings of what we now know to be marital mayhem, monumental moodiness on Bob's part, and mutinous misgivings felt by all parties alike.

Never the marrying type in the first place, Bob Dylan is a classic example landing deep in the heart of the bad husband/good father department of matrimony. None of his 5 biological offspring, including his daughter Desiree with Carolyn Dennis (more on that later), have anything bad to say, at least publicly, about their father.

Facing reality eye to eye has never been a hallmark of artists of any milieu, and our friend Bob, ever fond of fantasy whether it be Hollywood, musical mirage, or serial sexual conquest, is certainly no exception. Residing in never-never land, on the other hand, makes for excellent and unending fodder for musical muses, you gotta admit.

#14

Bob Dylan's Greatest Hits Volume 2

A mere four years after *Volume 1,* on November 17, 1971 out came *Bob Dylan's Greatest Hits Volume 2,* over which, this time, Bob possessed sole authority and responsibility. Again we find Bob facing the prospect of no new material on the horizon, but with an unprecedented opportunity to capitalize on all the publicity surrounding the film and album versions of George Harrison's *Concert For Bangladesh,* at which Dylan contributed a last-minute-arrival set hailed as an unadulterated return-to-genius form. This was, of course, in the wake of the *Self Portrait* disaster the year before. Beyond the purview of public eye, of course, we now realize that Bob really never left form in the first place and that he was engaged in a prolific period of songwriting in terms of both quantity and quality. I say this after in 2013 hearing *Another Self Portrait* and its amazing *Nashville Skyline, Self Portrait,* and *New Morning* outtake recordings. Until then, who knew?

Putting out a greatest hits volume two certainly was not a matter of brain surgery, for merely deciding a song list and sequence, given Bob's incredible 1960s back catalogue, was like taking candy from a baby. Yet, one small issue. Columbia higher ups would have none of Bob's inclination to include songs that had been bootlegged on *The Great White Wonder* because the audio attributes from Big Pink in '67 just did not pass their requisite muster for association with the Columbia brand name.

Thus, in September of '71 Happy Traum and Dylan re-recorded **I Shall Be Released, You Ain't Goin' Nowhere,** and **Down In The**

Flood to suit the suits at Columbia. Bob took this opportunity to get in some good-natured digs at Roger McGuinn by pointedly mentioning McGuinn's name in the lyrics of **You Ain't Goin' Nowhere** just at the point where Roger goofed up the original lyrics on the Byrds' cover of this country classic on their 1968 album *Sweetheart of the Rodeo*. Though Bob Dylan can be criticized for taking himself and his music too seriously, especially on records like **Street Legal** and **Saved** and in live performances like at Farm Aid in '85, more often than he is given credit for he is found lightheartedly mucking it up and taking good natured jabs at others and himself.

In addition, the opening track on *Volume 2*, **Watchin' The River Flow**, is a previously unheard composition that Bob reckoned was one of his greatest hits whether you liked it or not. It constitutes a great slide guitar song that does not appear anywhere else in Dylan's discography, with Jim Keltner's first Dylan appearance on drums as well as rollicking piano and superb sound production by Leon Russell. **Watchin' The River Flow** would go on to be covered by a slew of other well-known recording artists and grace many a Dylan live show set list over the ensuing decades. Also recorded March 16 to 19, 1971 in tiny Blue Rock Studios in New York City and added to *Volume 2* was the *Self Parody* outtake and subterranean cult masterpiece in its own right, **When I Pain My Masterpiece**. Lastly, we got treated to a 1963 Town Hall concert jewel, **Tomorrow Is A Long Time**, one of seemingly countless and forgotten '60s Dylan treasures that went practically unnoticed but that would have exemplified career highlights for most any other artist.

The rest of *Volume 2* is just loaded with fine studio album inclusions that are sensationally sequenced. The outcome is stunning. Try this masterpiece some quiet winter evening with all the lights turned off. Holy camoly, it'll blow you out the window. The brilliance. The effortlessness. The sheer talent. The down home fun you will experience. If you don't say it then, I'll say it for you now to save you the trouble. "Thanks, Bob. How can we/I ever thank you enough for the beauty you have wrought forth to make this world a better place."

Rounding out *Volume 2* were the following 16 heretofore unmentioned beauties: **Don't Think Twice, It's Alright, Lay Lady Lay, Stuck Inside Mobile With The Memphis Blues Again, I'll Be Your Baby Tonight, All I Really Want To Do, My Back Pages, Maggie's Farm, Tonight I'll Be Staying Here With You, She Belongs To Me, All Along The Watchtower, The Mighty Quinn (Quinn, The Eskimo), Just Like Tom Thumb's Blues, A Hard Rain's A-Gonna Fall, If Not For You**, and last, but not least, **It's All Over Now, Baby Blue**. Lumped together, these tunes pretty much aptly cover the wide spectrum of hues and hybrids of poetic country, folk, rhythm and blues, gospel, and rock accessible on Dylan's 1960s palette. On the other hand, mind-bogglingly, an entirely different song list is imaginable and could have served just as well.

Would Dylan's career turn into one big retro compilation? One had to wonder during the interminable gap of over three years between *New Morning* and *Planet Waves*. On the other hand, a solid soundtrack and confounding cover LP were about to keep those of us who didn't abandon ship on the edge of our seats.

#15

Pat Garret and Billy the Kid (soundtrack)

From springtime 1970 to September 1973, for around 39 months, Bob Dylan enjoyed a recording sabbatical (well, compared to his track record) as he and Sara adjusted to raising their four youngins in their brand new Pacific coast mansion on the beaches of Malibu. A far cry from the Manhattan house where the Dylans perpetually fell prey to nut jobs such as garbage can diver A.J. Weberman and unethical nosy paparazzi, a gated California estate protected by oceanfront property and 24/7 security guards furnished a secluded setting more conducive to the domestic solitude full-/time fame had long since absconded with. Born again recluse Bob had heeded well the friendly, but stern, warning from Tony Curtis that fame is a full-time occupation. Now, away from the harsh winters and burdensome baggage of New York and Minnesota, life could take on some semblance of normalcy and enjoyment of the perks of financial independence and the call of fatherhood.

One day the proverbial phone rang, and on the other end was a mere previous acquaintance, Rudy Wurlitzer, requesting a couple songs for an upcoming Sam Peckinpah film, *Pat Garret and Billy the Kid*. Ever the venerator of characters outside the law, Bob must have figured a couple of laid back background cowboy melodies sounded like falling off a log. Upon hearing firsthand a moving rendition of **Billy**, Peckinpah himself invited Dylan to act in the film right on the spot. Consequently, the Dylan clan packed up in November '72 and took up residence in Durango, where Bob played the supporting role of Alias to aid and abet Kris Kristofferson and James Coburn in their lead roles depicting a pair of true-to-life historical figures, fun-loving 19th century gunman and notorious killer, Billy the Kid, and Lincoln County sheriff, bartender, and customs agent, Pat Garret.

After shooting his assigned scenes, in January 1973 Bob recorded **Billy 7** at a CBS studio in Mexico City, and the following month in Burbank came up with the trans-Atlantic commercial hit, **Knockin' On Heaven's Door**, along with a handful of **Knockin'** riff spinoffs, which gradually accrued titles such as **Cantina Theme** (distinguished by Russ Kunkel's bongo groove), **Final Theme** (featuring flawless flute from Gary Foster), **Bunkhouse Theme** (piloted by downright gorgeous 12 string guitar by Carole Hunter), and **River Theme** (a country hymn hinged on Bob's happy-go-lucky humming). Rounding out the film score is an incredibly clean bluegrass shuffle, **Turkey Chase** (featuring beautiful banjo by Jolly Roger).

Although what Dylan composed for this spaghetti western, which more than stands the test of time, mostly revolves around **Billy** and **Knockin' On Heaven's Door**, he did manage to fulfill Wurlitzer's original wish for a couple melodies, and from there an entire film score was not far out of reach. Even though the landscape, vistas, and cinematography in the movie did a lot of the talking, with **Knockin' On Heaven's Door** Bob still managed to ingeniously musically merge the good-guy bad-guy plot with what turned out to be the biggest western movie musical hit since Tex Ritter's 1952 version of **High Noon** in the film of the same title. **Knockin'** went on to be covered by gee-tar aces Eric Clapton and Guns N Roses and to grace hundreds of Dylan live concert set lists, much to the pleasure (I'm here to tell ya) of Dylan audiences all over the planet.

Assisting in the recording process were big names Booker T. Jones on bass, Roger McGuinn on electric slide on **Billy 7**, Jim Keltner on drums, and acoustic guitar buddy from way back, Bruce Langhorne. Despite minimal effort on Bob's part, in line with his self-determined hiatus from employment at the time, not only did the whole movie work, but the limited objective(s) of the soundtrack were more than sufficiently met. This, in spite of unreasonable and unreliable press reports describing Dylan's soundtrack as inept and embarrassing like *Self Portrait* and another Dylan effort to deliberately court commercial disaster. Chalk these and countless other mercilessly critical reviews of Bob Dylan up to an unwillingness in fans and the media to allow the man to artistically evolve outside a narrow box that Bob never felt confined by in the first place. The soundtrack for the movie, after all, reached #16 on the U.S. album charts, an almost unheard of achievement for a film soundtrack, especially at the height of the music record industry boom of the 60s and 70s.

On the other hand, to be fair, the film itself, which is peppered with moments of pure cinematographic ecstasy, did not start to garner widespread praise until a 1984 restoration that elicited revisionist views on the matter. Part of the problem lay in the release date of the soundtrack, July 13, 1973, which coincided with that of Paul McCartney's album in support of the blockbuster *Live and Let Die*. Furthermore, the record ultimately got overshadowed by the holy hysteria over Bob's 1974 highly anticipated tour with the Band, the subsequent live album *Before The Flood*, and his next two stellar LP efforts, *Blood On The Tracks* and *Desire*. Regardless, the *Pat Garret and Billy the Kid* soundtrack is a gently refined piece of country devised to underscore a somewhat accurate, endlessly entertaining lightweight historical film produced by a great directorial stylist (Peckinpah).

Primarily instrumental music rough around the edges and beautifully simple, the score at moments reaches downright celestial heights that make the listener feel so small and humble that, if only this could go on all day, eternal beauty itself would surely be manifested in those red rocks of the desert southwest where Sheriff Pat and outlaw Billy once were friends until destiny proved otherwise. Forty years after the fact, a 21st century darkened room DVD viewing of *Pat Garret and Billy the Kid*, a mid-winter's night bowl of hot popcorn, and a warm blanket are the one and only certain recipe liable to drive into mankind's imperfect memory the virtuous treasure piece of Americana that Bob and his buddies created once upon a time.

#16

Dylan

The November 19, 1973 release of *Dylan*, an abbreviated compiling of traditional and contemporary cover songs, was a disingenuous corporate maneuver on the heels of the popularity of *Pat Garret and Billy the Kid* undertaken by the good ole boys at Columbia Records. Unilaterally compiled and issued without input from Dylan, 2 cover outtakes from the *Self Portrait* days and 7 from the *New Morning* sessions were squeezed onto 33 minutes and 22 seconds of vinyl once it became clear to Columbia executives that Bob had moved to Asylum Records (we'll get to that) to make *Planet Waves* before doing a world tour with the Band.

Even though it reached #17 on the U.S. charts, it never charted in the U.K., where it was dubbed *Dylan, A Fool Such As I*, and, at Dylan's insistence once he re-signed with Columbia much after the fact, was later never re-issued to the North American market when CDs became the favored technology of the day. In 2013 it was, however, eventually included in *The Complete Album Collection Volume 1* box set, a Dylan release that is deliberately omitted from this here book merely to avoid redundancy. Although just a couple hundred dollars or so, it contains 47 discs with 35 studio albums, 6 live albums, and a hodgepodge on 2 discs called *Side Tracks* – all of which is addressed in this here book. Once is enough.

Dylan was a puzzling anomaly that on the surface reeked of the stench of *Self Portrait* and begged the glaring question of motives on Columbia's part. The two most plausible objectives were to reap revenge, or more pointedly, sabotage Dylan in any way they could for being dumped for Asylum, not to mention cashing in along the way, of which only the latter succeeded. For despite Columbia's blatantly poor song selection, ignoring of far-superior outtakes on *Self Portrait* and *New Morning*, and appalling sound mixing, the album ranks as the best of all the bad Dylan LP offerings. Bob Dylan was, has been, is now, and will certainly always remain the ultimate Teflon musical artist, practically impossible to subvert, whether it be the dust of rumors like plagiarism charges, catastrophic forays into film-making such as *Eat The Document* and *Renaldo and Clara*, or merely horrible excuses for commercial music like *Knocked Out Loaded* in 1986. Just keep in mind one of the elucidating themes running through the course of Dylan's career, that the worst ice cream and pizza on earth are pretty good.

Lily Of The West, a traditional Irish melody, kicks things off with a classic boy kills lover's rival whom girlfriend prefers plot. This, musically, is a great take, though muddy recording, of a murder ballad with a cowboy western soundtrack feel. For starters, the bass track ought to be turned down slightly more than slightly, but this throwaway does not critically deserve any more sweat off the ole brow. Despite being a mere fun, capricious rendition of a whimsical melody, **Lily Of The West** was probably a good choice for the opening track.

The album was worth the money if only for the second song, a formerly rather obscure gem raised from the grave by Elvis in *Blue Hawaii* in 1961, **Can't Help Falling In Love**, with lyrics by George Weiss, Hugo Peretti, and Luigi Creatore put to a 1784 tune composed by Plaisir d'Amour. Why this was not on *Self Portrait* is anybody's guess, but Bob's committed, laid back vocal is just what the doctor ordered on a masterpiece melody so sublime as to be indestructible.

Rolling on, we find **Sarah Jane**, a traditional number that Flatts and Scruggs and the Kingston Trio covered. It finds Dylan singing his fun-loving heart out in a delirious state of marital bliss. Even obnoxiously loud backing vocals and foggy instrumentation cannot hold back the charming, unadorned tom-foolery in which the goofball in Dylan is fully engaged.

Peter LaFarge's **The Ballad of Ira Hayes** comes off as a badly mixed aimless warm up take narrating the tragic fate of an alcoholic Pima Indian World War II marine who in 1955 left this world for a better place. It illustrates as good an example as any of Bob Dylan's true patriotism. Musically, it is essentially a talking folk song that conjures up images of **Three Angels** on *New Morning*. Bob, again, seems to be having so much fun singing this thing that it somehow and paradoxically works well in a completely bad way.

Side two commences with Dylan tipping his hat to Jerry Jeff Walker with another terrific vocal on **Mr. Bojangles**, representing some of the best of Dylan's '69-'71 country crooning. A quite cool organ riff which is too functional and straightforward could have used some more improvisation by a guy like Al Kooper. Backing vocals too high in the mix, the calling card of *Dylan*, once again cannot kill the captivating kookiness being conjured up at the core.

Mary Ann, first published in 1710, is an arcane traditional song that is treated to a killer take and the all-too-familiar bland mixing and loud backing vocals that we have now come to know and tolerate. Leave it to Bob Dylan to record a song that sounds so dead but still totally works.

A trite Joni Mitchell hit, **Big Yellow Taxi**, is deservedly treated as a throwaway, complete with a most fitting crash ending that is unnoticeable because the song has long since become unlistenable. Yet, a steady musical groove which honestly cannot be denied is actually occurring and Mitchell's acid humor about the risks of so-called urban progress rings true.

Bob's *Nashville Skyline* ensemble is at its very best on **A Fool Such As I**, a Bill Trader composition that gets a funky gospel-edge groove and a lead vocal rather low in the mix. Although *Dylan* tanked in Europe even more than in the states, **A Fool Such As I** ironically did well commercially as a single in the U.K. Who would have thunk?

Dylan's versatility as a singer shines on the finale, **Spanish Is The Loving Tongue**, which is based on a poem entitled "A Border Affair" by Charles Badger Clark in 1907 and was put to music by Billy Simon in 1930. Here we find Bob turning a deliberate dirge into a romping waltz in the third verse and delicately delivering disarming sweetness in the way that only Bob Dylan can.

Dylan is an album that is so bad in a wonderful way that it undoubtedly merits a casual monitoring every ten or twenty years at the very least. At most it comprises an embarrassment to the universe which, much to the chagrin of those at corporate Columbia who slimily set out to do so, utterly failed to slay the dragon of Bob Dylan's captivating hold on the imagination of the human race.

How can a musician be soooooo bad that he charms us to death and comes off, to varying degrees, as a cool, clever, creative, comforting, credible, captivating crooner? Go figure does not begin to answer this enigmatic dilemma. There's gotta be more to it.

Sacred clown!

#17

Planet Waves

Historical context is essential to grasp *Planet Waves*. Hence, please strap yourself in for the next three pages or so and indulge the following necessary (albeit incomplete and highlighted) contextual setting of the stage, as it were.

When *Planet Waves* was released on January 17, 1974, it constituted Bob's first proper album in 3.5 years, even though Columbia had released the album of cover songs, *Dylan*, and the film score from *Pat Garret and Billy the Kid*, which were at least shreds of publicly known evidence that Bob was still stirring somewhere in the background despite his self-imposed ban on live touring ever since his 1966 motorcycle accident. As a result, in the eyes of the world at large, the shroud of secrecy surrounding Dylan's whereabouts and activities once again spread like wildfire around the time that *Planet Waves* came out.

Even at the time of *Planet Waves*, it must be remembered that the Band, the backup musicians on the record, had collaborated with Bob on prolific levels during Bob's so-called public disappearance in what came to be known as *The Basement Tapes*, but none of the fruits of these endeavors had yet been commercially shared. In the meantime, the Band had in its own right rightly been crowned rock royalty based on their debut record *Music From Big Pink*, their live performance reputation, and their distinctive mixture of musical roots. Rumors of what Dylan and the Band had done on tour in 1966 and in Woodstock in 1967 in the basement of Big Pink exponentially fueled the public's appetite for hearing Bob playing with them live. Of course, eventually, *Before The Flood*, a double live album of the post-*Planet Waves* world tour, *The Basement Tapes*, and even a 1998 official bootleg compilation from the '66 world tour would eventually find their ways into record stores.

However, in January 1974, folks could not wait for *Planet Waves* to come out (understatement personified), and the subsequent tour had zero problem whatsoever completely and immediately selling out huge stadiums like Boston Garden and Chicago Stadium. In fact, the tour grossed over $92 million in checks and money orders, a world record at the time, more than making up for initial lagging record sales of *Planet Waves*, which nonetheless merited a quite positive, albeit muted, critical reception.

In September of '73 Robbie Robertson moved to the Malibu area, in the vicinity of the coastal estate Bob had purchased, and after Robbie and Bob had done some preliminary jamming on some of Bob's new songs deemed to be promising, Garth, Richard, Rick, and Levon one by one made their way to southern California in the fall of '73 to fill out the sound of what was starting to look like a new Dylan album. Just prior to their arrival, Bob escaped to his apartment in New York City for roughly 3 weeks, where he penned six additional songs that ended up on *Planet Waves*, his one and only non-Columbia (Asylum) release ever (well, two counting *Before The Flood*). When the boys were exposed to what Bob had written, the groove they discovered that eventually sculpted *Planet Waves* gave voice to their palpably sensual intuition that they could shadow Dylan in their sleep. The record is just more living proof of the magic between Bob Dylan and the Band, an artistic conspiracy essentially constituting a musical genre all its own.

On the business end of things, we find the actual commercial dollar profit impetus for *Planet Waves*, for much was transpiring during Dylan's disappearing and doing-a-movie stage. Chronologically, it all sort of started with an ending, that being Bob's contractual obligations to his manager from 1962 to 1971, Albert Grossman. Somewhere along the line, exactly when will probably never be known, it dawned on Bob that Albert had rights to 50% of his song publishing rights. Since Dylan's legend and popularity was so widespread, mostly due to what can be called his back catalogue (roughly albums 2 through 7 from '63 to '66), Bob was losing what amounted to millions of dollars to Grossman just as the result of sales of Dylan songbooks to parents of little kids learning to play guitar alone. Can you say fed up with being fed up? Thus, after Bob was finally able to formally ditch Grossman in July 1970 (the feeling was essentially mutual), he was on his own in dealing with the sharks at Columbia.

He immediately came out with *Self Portrait* and *New Morning*, and legal connections to Columbia concluded, at least temporarily, after Dylan's 1971 *Greatest Hits Volume 2*. Bob did appear at the *Concert For Bangladesh* amidst great fanfare and publicity, which kept him in good favor with his legendary status and the public, but then he retreated more than ever, and right around the time he got involved with *Pat Garret and Billy the Kid*, Columbia fired Clive Davis, about the only guy at Columbia whom Dylan trusted, so Dylan wisely made Columbia purchase rights to produce and sell the soundtrack. Meanwhile, for years Bob had been feeling that Columbia was just going through the motions of putting out his records and that the corporate monster itself cared little for his art or him personally. All the while, business novice Bob was beginning to get it into his skull that, for countless reasons too obvious to enumerate, his name would add unspeakable luster and prestige to any record label under the sun.

Alas, we find David Geffen (hotshot Hollywood record producer) entering the scene, promising Bob double the volume of record sales Columbia had achieved, plus his own record label on which Dylan could sign other artists in addition to himself. In the meantime, Dylan was being courted by Warner Brothers/MGM and Atlantic Records legend Jerry Wexler, but the deal killer for them was Columbia's authority to still release Bob's official bootlegs from 1961-66. Nonetheless, Gefen's astonishing pitch won out in the end, which began to make more sense to Bob because Gefen was on line to mastermind the long-awaited live tour which Dylan had deprived the planet for eight years.

In short, Gefen brainwashed Bob, or whatever, that a tour demanded an album of new material in stores, and another live album would be required after the tour for reasons of popular demand and financial profit. Such elaborate scheming necessitated tight time lines that boxed Dylan and the Band into impossibly short recording scheduling. Into Village Recording in Hollywood the boys went on November 5, 1973, and considering Bob still was writing material and after three days of hastened proceedings, what came out on *Planet Waves* is truly no less than miraculous.

Businesswise, as an aside, Asylum was a short-lived two-and-out record deal for Dylan, in spite of Geffen's grandiose long-term fantasies. This was partly due to Dylan being more than irked by public claims by Geffen that he successfully swayed Dylan's choice to dump Columbia and go to Asylum, a feat that countless had failed to achieve, through no lack of trying, ever since Dylan teamed up with John Hammond back in '61. In short, the truth is that Dylan was quite pissed at Columbia long before he ever talked with Geffen, and nobody was about to share Bob's dirty laundry in public, let alone legally pull the wool over his eyes and control his puppet strings.

As for what ever happened with and to Albert Grossman, in 1979 Dylan ceased paying him for all the back catalogue publishing and record sales, so in 1981 Grossman responded by suing Dylan and claiming he had received less than his share of contractual entitlements to back catalogue royalties. Resolution did not come until 1987, a year after Grossman died, when Dylan agreed to pay $2 million to Albert's estate, a stinging blow indeed, for 1987 cannot be described as a high point in Bob Dylan's life on any level. Just another sad, cut-throat episode in rock and roll history.

La-de-da, back to *Planet Waves*, the album in question. This batch of songs is twisted, spare, and raunchy. With 20/20 hindsight, it is now evident that at this time in Bob's personal life he was only starting to discern a dilemma that was both practical and aesthetical.

The immense emotional debt he owed to his wife, Sara, was beginning to conflict with his rock star ego, for lack of a better word. How on

God's green earth could Bob answer the call of his inner artistic muse, which he had largely muzzled while fathering four children in upstate New York in the late 60s and early 70s, and at the same time not abandon his need to repay his wife for giving him the family he had always yearned for. Certainly Bob was in a having-his-cake and wanting-to eat-it-too predicament. Only a year after *Planet Waves*, on *Blood On The Tracks* the marriage had apparently gone south, but on *Planet Waves*, one gets the feeling that Bob is hanging onto his marriage for dear life. His mixing of marital bliss with resigned hopelessness is, in retrospect, raw, innocent, pathetic, and distressing, for starters.

On A Night Like This is the initial instance of the sundry of domestic themes running through the album, and Garth Hudson's whimsical accordion underscores Bob's utter glee over what he and Sara had accomplished. Instantly, however, in **Going, Going, Gone**, which, by the way, is a wonder of ensemble playing, Robbie's choked guitar entrance signals an unrepressed suicidal subterfuge defined by suspicion and self-hate. All the while, the outright beauty of the music masks the reality of Dylan's perplexing quandary. **Going, Going, Gone** just might be the first hint Bob revealed of a tumultuously dark chasm in his life that arguably persisted for over twenty years.

The best jamming on the record follows on **Tough Mama**, on which raunchy vocals plead for mercy as Bob has found bread crumbs of recognition but has lost his appetite, or shall we say, patience, with the whole marriage thing. A clue that Bob is or has been venturing out of his marital bond to medicate his neediness is provided in **Hazel**, lulling the listener with a concluding angelic harmonica covering up the mess Bob has found himself in. **Something There Is About You** places Sara back on her pedestal, where Bob can comfortably wallow in his newly-discovered self-inflicted lower-than-whale-shit self esteem.

The slow version of **Forever Young** concludes side one, a recording that did not come easy for the boys, which frustrated Bob because after this song had been in his head for years and years, he could not confidently choose how he wanted to record it. Was it a waltz or a straightforward folk rock ballad? He changed his mind on this matter multiple times, and eventually decided to put two versions of the same song on the same album, another instance of the I-can-do-whatever-I-want spirit of Mr. Zimmy. It worked.

Side two commences with the fast version of the aforementioned tune, which had its genesis as a musical ode to Bob's children and ended up alluding to virtually any human relationship whatsoever. Suffice it to say, this song became the one most associated with *Planet Waves*. A seeming waltz wanna be, yet in 4/4 time, **Forever Young** injected a musical mystery into the recording studio, but at the same time stands as a heartfelt hymnal uttered by the father archetype in Dylan, as well as a classic example of a song that has long stood and will always stand the test of time. Live renditions spanning the last 40 years bear this out.

Dirge constitutes Bob's most twisted song since the motorcycle accident as he commences to comfort himself with his own brand of elementary piano banging in order to assuage the dirty rotten shame of loneliness, suicidal thoughts, hopelessness, his lack of gratitude and forgiveness, and endless remorse. Robbie's tasteful 12 string guitar lead punches accentuate the hollow place where martyrs weep and angels play with sins. Bob Dylan is getting tired of the mere moment of glory that fatherhood delivers, a haunted man too discouraged to stand up and take action.

You Angel You sneaks in a romantic romp of an interlude, a hangover of the good ole days with Sara and the kids when he gladly allowed her to take him under her wing, or more aptly, place him in her back pocket. **Never Say Goodbye** leaves claw marks on Bob's domestic dream, which Bob stubbornly refuses to let go of, a gut-wrenching don't blink-or-you'll-miss-it ditty set on a frigid lake where Bob's dreams of iron and steel go unrealized on a beach being pummeled by crashing waves where he drowns while waiting for Sara to fill his void within.

The album screeches to a halt with **Wedding Song,** on which the Band is not utilized in Bob's only solo effort on the record. Autobiographical to be sure, despite some claims to the contrary, this uncharacteristically forced narrative sketches a glimpse of the ornate fantasy Bob had designed inside the inner landscape of his mind in order to do what needed to be done in his private life from 1966 to 1974.

Once the world tour with the Band launched in Chicago on the heels of *Planet Waves*, the beginning of the end of the Sara and Bob act was like the wave crashing on that forlorn beach in **Wedding Song** where Bob's impatient, self-absorbed, restless, irritable, and discontent nature lay waiting to hijack his sub-conscious professional karma and personal dreams which he had ignored, repressed, hidden, and denied ever since the motorcycle crash.

Whoever Bob Dylan had become as a husband, father, and former 20th century avant-garde messiah, it wasn't working for him, and countless self reinventions over the next twenty plus years wouldn't serve much better. As far as the rest of the world, they all just, individually and collectively, wanted Dylan to be whoever they fantasized him to be. Not likely, of course, but that train'll be riding the rails long after Bob Dylan is released from earthly bondage.

#18

Before The Flood

The first live album in Bob Dylan history, but certainly not the last, *Before The Flood*, came out on June 20, 1974 on Asylum Records. Dylan's world tour with the Band had just broken all box office records in the wake of *Planet Waves*, which was all but ignored in live shows and was entirely ignored on *Before The Flood*. Instead, we were treated to what amounts to a worthy but, in the end, unessential item in Dylan's discography. Six of the 21 tracks are works written and performed exclusively by the incomparable Canadian quartet and a hillbilly, with the remaining majority of the double vinyl platinum powder keg consisting of mostly Dylan war horses. *Before The Flood* concludes the four distinct, virtually unrelated musical styles which the Band and Dylan concocted between 1966 and 1974 (the first three being the '66 world tour, *The (Complete) Basement Tapes*, and *Planet Waves*).

All analogous live albums up to that point in time fell flat in comparison. In 1974 *Before The Flood* was some of the craziest and strongest rock and roll that had ever been recorded. Highlights include **It's Alright Ma, I'm Only Bleeding** on which Dylan personally invests a stake in the deal, **Like A Rolling Stone** as a two-step treat vocally echoing 1974's **Billion Dollar Baby** by Alice Cooper, a more-than-decent **Blowin' In The Wind** somehow spliced together from two different cities, and an especially inspired, energetic **All Along The Watchtower**. Epochal rock at its limits for its time, *Before The Flood* finds Dylan singing with what seemed like malevolent energy the winter of 1974, aggressively upping the tempo while simultaneously borrowing voltage from the Band, who never abandon their enormous technical ability. The boys sound undisciplined, threatening to destroy their reckless momentum at any moment in the proceedings, but never managing to quite pull that off. It is called talent wrapped in mayhem.

The test of time, on the other hand, has not been so gracious to *Before The Flood*. **Knockin' On Heaven's Door** reeks of artificiality, **It Ain't Me Babe** suffers from an annoying unk-cha syncopation, **Ballad Of A Thin Man** might be spooky but is dispirited, **Lay Lady Lay**'s attractive chord changes sound jarring, and **Rainy Day Woman #12 and 35** is not dull – it lacks any cutting edge whatsoever.

Recording and mixing engineer Rob Fraboni did a good enough job to be called back on *The Basement Tapes* in '75, by which point Dylan had already returned to Columbia at the behest of its returning president, Goddard Lieberson, who waged a determined campaign to get Bob back. The whole point of the Dylan/Band world tour in the first place centered around the concept of nostalgia, yet this very characteristic is fought every step of the way on *Before The Flood*, which is, more than anything else, memorable for its stormy re-workings, reinventions, revivals, rearrangements, and reinterpretations.

Reefer, a given in the 70s, was reportedly, and rightfully, in the mix. No revelation there.

#19

Blood On The Tracks

An overriding irony running throughout a book about 61 records is that sometimes words just get in the way. Obviously, these records must be heard without any mind clutter. In even uttering in print a single word about *Blood On The Tracks*, I almost feel the need to apologize. The English language might only serve to betray the artistic ingenuity of what I venture to say is Dylan's greatest novel put to music. What more can, or needs to be said?

I will start with this. Dylan changed the industry and direction of music with six albums in three years from 1963-66, culminating with *Blonde On Blonde*. Then, in the wake of 8.5 years (1966 to 1975) and merely four albums of truly new material, *Blood On The Tracks*, laced with universal heartfelt grief over the on-going collapse of Bob's marriage to Sara, despite his consistent denials of this certainly unquestionable fact, absolutely embodied the comeback album that was hoped to loom within the vaults of Columbia's accumulation of Dylan's domestic-period material.

After the '74 tour with the Band, Bob began pursuing art classes in New York with 73 year-old Ukrainian American Jew Norman Raeben, who Dylan later credited with having restored his songwriting ability. Whatever happened in Raeben's studio on the 11th floor of Carnegie Hall from May to July 1974, it profoundly influenced Dylan to the point that Sara no longer even understood where he was coming from.

After Raeben died in 1978 Dylan implied that this was even a factor in the collapse of his undeniably fulfilling, but doomed, marriage.

Be that as it may, or not, *Blood On The Tracks* happened to be Bob's first album after becoming a pupil of Raeben's artistic emphasis on feel and intuition and rejection of conceptualization. Begun in New York at A and R Studios (formerly studio A at Columbia where Bob laid down the bulk of his 60s masterpieces) and re-done in Minneapolis as little as 3.5 weeks prior to its release, with the help of Bob's brother David, who miraculously assembled what turned out to be an magical ensemble of unknown studio musicians, *Blood On The Tracks* quickly became the sort of college dorm student staple that Bob's pre-motorcycle accident releases had been.

3 of the *Blood On The Tracks* Minnesota backup musicians with Bob, late December 1974. Photo by author of a photo by an unknown photographer.

Credit Minnesotans Bill Peterson on bass, Bill Berg on drums, Kevin Odegard and Chris Webber on guitar, and Greg Inhofer on keyboards for capturing magic in a bottle in only two days and 14 takes in Sound

80 Studio in Minneapolis December 27 and 28, 1974. Had Dylan not secretly run off and re-recorded five of the ten songs at the eleventh hour, these cats would have been correctly credited on the liner notes. They took what now seem like mediocre recordings in New York and turned them into Minnesota gems on **Tangled Up In Blue, You're A Big Girl Now, Idiot Wind, Lily, Rosemary, and the Jack of Hearts**, and **If You See Her, Say Hello**. Likewise, back in New York, kudos to Tony Brown of Deliverance, who was just what the doctor ordered and particularly stands out for his lone bass accompaniment on **Simple Twist Of Fate, You're Gonna Make Me Lonesome When You Go, Shelter From The Storm**, and **Buckets Of Rain**.

Whether the rambling narrative of **Tangled Up In Blue**, the haphazard encounters in **Simple Twist Of Fate**, the angst of pining to the goddess in **You're A Big Girl Now**, the venomous cursing of his muse in **Idiot Wind**, or the sweet, tender sentimentality of **You're Gonna Make Me Lonesome When You Go**, the entirety of side one is one of those grab-you-by-the-throat, wee-hour plots taking the listener into the chasms of dark, shadowy, sub-conscious delights of lyrics such as, but not limited to, "I kissed good-bye the howling beast on the borderline that separated you from me." Both dumpers and dumpees (great non-word) can relate to this imagery, don't you reckon?

We hadn't heard Dylan be this compelling since *Blonde On Blonde*. Nevertheless, side one pretty much leaves us with our jaws dropping, inside a novel thick in the middle of a plot that screams for patience to change that ole vinyl to side two to discover just where else this tale is headed.

The bluesy 12 bar **Meet Me In The Morning** gives us a hunch, but no clue. It was the only song on *Blood On The Tracks* actually recorded by liner note creditees (wow, another non-word) Eric Weissberg and Deliverance. Buddy Cage somehow makes an overdubbed fuzzy steel guitar sound exactly like a saxophone, and outstanding drum kit support is provided by Richard Crook, who also did not get liner note credit.

Lily, Rosemary, and the Jack of Hearts ups the tempo, immediately lightening the air as Big Jim, the girls playing five card stud, and the rest prove to be no match for that red heart relentlessly trumping every trick in the trade offered up by an entirely luckless cast. The pensive, sole-surviving Lily transitions her thoughts into the sublime **If You See Her Say Hello**, sure to jerk tears out of even the coldest heart of stone this side of the wide Missouri. Will I ever forget my sad sack December 1976 train ride from Rome to Tangiers, Morocco after leaving an Italian lover behind, serenading my grief with this song's opening line?

Shelter From The Storm detours from the skeptical if not cynical to the romantic pedestalizing (relax dude, that's an operative non-non-word) of that moving-target muse initiated on side one. **Buckets of Rain** leaves our lover on the doorstep of neurotic, needy nostalgia and our listener locked and loaded to flip to side one again, muttering, "Whaaaat?"

Surprisingly, only **Tangled Up In Blue** and **Simple Twist Of Fate** have ever become staples in live performance set lists over the years. This is yet again a testimony to the shear seemingly endless quantity of outstanding songs in the vault of Bob Dylan. Man, I actually know a heavy metal drummer whose favorite all-time Dylan song is **You're A Big Girl Now**, another Dylan song that has rarely been played live. Granted, **Idiot Wind** was given one of Dylan's most tremendous vocals ever in the Rolling Thunder Revue days, notably in the Fort Collins effort that NBC recorded for its 1976 Bob Dylan special, now a sought-after classic bootleg video replete with now comical commercials for 1970s audio equipment.

On the other hand, why in the scheme of things **Lily, Rosemary, and the Jack of Hearts** has never been rendered live audience treatment will likely remain a Dylan mystery that will go to his grave. Perhaps the overplaying of **Tangled Up In Blue** on the never-ending tour only furthers these *Blood On The Track* and other Dylan album riddles keeping Bob freaks spinning in their sleep dreams about why this, why that about everything from song arrangements, in-studio production levels, timings of album releases, and you name it. I resemble that comment!

Sound engineer Phil Ramone, as well as all the boys involved in Minnesota, regard *Blood On The Tracks* as essentially a broken-hearted man revealing his soul on tape. After an initial lukewarm response from the public, once it started selling like hotcakes, Dylan himself wondered how in the heck people could enjoy such pain. As though his hand is being caught in the proverbial cookie jar, Bob's consistent denial that *Blood On The Tracks* is autobiographical might be his most dubious bald-faced lie of all time.

After the magnitude of that last sentence, I'm not sure I can go on. Nonetheless, somebody's got to do it.

Speaking from firsthand experience, suffice it to say that *Blood On The Tracks* legitimized Bob in the marijuana minds of late baby boomers slightly too young to catch Bob in real time in his heyday of the 60s. Surely various and countless more commercially successful 1970s acts sold more records than Bob on the coattails of the massive music recording industry launched by the Beatles. However, this was true in the 1960s as well. *Blood On The Tracks*, on the other hand, reminded 60s hippies and clued in their 70s counterparts why Bob Dylan was not to be underestimated. Record sales, amazingly enough, have never been the measure of Dylan's cultural impact, importance, or incomparable influence. Still, *Blood On The Tracks* eventually went double platinum, becoming his best selling studio album, not counting *Greatest Hits Volume 1*, which has now gone quintuple platinum (i.e. over 5 million sold).

Blood On The Tracks was more of a musician's record, as well as an intellectual's, solidifying Dylan as a towering Americana literary figure showing up in poetry books on college campuses far and wide. I recall taking a 300 level poetry class at Loyola University of Chicago in the spring of 1976. **The Times They Are A-Changin'** and **Blowin In The Wind** were in the anthology that served as one of our texts. I recall many a Saturday night buying 69 cent quarts of Meister Brau at Bruno's Liquors across the street from the dormitory where I lived, reading poetry, smoking skinnies, listening to *Blood On The Tracks* and *Desire*, and marveling at what an intellectual I had turned into. Ahhhh, the 70s seem like yesterday, and I don't even remember them.

One word that comes to mind is clever. *Blood On The Tracks* is nothing if not shrewd. Without much fanfare or any big sticks or electric guitars or anything, Dylan took whatever lyrical and musical greatness he could possibly muster in himself and somehow refuted critics who insisted his days as a spokesman were long gone. It is, if you will, Bob's album of the 70s, which is saying a lot, given the material that preceded and followed it.

One dice had come up comeback, the other understated masterpiece. The public knew it. Bob Dylan knew it.

#20

Desire

Bob was now a father of five (one stepchild and four biological), and trouble was brewing on the home front, as had been made plain and clear on *Planets Waves* songs such as **Tough Mama**, **Going, Going, Gone**, and **Never Say Goodbye** as well as *Blood On The Tracks* tracks like **Idiot Wind**, **Buckets Of Rain**, **You're Gonna Make Me Lonesome When You Go**, and **If You See Her, Say Hello**.

On the heels of *Blood On The Tracks*, Bob had quite a year of music making leading up to the January 5, 1976 release of *Desire*. Much of the year was spent formulating the Rolling Thunder Revue, and the rest consisted of an amazing, rollicking, meant-to-be, rare, synchronistic, and short-lived collaboration with Jacques Levy writing the songs for *Desire*. The two just clicked for a time, and that was it.

Bob had only met Levy (sometime in '74) one year before they reunited at The Bitter End, a Greenwich Village nightclub where much of the Rolling Thunder concept came to life somewhere around July 1975. It was also at this time that Bob began working with Levy, who was a relative unknown except for his co-authorship of **Chestnut Mare** with Roger McGuinn, which was one of the last of the Byrds' hits. Levy and Dylan holed up together in the Hamptons in the dog days of summer of '75 and wrote all of the songs for *Desire* in approximately four weeks.

Desire was essentially sandwiched in between the first tour of the Rolling Thunder Revue in the fall of '75 and the second tour in '76. The recording sessions were legendarily chaotic as a result of the inexperience of Columbia's producer Don Devito and a parade of musicians that kept streaming in and out, numbering as many as 21 at one point. Bob eventually settled on a heedless crew that established the backbone of the Rolling Thunder Revue, including Rob Stoner on bass, Howard Wyeth on drums, and an absolute nobody on fiddle, Scarlet Rivera. Even though this carefree mass ensemble approach to recording *Desire* ended up working out quite well when all was said and done, Bob clung to this freewheeling approach with disastrous results on his 1980s LPs *Empire Burlesque, Knocked Out Loaded*, and *Down In The Groove*, all of which lacked the coherent artistic vision Levy and Dylan cooked up on *Desire*.

Fascinatingly, Scarlet was spotted by Bob while walking down a New York sidewalk carrying her violin case, and Bob had his limo driver stop so that he could talk to her, simply because she looked intriguing. Lo and behold, when she accepted Bob's invitation to stop by Columbia to informally audition, she could actually play her instrument to Bob's satisfaction, and the rest is history.

Scarlet's version reveals that she received Bob's approval to collaborate with him in the form of a wry smile after several minutes of her demonstrating her trademark gypsy fiddle act. She also insists that while on tour with the nutty Rolling Thunder Revue in the wake of the *Desire* sessions, her sweet, unpretentious innocence was closely guarded and respected by not only Dylan but his free-spirited fellow troubadours, which is a rare and charming anecdote relative to what else purportedly went on during that particular and particularly zany tour.

Rounding out the supporting cast on *Desire* was Emmylou Harris, whose solo career at the time was taking off due to the fact that she could flat out out-sing anybody in Nashville. Nevertheless, she did make the time to help out Bob in the little time that she had to offer the project.

Scarlet's fiddle is the first sound audible on track one, **Hurricane**. Narrating the framing of Rubin Carter, a well-known professional middleweight boxer, on a murder charge back in 1964, Bob brought Carter's plight to public consciousness in a big way. Not only did this song open *Desire*, but Bob performed two benefit concerts during the Rolling Thunder days on behalf of Carter, one at Madison Square Garden and the other at the Houston Astrodome. Furthermore, on December 5, 1975 Bob performed right at Clinton State Prison, the minimum security jail where Carter was sitting like Buddha in a ten foot cell. Carter had sent Bob *The Sixteenth Round*, his autobiography, written in confinement, in hopes that Dylan's 1960's civil rights background might lead to the much-needed attention Carter was seeking in order to get himself exonerated. Eventually, in 1985 the murder charge on Carter was dropped, he became a free man who tirelessly advocated for the wrongly imprisoned, and *The Sixteenth Round* was heavily utilized in the screenwriting for Norman Jewison's 1999 film starring Denzel Washington, *Hurricane*. So, really a win-win for all involved in the long run.

Rubin Hurricane Carter at Bunker Hill Community College in
Boston on March 24, 2011. Photo by Michael Borkson.

Next came **Isis**, a rambling symbolic travelogue of sorts about a man who sets out to search for treasure after getting married to a woman whose loyalty he takes for granted. A circular, hypnotic, alluring three chords and a cloud of dust arrangement finds Bob pounding the 88s surrounded by quite effective free-spirited fiddle fills by Rivera. **Mozambique** finds Ronnee Blakley backing Bob's vocals with exotic shadowing of each word as Rivera's violin dances around the melody like a flickering flame inj a gentle breeze. Levy and Bob playfully came up with the idea for **Mozambique** by staging a contest to see how many rhymes they could come up with for "ique", a poetic ploy which, from me, gets a thumbs up critique.

One More Cup Of Coffee tells the tale of a gypsy family cursed with abandonment, featuring a middle eastern flavor as well as fiddle to boot, all of which dovetails with the world music vibration introduced by the Caribbean mojo of **Mozambique**. A delightfully hypnotic melody, **One More Cup Of Coffee** has been covered by first rate artists such as Robert Plant and the White Strips, not to mention the version by Sertab Erener that became a sort of thematic soundtrack for Bob's bizarre and wholly underestimated 2003 film, *Masked and Anonymous*.

Side one comes to a wonderful climax with **Oh Sister,** in which Bob, for the first time in his career, invokes God to woo a woman. This discourse on the fragility of love, with lovely backing harmonies by Harris overdubbed as an afterthought, became a popular set list staple on the Rolling Thunder Revue even before *Desire* was released. One of the few overdubs on *Desire*, Emmylou's contribution here plainly makes the song pop.

Side two commences with **Joey**, an 11-minute, 12-verse epic ballad concerning the tragic fate of vicious Mafioso Joey Gallo, who was gunned down in 1972 in Umberto's Clam House in Little Italy. Jacques Levy portrays Gallo as an outlaw with morals, much as Woody Guthrie did with his song about Pretty Boy Floyd, despite irrefutable evidence that Gallo, in actuality, was a brutal jerk. That did not stop Levy from making him out to be a martyr that refused to kill innocents, shielded his family from his mortal bullets, and made peace with black men. For this transgression Dylan, not Levy, was unjustly and roundly criticized by critics and fans alike even though Levy wrote all of the lyrics to **Joey**. Emmylou again adds killer haunting backup support, just what this dark drama requires. **Joey** is a good example of a lyrics-driven song on a lyrics-driven album. Although casual music fans may not pick up on some of the finer nuances of songwriting, a focused musician with a good ear can tell that Dylan came up with music for **Joey** after, not before, Levy had written the words.

Listen to *Desire* again, and imagine this being true, for it is on most of the songs. This can be chalked up to the peculiar way that Dylan conspired with Levy as his co-writing comrade on an entire LP, an isolated but not unheard of endeavor for Bob. Robert Hunter, for instance, wrote the lyrics for the 1988 **Silvio** on *Down In The Groove*, a most decent rocker that saw a long run in the #6 spot in mid-1990s live set lists.

We then head south of the border to another song with a strong ethnic and outlaw flair, **Romance In Durango**. This southwestern Colorado fugitive and his little lady will not let reality stand as an obstacle to their enchanted fantasies. One can imagine Levy and Dylan structuring an entire song around the hook of rhyming Durango with fandango. Clearly Bob and Jacques had a grand time in the creative process.

Black Diamond Bay, taken out by a superb harmonica break, is a clever account of a tiny island being destroyed by a volcano, full of ironic futility and hapless characters, quite probably inspired by Polish author Joseph Conrad's novel *Victory*, one of a myriad of cases in point evidencing that Bob Dylan has always been an extremely well-read artist.

Parenthetically, further evidence of this is borne out by his well-written 2004 memoir *Chronicles* and the frequent sightings of Dylan purchasing large numbers of books, especially fiction, while seeking refuge from the ravages of touring and wearing his trademark hoodie disguise and hanging out in bookstores far and wide. I was not there, but a buddy of mine spotted our bookworm rock star purchasing an armful of novels in Old Town's Barbara's Bookstore on Wells Street in Chicago on Sunday afternoon December 14, 1997, the weekend Bob did two killer shows at the Metro. Such firsthand tales go a long way in explaining how the heck Bob Dylan comes up with all those darn fascinating lyrics. The man is an extremely avid reader.

Desire is closed by the song that reveals more about Bob Dylan's actual real personal life than any other song in his lexicon up to that point, **Sara**. This public display of raw nerve transparency is a clear snapshot of Bob's fevered cry of loss of his wife, Sara Lounds (sometimes incorrectly spelled Lowndes, by the way). However, it also displays Dylan in an emotional posture of sincere devotion to the goddess that Sara represented to him then and possibly still does. I mean, the strength of her character is evidenced not only by her raising of a daughter and three sons, often in Bob's absence even preceding their divorce, but by her staunch support of Bob on every level imaginable going all the way back to 1965, especially guarding his personal privacy every bit as much as he has done so himself, which is saying a lot. She even co-starred in *Renaldo and Clara*, which rhymes with Sara, by the way, right in the midst of their marriage going down the toilet, which is an apt metaphor in any sentence mentioning that particular cinematic catastrophe. Now, that's what I call a trooper.

About a year after *Desire* came out, Sara legally filed for divorce from Bob, which was not half as bad as the child custody case that followed, but she did manage to show up in the recording studio at Columbia, at Bob's request, for a firsthand witnessing of the one take needed to capture this homage to love, loyalty, and forgiveness. Listening to **Sara**, and even imagining the dynamic of Bob's then estranged wife being physically present, is enough to turn a heart of stone into an open wound. It was as if the always-restless Bob Dylan knew his marriage was over, and the Rolling Thunder Revue became a creative outlet, an escape if you will, from the pain that touring medicated.

However, nobody could ever argue with the results. Add a little heartache to sex, drugs, and rock and roll, and the results are obvious in the *Bootleg Volume 5* release that documents some of the best of the Rolling Thunder Revue. Or take a look at the NBC TV Dylan special in the fall of '76. Here we encounter thoroughly thrilling, tumultuous theatrical thunder threatening to teeter-totter into totally topsy-turvy tyrannical turmoil. Our friend Bob not only thrives on pushing the envelope, he seeks to do so each and every time he straps on a guitar or sits down at a piano and will have it no other way.

The point is that the music Bob was making away from the recording studio in the immediate post-*Desire* era rivals some of his best stuff ever. Just as his personal life was bottoming out, Dylan was pushing the limits on pretty much all levels on the Rolling Thunder Revue. Gracefully watching the tilt-a-whirl while riding the roller coaster is a risky magic trick done gracefully by the very few, and it eventually cost Dylan his marriage and millions in mullah.

#21

Hard Rain

*H*ard Rain, Bob's live album of the Rolling Thunder Revue tour, came out on vinyl on September 13, 1976. Although it presents some fascinating intellectual conundrums, in hindsight the record never had a chance.

We now realize that by May of '76, when the Fort Collins and Fort Worth shows were chosen for professional recording, the Rolling Thunder Revue had largely run out of steam. Hence, rather than memorializing this traveling circus of troubadours, *Hard Rain* demystifies it. In addition, the fall 1976 Rolling Thunder NBC TV special was not well received for similar reasons. Oddly, however, the Fort Collins video is a major step up in entertainment from *Hard Rain*, if only because the Rolling Thunder Revue was a live theatrical production that truly has to be SEEN to be fully appreciated. One can only hope that the 2010 rumored *Hard Rain* DVD will someday come to fruition and will entirely exclude 1976, or else miraculously re-master and remix the whole shebang. In today's digital age, nothing is impossible if you believe in God. Or even if you don't, for the atheists I have met who have deeply thought about it are some of the most open-minded human beings I have ever met. Whew, now THAT was a tangent.

Even though Dylan is fairly spirited throughout on *Hard Rain*, and the album is surely not an abject failure, only a few selected song selections hit home, and none hit home runs. Furthermore, although the 2002 *Bootleg Volume 5 Rolling Thunder Revue* averts the melody dismissals, inconsequential solos, and haphazard vocals on *Hard Rain*, and thereby is worthy of having gone gold, *Hard Rain* finds Dylan defying audience expectations with utter mulish obstinacy (did you know that obstinance is not a word – I didn't!). I mean, when mulish obstinacy worked on the '66 world tour, that was another animal!

Did we really need another lame **Lay Lady Lay** like on *Before The Flood*? Audio and video accounts of Dylan on the Rolling Thunder Revue's second leg accurately portray him as so self-absorbed so as to be naïve and unaware that all he was doing was not of interest. Furthermore, Bob's collaboration with Don DeVito on sound production is truly the final nail in the coffin of *Hard Rain*. The band sounds like it is far off in the distance, so Bob's fervent, fierce vocals end up too high in the mix. The net results are sadly and avoidably atrocious.

Having said all that, and without minimizing the shortcomings of *Hard Rain*, this can be said. **Idiot Wind** was comparably completely out of place on *Blood On The Tracks* and fits in perfectly on *Hard Rain*. Despite key verses being cut from **You're A Big Girl Now** and **Memphis Blues Again**, they both rock and reflect the spontaneous magic Scarlet Rivera contributed to the rhythm section black magic of bassist Rob Stoner and percussionist Howard Wyeth.

Plus, just Ken Regan's cool close-up cover photo of Dylan in black eye shadow alone can be credited for this one eventually going gold. Or, at least being worthy of framing.

So, not a complete failure by any means.

#22

Street Legal

Ahhh, another Dylan album marinated in ponderings, head scratching, quandaries, labyrinths, knotty intricacies, dilemmas, bewildering puzzles, and unending enigmas. Whew, take a deep breath – here we go.

This one hit record stores as I was embarking on a two year sojourn in the Peace Corps in the Eastern Caroline Islands of Micronesia, and I vividly recall purchasing it in audio cassette form on the rather surreal island of Guam in Gibson's, a department store in the concrete jungle section of Guam adjacent to an American airbase. Upon first listen in Gibson's, a combination of severe culture shock and bewilderment over what I was hearing left me scratching my head in dumbfounded bafflement. Let's see what we can sort out, one clue at a time.

Well, first, my friend, *Street Legal* absolutely shocked Bobdom June 15, 1978 with yet another bullheaded effort at reinventing himself, an accusation haunting Bob, not entirely without merit, ever since *Blonde On Blonde*. This strained effort, replete with thick apocalyptic themes, Elvis-esque extravagance, female vocal backing, and mysterious biblical finger-pointing, suffered from the great divide separating chasms of slick sound production yearning to blend with dense lyrical overtones. On the other hand, what a killer album.

Wait, let's first crown this baby with the weirdest Bob Dylan album of all title. I know, I know, how can I say that? On the other hand comma, I just did.

Although the album soared over the heads of Bob's less sophisticated American listeners (I can say that – I'm American!), it managed to climb to #2 on the billboards in the U.K., where it is to this day his best selling studio LP ever, indicating how much more popular Bob has always been across the pond. It must be emphasized that *Renaldo and Clara*, Bob's excruciatingly epic, spontaneous, surreal film without a plot or pre-written dialogue shot in 1975, hit theaters just before *Street Legal* was released in 1978. Bob was in a state of incessant annoyance helplessly defending his movie in addition to his child custody rights as he assembled a touring band to hit Japan in early '78, willy-nilly composing the eventual set list for *Street Legal*, unmercifully subjecting a parade of studio musicians to marathon rehearsals in Rundown Studios in Santa Monica, and evidently bottoming out personally, emotionally, and metaphysically. *Street Legal* finds Dylan at his most wordy, an independent clause that is more than a mouthful, seemingly bucketing out his inner agony via a grandiose musical catharsis.

Data plainly indicates that after Bob's divorce settlement was reached in 1977, the looming custody battle was salt in the wound that, in a broad sense, and for whatever reason, led to an overtly Christian period in Bob's music and heartfelt, holy ticker for the ensuing four or five years. *Street Legal* is only comprehended in the grasp of the depressive vortex that was simply veering Bob Dylan into the space between this galaxy and the next, transforming his peculiar brand of spirituality into a righteous evangelical dogmatic gospel creed. Bob's pathetic human nature gloriously rose to lift himself, and not just a few fans, into self-introspection, striving to avoid the pits of spiritual bankruptcy. As hard as any of this was to understand, it is even more difficult to imagine the emotional pain fueling all this. That his children would legally remain partially accessible in southern California might have been the only shred of glad tidings preventing, well, let's not even go there.

Thus, can we all muster up the compassion needed to cut Mr. Dylan a mere fragment of slack prior to ripping him for *Street Legal*? Early critiques clearly could not, but little did these same critics realize the dark night of the soul (which we are all subject to and familiar with) Dylan was experiencing in 1978. Yet, the album passes the test of time with flying colors. The 2003 re-mixed release by Columbia, an audio marvel of the modern age, underscored this commonly-held conclusion in spades.

Back in 1978, a case in point is pertinent. However, heads up. 93-word sentence incoming.

As this writer resided in what seemed like the end times on a Pacific atoll in the Eastern Carolines with a population of 225 and 1.5 square miles of coral and sand, cut off from civilization for months on end while serving as a Peace Corps volunteer, the opening tune, **Changing Of The Guards**, laced with warnings of the burning of Eden and bracing for elimination, brought great sympathy for the otherwise unbearable loneliness, depression, and ambiguity of severe culture shock, a bland diet of unprocessed food, nobody to speak English with, and a lack of alcohol, drugs, and available sexual partners to medicate the pain of it all.

The album had more than merit even in its time, I am here to tell you. Slapped in the face by a big boy's dose of reality and only a couple barely-functioning audio cassettes to my name, my only sane recourses were repeated listenings to both Dylan's *Street Legal* and Willie Nelson's *Stardust* LPs. Somehow relevantly, *Stardust* would go on to help partially inspire 2015's *Shadows In The Night*, Dylan's salute to Sinatra and some oldies but goodies like we find on *Stardust*. Go figure, Dylan and this writer share similar tastes.

As intriguing as the lyrics are on *Street Legal*, and they unquestionably are, they might have to take the cake for the most hopeless, depressing, and desperate, not to mention way-out-there songs Dylan has ever bunched together on a single LP. Given the dire straits (pun intended) and third world village I found myself in, it was not much of a stretch for me to go to the desperate, dejected doldrums where Dylan was venturing. It was either that or listen to Willie Nelson pining about moonlight in Vermont, blue skies, the sunny side of the street, and/or the lack of peace in Georgia. Hey dude, you don't know the troubles I got. I was more interested in Dylan moaning about some chick he longed to touch who he misses so much drifting like a satellite in a neon light ablaze and smoky haze bathing in a stream of pure heat. Hey, that's just where I was at. Finding myself by losing myself.

On song two, sick images of bestiality on **New Pony** brought the tone into Dylan's nasty snot of sexual perversity at its worst (a theme embellished upon more three Christian albums later on *Shot Of Love*), setting up for **No Time To Think**, on which Bob shouts about some poor lost soul stripped of all virtue while crawling through the dirt, completing a dark, dreary descent into shear shadow. **Baby, Stop Crying**, a hymn to the wounded female archetype, inspired by Robert Johnson's **Stop Breaking Down**, fittingly sets up the polar opposite in the male chauvinistic, sexist, as well as ode to martyrdom, **Is Your Love In Vain?**, a ballad sung at the altar of male ego neediness. Both Bob and every woman serving as his muse or goddess or idealized lover seem to be caught in a lose/lose merry-go-round of incurable constant mental torture situated in a bed of psychological quicksand. Whew! What heady and heavy stuff! Brings back such splendid, cherished recollections. Wait a minute, am I getting sarcastic again?

On side two, **Senor** kicks things off with a trip to the book of Revelations, painting a tale of a female martyr locking heads with a resentful guy desperately looking at the man in the glass for the first time in his life. "This place don't make sense to me no more," alright. You won't get any argument from me, senor. Is the senor addressed over and over again Bob himself, almighty God, or just some other guy, perhaps with some elder wisdom which Bob appears to desperately need here? Is it just me, or is this song not the most obvious suggestion of early rumblings of the spiritual quest that would find its answers in Jesus Christ in Bob's next three LPs?

True Love Tends To Forget underscores yet another variation of the victim role, placing the iron cross around the neck of the male this time. Lost in the wilderness, drifting in infinity, and stuck with some tear jerker baby on a weekend in hell — sounds to me like for some reason Bob is immersing himself in the most depressing poetry he can possibly come up with. This ain't no happy camper, pal.

Next, in **We Better Talk This Over**, the deadly warfare escalates into hopeless exile as the lovers lose themselves in the haze of their delicate ways with both eyes glazed. **Where Are You Tonight?** fittingly terminates the bloody slippery slope of self escape only to be found out all along by an invisible lust object with 20/20 vision.

Dylan in Rotterdam on June 23, 1978. Photo by Chris Hakkens.

Is it no wonder that Bob Dylan picked up a silver cross tossed onto a sweltering Montreal stage in late '78 and subsequently had a sort of white light experience in a Tucson hotel room, leading to enlisting in a four-day-a-week three month bible study course at the Vineyard Fellowship near his Malibu estate? These events in the months after *Street Legal* solve more than a few of the riddles surrounding it as well as Bob's next three so-called Christian records. I mean, if *Nashville Skyline* and *New Morning* were expressions of the rapture of Bob's domesticity with Sara, *Street Legal* is his (not Sara's, mind you) novel narrating his own naked, nerve-racking, neurotic neediness.

The dust of rumors doubting Bob as an abidingly creative artist hit another peak after *Street Legal*. This can be chalked up to arrows shot into Bob's back by casual listeners that he has never been fully able to shake ever since he (figuratively speaking) met Phil Spector in the under or over produced, take your pick, album strangely titled *Street Legal*. It did not help that Bob began wearing black eye shadow and white sparkling Elvis jump suits on stage in 1978. He also shamelessly marketed *Street Legal* at live shows, a somewhat disgusting irony given the 1963 goody-two-shoes folkie bronze mold that some fair weather fans will never, ever let Bob grow out of. Bob's evolutions of self, by 1978, had been so many and so varied that constant reminders are needed to recall that the guy in short sleeves who blew away the Newport audience in '63 was the same wandering troubadour still persistently pushing the boundaries of rock in the late 70s.

Consequently, many followers of Dylan permanently abandoned ship in 1978, even before Bob went all "Christian" and everything, depriving themselves of another 36 years and counting of some of Bob's best material. This, of course, constitutes a rightly-deserved tragedy for them that eternal artist Bob Dylan himself has scarcely ever even noticed.

Yet, what B movie were we watching, by the way? Had our skin-shedding chameleon made one too many character costume changes? Were we unable to keep up, or was he just lost on a road going down a despondent toilet of a vortex?

Man, this is starting to sound like the end of the first episode in a two-part Batman TV plot. I guess all we can do is stay tuned!

#23

Live At Budokan

Recorded roughly 3 months prior to the release of *Street Legal*, no less than a shocking sacrilege, *Live At Budokan*, was unfortunately, pathetically, and shamefully released on April 23, 1979. Its only redeeming grace was that it provided terrific band rehearsals for the ladies singing backup and the gents in the studio band on *Street Legal*. Thank the Lordy in the sky that I was stationed on that God-forsaken atoll in the paradise paradox of the Eastern Carolines doing my remotely-stationed-to-put-it-lightly Peace Corps thing, or else on this live LP nonsense I surely would have wasted whatever newly released vinyl albums and audio cassettes were going for toward the end of the 70s.

Live At Budokan is pretty much 20 greatest hits, **Going, Going Gone**, and **Is Your Love In Vain?**, the only number from the extraordinarily and wonderfully bizarre and out-of-character *Street Legal*. February 28 and March 1, 1978 at Nippon Budokan Hall in Tokyo was the scene of this first class misdemeanor in rock and roll trivia.

Misguided profit motives deservedly led to some of the worst reviews Dylan has ever received, and that is saying a lot. Did somebody say, "I need some money to pay for my divorce?" These songs feature a hit-or-miss, contentious, fire and brimstone effort by band and Bob alike method. Did somebody else say, "Too much brass?" Though slick and sterile sounding, somehow *Live At Budokan* went platinum. Even if moments and snippets work well, at best they do so only marginally. It sounds like a bunch of pretty good hacks (I should know – I AM one) on their best night ever. The nine, count 'em nine, members of this musical assortment, not counting the female backup vocalists, had just not gotten it together yet and found the groove they would go on to contribute to *Street Legal*. It's called a cluster "F", folks.

I suppose *Live At Budokan* is worth one good listen, but it badly fails the test of time and truly is a bit much even for diehards like yours truly.

#24

Slow Train Coming

*S*low Train Coming was more like slam on the breaks, screech, spin around, peel out, and 180 degree u-turn. Nobody was still quite sure what to make of *Street Legal*, with its weird-even-for-Dylan one-of-a-kind sound, and now this? Whew…what the hell was going on in Bob Dylan land?

Picture 1979 Dylan fans filing through sections of vinyl records in their favorite music stores, staring at the cross on the cover of Bob's new Columbia release, asking the hippie behind the counter to play a sample on the store turntable, scratching their heads, and thinking, "Wow, this stuff sounds incredible with whoever is playing that killer lead guitar! An evangelical Christian message never sounded THIS good before." Meanwhile, sub-conscious messages floating to the surface, like, "Geez, without the political party, or better yet, the pathetic 1970s television fund-raising component of modern day Christianity, some of this stuff really hits home." The release of *Slow Train Coming* on August 20, 1979 underscored the irrefutable ever-recurring reminder that Bob Dylan albums, when all the fog has lifted, never lie.

The above account actually occurred to me on the Polynesian paradise of Fiji about 6 months after *Slow Train Coming* came out on August 20, 1979. At the time I was experiencing neon lights for the first time in 20 months. I was ecstatic over the sound of the record, likely due to being restricted to *Street Legal* as my only Dylan audio cassette while I lived with 22most friendly, quite spiritually grounded Micronesian natives of Piis-Losap Atoll 6 degrees north of the equator (one google map of that scene and you'll catch the drift), where 8 Korean-manufactured D cell batteries powered the JVC boom box that kept me in extremely slanted, bizarre, completely surreal, propagandistic communication with the outside world via short wave radio stations such as Radio Australia, BBC Radio, Radio Moscow, and last, but certainly not least, the lovely Voice of America. In addition, the devout Christian community on the island where I had been residing, looking back, was a set up to open-mindedly hear Dylan's gospel/evangelical tidings on *Slow Train Coming*. Late 70s contemporary, current music releases (not that I was missing all that much given it was the tail end of the disco era) were simply not on my Pacific isle radar during the height of Dylan's "Christian" era. I truly figuratively, but not literally, bought *Slow Train Coming* hook, line, and sinker, as the east Indian Hindu manning the store in Fiji only had vinyl copies, which were unplayable on Piis-Losap, where audio cassettes ruled the day. I can safely say that hearing this record just once in that record joint on the main island of Fiji irrevocably changed my life in ways too numerous and nuanced to detail at this point, but watch for my next book for further elaboration.

Each song on *Slow Train Coming* stresses the importance of Christian teachings and philosophy, which both drew countless Christians forever or temporarily into Dylan's fan base, on the one hand, and alienated a few of the Dylan faithful, either for the time being, or in some extreme cases, permanently. Even now, 35 years after Dylan's debut Christian record, just the mere mention of Bob's name will prompt some folks to moan, "Is Bob Dylan still preaching the message of Jesus?" Don't you just love that question? It's right up there with asking if Dylan has kicked the bucket yet!

No fewer than 10 all-over-the-place albums of new material have materialized since then, but for some, once you are in the Christian or any other religion box, you never leave. On these ten albums, Bob's message has never wavered far from his ever-present references to an inner search for peace of mind, which can also be traced back to 100% of the music he has released commercially going back to 1962. Hence, the only distinction of *Slow Train Coming*, when held to the light of the rest of Dylan's lexicon, is merely its outright, unmitigated biblical evangelicalism. Neither Bob nor any other commercial rock star had ever gone THERE.

Some of the facts are these. *Slow Train Coming* reached number 2 on the billboard charts in the U.K. and number 3 in the U.S., was extraordinarily well-received in the secular press, was years later voted number 16 in a ranking of the greatest 100 Christian albums of all time, outsold *Blonde On Blonde* and *Blood On The Tracks*, and received a 1980 Grammy for best male rock vocal for **You Gotta Serve Somebody**, the opening number. So, say what you will.

The album starts with a funky riff of organ, drums, and bass prior to Bob coming in with an eerie sneer suggesting a series of hypnotic propositions of the what-if game culminating in the unavoidable conclusion that no matter what you do, who you are, or how others perceive you, your fate is destined to the necessity of serving somebody. Just who is not made clear. Perhaps Him, Her, or It, or whatever name you use for the divine. Granted, Bob proposes that it will either be the Lord or the devil, but the wording of the lyrics leaves just enough wiggle room for any spiritual sojourner to feel free to shake off the Jesus Christ righteousness Bob is spitting out, if he/she chooses to do so. Uncannily ingenious, if I do say so myself. Wait a minute, I just did.

Most fittingly, the recording studio used for *Slow Train Coming* was the legendary Mussel Shoals, Alabama scene, so Memphis Horn and Mussel Shoal sessionists, drummer Pick Withers, bassist Tim Drummond, and keyboardist Barry Becket backed up lead guitarist extraordinaire Mark Knopfler of Dire Straits. Bob had met Knopfler backstage at a Dire Straits concert in L.A. in early 1979 and asked him to play on his next record. Little did Knopfler know when he instantly accepted this invite that Bob's next album would come right out of the *New Testament*. In any case, the rock and R and B sound these folks came up with stands testimony to what great musicians can do with good music.

Precious Angel is next, offering Knopfler his best chance on the record to stretch out his lead fills on the *Slow Train Coming* tune with the most popular sensibility. Bob seems to be singing directly to his lover and passionately urging her to not sway into the darkness of the flesh and the material, disclosing his heartfelt hope that the light of Jesus might keep their relationship on the straight and narrow. Inexplicably, sadly, and parenthetically, the gripping **Precious Angel** has not been included once in Bob's live concerts since the fall 1980 apocalyptic tour dripping with righteousness, self and otherwise. Yawn, ho-hum, go figure. But, "Rats!!!," nonetheless.

I Believe In You abruptly slows things down, giving Bob the floor to expose himself nakedly at the altar of Jesus, repeating over and over that his faith is unshakeable even through the tears, laughter, loneliness, rough times, betrayals, inevitable diversions of life, criticism, and the darkest hour before the dawn. Bob lays bare his personal relationship with Jesus, fervently delivering each syllable of his vocals as if to glorify, worship, and adore the creator written about in *The Holy Bible*. Whatever reluctance he ever possessed to candidly expose his deep inner guts to the public, which began to disappear with **Sara** on *Desire*, is now obliterated on *Slow Train Coming*. **I Believe In You** is the first clue standing testimony to this auspicious shift in the music of Bob Dylan. The man behind the shades now not only has his dark sunglasses off, but he undresses himself and stands naked, much like the president of the United States he mocked so scornfully in **It's All Right Ma, I'm Only Bleeding** 15 years before.

Slow Train Coming, the title track, finds Bob metaphorically throwing up his hands in a futile gesture, for he does not seem to know what the world is coming to. He cannot fathom how the human race can remain so blind to the undeniable holy force running the show out there. Mankind is lost in its egotistical choice to do spiritual warfare with Satan. Bob is searching for somebody who knows how to actually live brotherly love. This cathartic release of Dylan's hopelessness ironically constructs a sense of purpose. There seems to be a character developing in the course of the album *Slow Train Coming*, and particularly in the song **Slow Train Coming**. Bob Dylan steps to the plate and announces that he is a man with a mission. Nothing, no matter how evil, is going to stop this guy we did not know existed.

Gonna Change My Way of Thinking utilizes a catchy cow bell to sustain the bad-ass backbeat of a sizzling rock groove in a song that required a re-dub of Bob's vocal. Here we catch glimpses of where Bob has gone wrong, but no matter, for he is determined to be ready for the return of Jesus when the world ends. **Do Right To Me (Do Unto Others)** showcases Pick Withers tenderly brushing his drum kit and Barry Becket on keyboards as Bob underscores the golden rule with some serious soul.

When You Gonna Wake Up reiterates the righteous slap in the face Dylan imposed on humanity on *Slow Train Coming*. Here he seems disgusted, even hateful. These, folks, are not endearing characteristics on any level. On the other hand, has Bob Dylan ever cow-towed to record companies, his fans, or anybody else? Has he ever been the type to sneak out of town when the shooting starts? The Memphis Horns punctuate this gospel version of scolding a child from the pulpit. Despite this being a wonderful composition, you gotta figure this one can be blamed for some of Dylan's legions abandoning him. The word unpleasant might understatedly say it all here.

Bob's affinity for children's nursery rhymes is at the roots of **Man Gave Names For All The Animals**. Featuring riveting low end bass, drums, and a keyboard that serves as a second bass, this playful little ditty is quite the change of pace from the previous song's vitriolic and bitter refrain. Although the song ends on a sinister note, it is practically comic relief when juxtaposed with the grave enormity meandering through fire and brimstone in every other song on *Slow Train Coming*.

If **I Believe In You** unclothed Bob, the finale, **When He Returns,** cloaks Dylan in a robe on a platform where his inner rabbi shines through. His earnest singing of the song might be his most unburdened vocal of his career, or at least since **Visions of Johanna**. One gets the sense that Dylan is a man comfortable in his own skin and letting it simply rip. This is a trustworthy, humble conveyance of the biblical gospel trumpet, not an annoying door-to-door missionary talking down to the resident whose intelligence is underestimated.

So, now that the album is over, what to do. Certainly that intrusive sanctimoniousness does NOT deserve another listen, but that music surely DOES. Hence, *Slow Train Coming* is one Dylan record on which the music completely trumps the plot. Of all the Dylan albums which bear repeated listening before the novel grows on you, *Slow Train Coming* probably takes the cake. First listen, vomit, or at least bewilderment. 11th listen, one of the finest records Dylan has ever made. A recurring Dylan theme ever since the 60s.

The fall tour in '79 was noteworthy in a number of respects. First, no old secular material was included in the set lists, and Bob insisted on lecturing about Jesus Christ from the stage. The minority of hecklers did not seem to bother him one iota. In November Bob carried out two weeks-worth of live shows of completely Christian music at the Fox Warfield Theater in San Francisco, bootlegs of which later became highly sought after staples in the collections of Dylan freaks. More than 30 years later these recordings stand the test of time and are a must in any curriculum of Bob Dylan 300 level courses.

Finally, credit is due where credit is earned in the case of producer Jerry Wexler. Bob picked this 62 year old confirmed Jewish atheist to bring out his Christian best in the recording studio in Mussel Shoals. Dylan had finally realized that the cluster f!*k that occurred on *Desire* and *Street Legal* needed to be avoided on this album. Bob might be bullheaded as hell, but he occasionally admits defeat and changes course. Wexler's background with Atlantic records in the 60s with artists like Percy Sledge, Dusty Springfield, Wilson Pickett, and Aretha Franklin was just the right mojo required to achieve that famous Mussel Shoals sound. Helena Springs and Carolyn Dennis must also be credited for excellent backup singing on *Slow Train Coming*.

On an important side note which remained secret from the public long after the fact, Dennis stuck around in Bob's touring band for years after this and married Dylan after having a daughter, Desiree Dylan, with him in the mid-80s. This marriage eventually broke up, but by all accounts no bitterness exists between Bob and his second ex-wife and daughter. Even Dylan's 4 children with Sara have nothing bad to say publicly about their father. Dylan apparently falls into the terrible husband, good father department. Worth reiterating only because it might be the most significant shred of positive evidence to support Bob Dylan's private persona.

The cosmic question after *Slow Train Coming* was, obviously, what would this born-again Jewish Christian do next. Would he remain on the gospel carnival circuit? To find out the answer to this and other perplexing quandaries about Bobby, Zimmy, Archie, or Ray, whatever you might choose to call him, read on.

But you're stiiiiiilll gonna have to open your mind.

#25

Saved

Speaking of an open mind, *Saved* requires one.

Dylan's follow up to *Slow Train Coming* was an even further embrace of the virtues of *The Holy Bible*. Coming out June 23, 1980, just as I was about to return to the U.S. from 25 bizarre, surreal, exotic-as-hell, mind-altering, and mind-altered months in the Truk (Chuuk) Islands, *Saved* comprised an open declaration of Dylan's deepening faith. This precisely mirrored my own fervor for Jesus after attending church virtually daily (often at both dawn and sunset) in the missionized Christian community where I was stationed as a Peace Corps volunteer.

Dylan's mixed up confusion (whether you will pardon the pun or not) on *Street Legal* reverberated through my brain for two years in Truk due to the miserable fact that it was the only audio cassette of Dylan stuff I possessed at the time. It was just the wrong befuddling, baffling, and disturbing Dylan album to comfort me through my severe culture shock in a primitive third world village characterized by a diet of relentless fish and rice and an utter lack of a single stick of furniture. However, I had no alternative, except for a lame AM radio station 65 miles north on the district center mountainous island of Moen (or Wolle in the local vernacular) which statically trumpeted the hands-down most pathetic folk music I have ever encountered. I was left to wear out, for this lost soul of a Peace Corps Volunteer, the fascinatingly disheartening *Street Legal*. I think it set me up for a 1980s slump! Yeah, that's it – I'll blame Dylan for my underperforming decade because at the time I took responsibility for nothing in my life, as in zilch, nada, and/or not squat.

As a result of the mess I was, when Bob started coming out with all this gospel stuff, the then-clear-eyed-and focused Dylan became sort of like my own messiah or alter ego, if you will. I sub-consciously yet desperately wanted the clarity Mr. Bob had. On the other hand, it is also partially true that I was already guilty of losing interest in Dylan in the early 80s like so many others. Life is complicated. Thank God I ended up finding some simple solutions, but again, that's getting into my next book, though utterly vague its outline seems at this time.

The early, initial versions of the *Saved* album cover painting by Tony Wright depicted several human hands reaching up to what is clearly the hand of God reaching down from the heavens, but Colombia executives later chose to pull these copies in favor of cover art representing a painting of Bob performing on stage during this era. It was correctly felt that Dylan's exclusively religious themes would hurt sales. Columbia did everything in its power, which was not much, to downplay the overt nature of Dylan's falling under the Christian spell.

On the other hand, even the liner notes contained the following inscription from Jeremiah 31, which seemed more akin to something one would find on the inner sleeve of a bible than a Bob Dylan record: "Behold the days cometh, sayeth the Lord, that I will make a new covenant with the house of Israel, and with the house of Judah." Bob Dylan was outspokenly telling his audience, believe it or not, that his religious conversion was not a passing fad, and he did not seem to be bothered by the pragmatic, troublesome obstacle that his religion was overshadowing his music. On *Slow Train Coming*, many were willing to cut Bob some slack because the music was compelling enough to not get buried by Bob's righteous rhetoric. Unfortunately, this was not at all true on *Saved*.

Here was an album whose nature was oddly muted and at times chilly and graceless. It lacked the Knopfler lyrical guitar lines on *Slow Train*

Coming as well as *Slow Train's* rhythmic exuberance and supple backing band. Nonetheless, somehow, someway, the only real miracle on *Saved* was the fact that it achieved an artistic triumph over its dogmatic theme. Regardless, it is inspiring to listen to, despite being, other than perhaps *Self Portrait*, the flattest and most pedestrian Dylan album up to that point in time. Making things only worse was its talking down and sermonizing to unbelievers. Still, there are moments on *Saved* when the human nature of the listener is unquestionably pole vaulted onto the threshold of none other than the pearly gates themselves.

One of Bob Dylan's uncanny talents is evoking phantom strains of traditional American music, which on *Saved* took the form of black American worship music. The venue for recording reverted back to Muscle Shoals, which, granted, was only appropriate. Despite *Saved's* routine songwriting according to Dylan standards, the posse behind Bob was too solid and experienced to be held in check for an entire album.

Back to produce was Jerry Wexler, aided by Barry Becket, as were Spooner Oldham on keyboards and Tim Drummond on bass. Carolyn Dennis and Clydie King were joined by Monalisa Young and Regina Havis as the girl-group backup quartet, Fred Tacket replaced Knopfler on lead guitar, and rock legend Jim Keltner took over on drums for Pic Withers. The rhythm section, thanks to Keltner's masterful shadowing of Drummond, is less metronomic than what Withers contributed to *Slow Train Coming*. I guess what they came up with in only five, **yes 5**, days of putting their noses to the grindstone was pretty remarkable, but, c'mon man, five days?

The album opens with Bob conjuring up Americana's heart with just a couple guitar chords on the traditional folk anthem **A Satisfied Mind**. It is nearly impossible to resist being pulled down into the descent into darkness that Dylan is engineering with soaring harmonies swirling to fill his eccentric humming and brave phrasing that practically disembodies this folk classic, leaving only a winding pilgrim's path through a wailing tent show down by the river on the edge of town. This and all the songs on *Saved* were far better performed in live shows without the burden of the partially muted mix on the studio version.

Stepping up the tempo, the title track **Saved** lacks the presence and life it calls for, at least on the studio version. Relying on merely a piano to carry a fine melody over the driving low end of Keltner's spirited drumming and Drummond's too staccatic bass lines, the song seems to stall at the end of measures, sounding much too amateurish for such a quality ensemble. One almost wonders if *Saved* should not have been released as a live album to retain the feverish vibration of bodily worship so widely acclaimed in black American spirituals. After all, much of it was written, arranged, and perfected on the road on the American/ Canadian nothin'-but-gospel tour right after *Slow Train Coming*. It seems like the confines of a recording studio took much of the breath out of the material on *Saved*. But once again, that's just me.

The slow ballad **Covenant Woman** is somewhat of a return to 1960s Dylan chord patterns, but Bob's singing lays back a little too much and does not receive the backup support it screams for. Happily, this cannot be said about most of the renditions of this stellar song in concert.

What Can I Do For You suffers from yet another flat-footed delivery of a tune needing a faster velocity as Dylan proposes a series of inquiries into how he might ever repay his debt to the almighty. The song is, on the other hand, saved, if you will pardon the pun, by a wailing Little Walter harmonica taking it out. Side one closes with a sinuous barroom riff that is unabashedly syncopated on **Solid Rock**. At times one gets the sense that Jim Keltner on the drum kit is the only saving grace on an album that constitutes a sad could-be, wanna-be, should-be, would-be, just is/was-not-to and never-shall-be.

On to side two, serene gospel stoicism embodies **Pressing On**, a melodic descendant of Robbie Robertson's **The Weight**. Bob's vocal definitely and finally steps to the plate, as do the most exotic backup harmonies by the girl group on the record, saving this lackluster melody from disaster. There is, ironically, a whole lotta saving going on on *Saved*. Sometimes life preservers are tossed out by Keltner, other times by Dylan's singing, and when all else fails, the sparkle-adorned ladies in the background bring the necessary first aid. Almost pathetically, though, and certainly frustratingly, these musical breakthroughs invariably occur in isolation from one and other and never in fusion. This probably best explains why *Saved* as a studio album, catastrophically, fails the test of time.

In The Garden is no doubt a lovely, billowing arrangement sung with stirring conviction that could convert a non-believer based on its music alone. The gritty upward ascending bass lines and Spooner's meandering organ fills contribute a serious melodrama engendering an eerie fear of betraying or even questioning the Son of God. **In The Garden** is one of those potential pearly gate moments on *Saved*.

In The Garden is also a prime example of a song on *Saved* that here and there suggests that this record is actually salvageable, a judgment that could be made about virtually every song on the album. The problem is that when each song is saving the album, one has to question whether the record has any saving grace at all.

This, parenthetically, brings us to **Saving Grace**, on which Bob's vocal is the lone saving grace. What is being saved, who is being saved, and should Columbia customers simply skip this Dylan record in order to save some dinero? It gets weirdly confusing. Just when you want to label this stuff lame, it shows compelling promise over and over again. Promise to bring home the spiritual goods it is selling, but some of us are thick enough to still be waiting for delivery 35 years later.

Concluding this knotty dilemma personified, Bob takes us out with the mightiest R and B groove on *Saved*, **Are You Ready**, punctuated by another committed vocal, some more Little Walter harmonica that would make Muddy Waters proud, and regrettably claustrophobic production by Wexler, who should have known better if only for his successful achievements producing Ray Charles in his pre-country R and B heydays.

I can vividly recall the moment I finished listening to *Saved* for the first time. I was in the Johnsburg, Illinois second floor apartment of my older brother John. I was stoned. I felt my jaw drop. I hated it.

Still, I was drawn to the introspective salvation that Dylan was on fire about. The suckin' 70s were over, and I was, unbeknownst to myself, honestly a mess. Life on the moon in Micronesia was the beginning of an up and down roller coaster that was mostly down that would last throughout the 80s. Bob's Dylan's Christian albums, nonetheless, had planted mustard seeds on my spiritual path that would eventually reap tenfold rewards. Both Bobs, Dylan and Shiel, for better or worse, would first require hitting bottom. But not quite yet. Stay tuned, and we'll get there.

It can probably be argued that, looking back, *Saved* and *Self Portrait* constitute the only two Bob Dylan studio albums that do not stand the test of time, at least prior to Bob's mid-80s bottoming out, which at this point, is actually light years away in terms of the evolution of Dylan's music. On the other hand, the live shows from the fall 1980 tour bear witness to the proposition that *Saved* would have been a better live album than studio album. Despite being poorly recorded, there actually is nothing wrong with the music on *Saved* itself. Otherwise, 1980 would not be point blank legendary in the annals of Dylan's live performances.

Bob's self-righteous renditions of not only the songs on *Saved* and *Slow Train Coming*, but his covers of Peggy Lee's **Fever**, **Senor** from *Street Legal*, the bluegrass spiritual **That's All**, his own **Blowing In The Wind** all gospeled out, Dave Mason's **We Just Disagree**, the standard gospel **City of Gold**, or Dick Holler's **Abraham, Martin, and John** popularized by Dion – all stand testimony to the legendary, feverish rock solid energy he relentlessly showed up with on tour night after night right after *Saved* came out.

Where this on-fire version of the skin-shedding chameleon Bob Dylan was during the recording of *Saved* at Muscle Shoals God only knows. And why on God's green earth Columbia has not yet let loose of a live LP from Bob's gospel era is, at best, anybody's guess, and at worst, ethical justification for a lawsuit rooted in cruel and unusual disregard for mankind's welfare, greater good, and right to exposure to f-ing killer, inspiring art forms inherently self-evident in the human condition.

Oh, I forgot, that's why God created bootlegs.

#26

Shot Of Love

One summer after the comparatively lame *Saved*, Bob Dylan's *Shot of Love* album was released on August 10, 1981, completing a trilogy of three so-called Christian albums in precisely 24 months. Although the term Christian can, for critical purposes, be used to refer to these three records and this time period in the life of Bob Dylan, two things can be said. First, I challenge anybody to find a Bob Dylan album that contains zero, as in nada, spiritual references in general, and even Christian ones specifically. They all do. Second, other than the annoying broad-brush Christian labeling (which is up there with the inane insignia of Dylan comeback album) of *Slow Train Coming, Saved*, and *Shot Of Love*, it is virtually impossible to find much that they have in common. Contrasting them, on the other hand, is, as they say, similar to falling off a log, or do you prefer taking candy from a baby?

To say *Shot of Love* is my favorite of these three records would be quite accurate, at least until I happen to be in the right place and time to listen to *Slow Train Coming*, and then I end up on that merry-go-round of changing my mind ad infinitum. We are talking apples and oranges, folks. More on that later.

Shot of Love was Dylan's only and first record of these three most controversial albums to focus on secular themes such as love and hard times, let alone an ode to the subversive Jewish comedian, Lenny Bruce. Its music was more rooted in rock than gospel. It reached #33 in the U.S.

and #6 in the U.K., a lamentable statistic more attributable to the lingering hangover of *Saved* than to any *Shot Of Love* merit or lack thereof.

There were few major alterations in the studio musicians who played on *Shot Of Love*. Notable returnees were Tim Drummond on bass, Jim Keltner on drums, and Clydie King and Carolyn Dennis as backup singers. A notable addition was the extraordinary (and legendary) Donald "Duck" Dunn of Stax Records and Booker T. and the MGs fame, who is credited for having played bass on the album, but exactly where is not real clear (please do enlighten me if you can).

In any case, the first song is the title track **Shot of Love**, which interestingly, was produced by former Little Richard sound man Bumps Blackwell, who, rather unfortunately due to illness, could not stick around for the rest of the recording process. Thus, Jimmy Lovine is credited with producing the rest of *Shot of Love*, and despite his intense tension with both mixing engineering Chuck Plotkin and Dylan over minutia such as whether to use nice mixes or monitor mixes, Lovine is due exemplary credit for avoiding the sound catastrophe(s) reeking throughout *Saved*.

Noteworthy if only for Dylan later singling **Shot of Love** out as his most perfect song due to its capturing of the purpose of music to elevate and inspire the soul, much else is significant about this title track number in particular. Hence, it is deserving of special, slightly deeper scrutiny.

Here goes.

First, historical context is needed to grasp its heralding in a total turnaround from *Saved*. With **Shot Of Love's** opening electric power chords, one gets the impression that that whole muted nonsense on *Saved* has been thrown out the window. Hence, Bob is telling us in the first nanosecond of the first song that we are headed in a completely new sound direction, and the amps have been turned up from 6 to 8. Whew, thank God for that.

Furthermore, the complaint most heard about *Saved* was that the lyrics were too bald-faced and pointed in the messianic direction. Hence, **Shot of Love** set a tone for Dylan's clever delivery of the exact same gospel message by couching it in hidden, covert wording and images. Overall this song's use of the word 'love' is a reference most likely to the kind of love described in Corinthians 1:13, which famously describes in exquisite detail the many powers and virtues of a non-possessive giving and receiving of love, a harmonious love if you will, as opposed to the casual use of the word so often characterizing contemporary American English. Academics would likely call it agape. In the first verse of **Shot of Love**, Bob states that he does not need drugs like heroin, codeine, or whiskey to help him repent. Right here he diverts from *Saved*, which was too holier-than-thou to even mention such secular terms. Bob's spiritual dagger is still being hurled, yet he seems to have come down to earth, and his tone is both more human and humane, not to mention easier to swallow. Verse one is expressing that God's gifts are useless without loving other humans, which both more resembles the secular golden rule and conveys a much more universal message than that on *Saved*.

Moving on, verse 2 is possibly a by-product of 1 John 4:18, which teaches that love is not yet perfected in one who is still afraid. However, the images used are that of a doctor medicating patients, universal fear of human nature running rampant in the kingdom of the world, and putting a price on the head of Jesus. These types of worldly concepts are a 180 degree reversal from the righteous fire and brimstone lexicon on *Saved*. Verse 3 continues this pattern by using books, movies, and alibis as examples of useless illusions without the gift of love. Verse 4 emphasizes the need to love one's enemies and pray for one's persecutors, right out of Mathew 5:43-44. Verse 5 might be attributable to 1 Peter 4:8, which notes the ability of love to cover a multitude of Dylan's own sins. Dylan's humility, transparency, and willingness to admit personal fallibility marks a major turn in his rhetoric on **Shot Of Love** as well as on *Shot Of Love* in general. The bottom line brilliance of both the song and the LP is their avoidance of the vexatious sound and lyrical pitfalls of *Saved* while not wavering from a core Christian mojo. Not an easy trick to pull off, maestro!

Heart of Mine is actually Bob's first outright love song in years. Let's make that since *Desire*, so we are talking 5.5 years. Yet, this little Tex-Mex tune is firmly rooted in Jeremiah 17:9's warning that the human heart is more tortuous than all else, beyond remedy, and beyond reckoning with on a logical level. The version eventually making the album cut is slightly scattered and funky, unlike the one that Ringo Starr and Ronnie Wood came up with in less than ten minutes when they dropped by Rundown Studios in Santa Monica one day. The Starr-Wood more in-your-face rocked out arrangement remains a highly sought after bootleg in Dylan circles. Keltner's nuanced percussion on this one is remarkable for its weaving into and out of up and down tempos and chord-hanging measures. **Heart of Mine** is the first of numerous allusions Bob makes on *Shot Of Love* to his romantic department being at odds with his very soul.

On to **Property of Jesus**, which utilizes the chorus line "You've got a heart of stone" to sarcastically ridicule non-believers who sneer at faithful Christians. Highbrow Dylan satire at its best, **Property of Jesus** is a sharp, put-down song laced with vitriolic hatred, scorn, and vengeance, much as *Slow Train Coming's* **When You Gonna Wake Up** but without its off-putting superiority complex. **Property of Jesus** is a song that draws the listener toward its biblical broadcast. One gets the sense that it took Dylan three albums to figure out how to get his evangelical point(s) across without provoking his fans to vomit in sheer grief over his apparent loss of his once intangible talent for intuiting how to overlay lyrics onto music and/or vice versa and thereby elicit intellectual curiosity, not academic revulsion. **Property Of Jesus** has all the earmarks of quite the intellectual and spiritual triumph hidden on a relatively obscure Dylan LP. It has, in my mind, big however, always been overshadowed by the album-closing **Every Grain of Sand**, about which the same can be said and to which we will soon get.

Lenny Bruce, a gem taking Bob under ten minutes to write, underscores a bizarre tribute to one of Bob's martyred heroes with a sparse solo piano arrangement anchored tightly to gospel sensibility. Its lyrical tone is extremely secular in tone, however, which is, again, a refreshing switch from the strictly religious vibes on *Slow Train Coming* and *Saved*. Bruce is made out to be a hero who couldn't catch a break and had the guts to commit suicide in a 1966 drug overdose in the wake of his obscenity trial. In an odd way, **Lenny Bruce** is a throwback to Dylan's freedom and/or protest anthems of the 60s such as **Chimes of Freedom** and **The Times They Are A Changin'**. Bob paints Bruce as a victim of a hypocritical, unjust, and heartless society, a searing indictment and condemnation of the same gossipers and rumor mongers that he himself has been falling prey to ever since pretty much day 1 in New York City back in 1961. Contrast this to the messianic self-destructive psycho portrayed in the film *Lenny*. The truth probably lies somewhere in between, I reckon.

Watered Down Love harks back to the theme of **Shot Of Love** in its vague reference(s) to the 1 Corinthians 13 depiction of pure love. Not a bad number at all, it, on the other hand, could be the most pedestrian recording effort on *Shot of Love*.

Screaming around the corner, we are suddenly treated to the restoration of the power of Bob's voice, not to mention his slow-burning defiance, on **Groom's Still Waiting At The Altar**. Missing from the original vinyl release, it was wisely added to the compact disc re-issue. The groom character appears to be Jesus himself who is wed to his bridal flock (or his church). Secular lines such as "West of the Jordan, east of the rock of Gibraltar", to me, seem like a segue to some of the geopolitical overtones three years later on *Infidels*. Personal images like "Try to be pure at heart, they arrest you for robbery, mistake your shyness for aloofness, your shyness for snobbery" are not only interesting metaphorically, but Dylan seems to clearly be a man wrestling with himself and his own demons.

The reggae-tinged **Dead Man, Dead Man** is an evangelical warning against the devil's hold on the mortality of the physical body, evidently harkening back to Romans 7:24, which beseeches the almighty for immunity from the evils of the flesh. On *Shot of Love* Dylan repeatedly seems to be confronting his own personal demons related to sexual lust in light of his recent convergence to Christianity. There is a theme of conflict between Bob's troubled sexual relations and the demands of a higher calling. This actually comes off as rather refreshing in the wake of the aggravating, if not galling, holier-than-thou pretense on *Saved*.

In The Summertime intersperses a simple, lovely, wistful, introspective melody into the mix. A relaxed, upbeat change of pace, it has a lovely feel to it. To take it out Bob treats us to a harmonica that hangs there in a suspended state of sensual palpability. **Trouble** grinds out a gritty guitar-driven quintessential blues emphasizing the classic blues theme of tribulation being a universal and intrinsic aspect of human nature, complete with nasty gee-tar hooks and impeccable contributions by the rhythm section.

One of the most celebrated songs in Bob Dylan's entire discography, **Every Grain of Sand**, exposes the dilemma of Bob's disappointments, failings, human fallibility, as well as triumphs, and thereby brings *Shot Of Love* to a most introspective conclusion. All of these reality doses are either the result of God's delivering hand or Bob's words and actions. Dylan steps to the plate of accountability while simultaneously kneeling to worship an inexplicable force sitting in the director's chair, driver's seat, or on the throne. Take your pick. In any case, **Every Grain Of Sand** is worthy of the masterpiece moniker.

It was his most sublime work up to 1981, a summation of his numerous attempts to articulate the promise(s) of redemption. It is a fitting culmination of his Christian epoch, highlighted by idiosyncratic harmonica notes piercing the heart and moistening the eye. **Every Grain of Sand** contains a universality that has nothing to do with the rest of the LP, a sort of prayer in the same intuitive zone as **Blowing In The Wind** twenty years previous to it. It hits the heart like a hymn that has been passed down through the ages and that wrote itself, sort of in the vein of **Amazing Grace**, and a watermark in Dylan's songwriting maturation that, only in retrospect, can been pointed to as a mid-career bridge connecting shores that for some 25 years were separated by Bob's personal descent into the dark night of his soul and his slow but sure emergence into higher spiritual sagacity.

I would apologize for that 74-word sentence, but that would be entirely disingenuous of me. We are talking about perhaps Dylan's most re-markable composition which got lost in his 1980s obscurity but which is yet more reason for the folks in Stockholm to finally grant Bob a Nobel in literature.

Shot Of Love generated quite a few outtakes, or at least partial songs that were worked over in March and April of 1981 at United Western and Rundown Studios in Los Angeles, and a cherished bootleg record-ing fortunately snuck out, and right off the soundboard, too. Good stuff at high volume on a road trip! **Caribbean Wind** wound up on *Biograph* 4 years later and **Angelina** appeared on *Bootleg Series Volumes 1-3* in 1991. **Is It Worth It?** and **Magic** highlight a long list of fur-ther album rejects including **Hallelujah, You're Still A Child To Me, Wind Blows On The Water, All The Way Down My Oriental Home, We're Living On Borrowed Time, I Want You To Know I Love You, On A Rockin' Boat, Movin', Almost, Don't Ever Take Your Love Away** (a bossa nova), **Mystery Train** (this recording is so good it's scary), **Ah Ah Ah #1, City Of Gold, Need A Woman**, and **Thief On The Cross**. If Bob ever gets it in his mind to resurrect this stuff, he's already got 1.5 albums worth of really good stuff to serve as a foundation. I know, I'm dreaming, but it sure would be nice!

Many have asked what happened to end Dylan's Christian period of work. Who can really say, but the suicides of Bob's longtime friends Howard Alk, on New Year's Day 1982, and Mike Bloomfield, who was found dead from a drug overdose in a parked car in San Francisco, were no doubt incidents that touched Bob to the core. The death of Christian musician Keith Green may have also been a factor in ending Dylan's four-year run of an album a year pace of output. Instead of putting out another record in the summer of 1982, Bob closed Rundown Studios before signing another five year five album deal with Columbia.

He would record an album of duets with his sometimes-on sometimes-off lover Clydie King, but this remains unreleased because, according to Bob, it does not fall into any category CBS knows how to deal with. Bob retreated to Minnesota to spend more time with his 16-year-old son Jesse and frequented Minneapolis performances of X, The Clash, and Elvis Costello, while not touring again for two years. One theory with no lack of merit is that the commercial failure of *Shot of Love* was a blow to Dylan's passion to keep dipping into his creative wellspring, especially given what must have been his understandable weariness after releasing four quite laborious records in 36 months. Another well-documented point is that Bob and Sara made overtures to reunite and his son Jesse's bar mitzvah inspired a temporary return to studying the *Torah*.

I say forget it. Some questions do more damage than they are worth. When it comes to Bob Dylan's religious beliefs, the answer is always, "Yes," and the question is never, "Why?"

#27

Infidels

A potential but never-fully-realized masterpiece, *Infidels*, was released Oct. 27, 1983 after engineer Neil Dorfsman was charged by Bob to re-mix the whole shebang when producer Mark Knopfler exited the scene to tour Germany with Dire Straits, the rock and roll band of the 80s, which was coincidentally in its prime. Bob, who felt that technology had passed him by and thus did not trust himself to produce himself, felt that his poetry just needed music as a vehicle, so he turned to his multi-talented buddy Knopfler, who he deemed was more at home in a modern recording studio, after briefly entertaining an invitation to Frank Zappa to handle the studio sonics.

Although the album was not marketed by a fall tour, its sales persisted at a sizzling pace through the Christmas season and received almost universal praise by critics, once again fueling rise to that revoltingly common box labeled Dylan comeback album. On the other hand, Dylan was beginning to get a reputation for being a culturally spent force, a confused man trying to rekindle old fires, a hateful crackpot, an artist hell-bent on relentlessly putting out bizarre material his fans weren't sure what to make of, and/or an echo of his ludicrously-absurd Christians days. Perhaps *Infidels* truly made no sense, did not hang together, had no point, and did not even need to exist. Was Bob kneeling at the altar of his fans and handing out standard-lowering bread crumbs, or were members of his commercial audience worshipping a washed-out has-been and thereby demeaning themselves?

Either way, 1983 began a convoluted, contentious, confusing conflict, for lack of a better word, between Bob and the rest of the world that was a bumpy, dicey, under construction, and enter-at-your-own risk two-way street lined with potholes. Weird, enigmatic, and frightfully dark, this it-takes-two-to-tango co-dependent addictive bond between artist and audience persisted for the remainder of the 80s, and to make things worse, just after the darkest hour before the dawn, a leaky dike would give way to a black hole leading to infinity between this galaxy and the next. Without getting ahead of myself, the subsequent 3 albums would get progressively, and chronologically, worse and worse. However, I prematurely digress, as I am wont to do.

Infidels was hailed as a successful return to secular music, but the whole truth is that Dylan's music, from the beginning, has not once ever completely abandoned religious imagery. Yet, on *Infidels*, the themes turned largely to love and loss, the environment, and geopolitics. Moreover, the music comprises some of his best poetic and melodic work since *Blood On The Tracks*. On the other hand, his mostly outright, blatant, as well as in-your-face Christian albums preceding *Infidels* had received no lack of salute from evangelicals, atheists, and/or theological sojourners alike.

Consequently, go figure. What was Bob Dylan up to and where was he religiously? And who was this **Man Of Peace** dressed as Satan he keeps talking about? First, he's in the background, then he's in the front, and both eyes look like he's on a rabbit hunt. What the hell is going on here?

I was suddenly and unexpectedly back in the U.S. after 4.5 years in the Pacific Islands of Micronesia, trying to figure out who I was, how to plug back into American life and a job market that did not have any openings for a guy who knew how to spear fish, speak an oral dialect from a remote region of the earth, harvest breadfruit and taro, climb coconut trees, and generally make a mess of his life by depending on substances and women for his so-called sanity. And here was Bob Dylan veering away from overt Christian principles and warning of apocalyptic end-time geopolitical chaos going on. Okay, pulling in the reins, can we get away from mind-f-ing riddles that alcohol, marijuana, lust, and cocaine were constantly drawn to in the early and mid-1980s? Wait a minute, which Bob's life are we talking about? Bob, I mean I, always get that confused. Suffice it to say, what Dylan was saying in late '83 on *Infidels* made about as much sense as I did when I looked in the mirror. Again I found myself relating, in a non-rational but not irrational way, to all the scary secular nutty paranoia on *Infidels* that seemed to lure me deeper into my (repressed) fear and search for meaning.

I mean, here was our friend Bob, who assured us of his Christian ways for three albums in a row, grieving the trampling upon of the Torah and making Israel out to be a victim cloaked as a bully. Had Dylan turned his back on Christ? Or was he just preaching ecumenicalism? Or was he just confused? Or, worse, just plain nuts? In 1983, all this was something, really about the only thing, I could relate to.

What I do know is that *Infidels* surely gave birth to Bob's most debated outtake of all time, **Blind Willie McTell**, an undeniable Dylan career highlight, superior song, and even better take honoring all of those old bluesmen (not just Mr. McTell) he had been singing about ever since and especially on his debut album. In addition, **Foot Of Pride** was also cut in the fury of commotion surrounding the frenzied last minute re-mixing required to meet Columbia's release deadline. Both of these songs, folks, constitute material that any other God-fearing-or-not artist would give his right testicle to have come up with. To Bob, however, they represented recordings that simply fell short of his artistic vision and inherently dormant capability.

However, the general public also came to perceive *Infidels* as not measuring up sound production wise. The album unquestionably could have benefitted from more scrutiny in its polishing phase. Imagine what another six months of leisurely attention would have achieved, let alone dropping **Union Sundown**, a protest of imported consumer goods and greed marinated with backing vocals by Clydie King, and replacing it **Foot Of Pride** and **Blind Willie McTell**. These and other cosmic hypothetical riddles shall remain hallowed in the halls, minds, and quandaries of Dylan freaks into infinity.

Jokerman starts the ball rolling in the direction of a sly political protest. Dylan's fascination and embrace of the then-revolutionary 1980s trend of music videos led to an obscure, but quite cool and slick still slide show suggesting any number of personifications of the song's protagonist, ranging from Cesar Romero's 1960s Batman character, politicians in general, Cassius Clay, Ronald Reagan, Adolph Hitler, Bobby Kennedy, Dr. King, and/or even Dylan himself. Take your pick, Frankie boy, my loss will be your gain. Oh, sorry, man sorry, for that irrelevant lapse into quoting 1968's **The Ballad Of Frankie Lee and Judas Priest**. Sometimes I do stuff like that.

The rightly-judged-to-be-sexist **Sweetheart Like You** is next, with some killer chord changes, causing the secular label to be hurled onto *Infidels*. Some creative brainstorming pundits have thrown out the possibility that *Infidels*, in turning away from sheer religiosity, came from Bob's mourning of the church's deviation from spiritual truth. Did somebody say 1970s TV evangelistic greed? On the other hand, perhaps Bob's faze with born-again zeal had merely run its course, and at the end of its holy rainbow Bob had encountered a temporary dead end. Oh man, I thought we dropped this merry-go-round topic a few paragraphs ago. See how hard it is to resist wanting to understand Dylan's religious stances, phases, non-beliefs, meanderings, and other assorted contemplations? Let's not overanalyze. That just spoils the fun, and I ain't lookin' t' make nobody wrong anyhoo. Even if I were right, I already accomplished that once back in the 70s, or was it the 80s? I'm still waiting to finally be wrong once. Not!

The ensuing **Neighborhood Bully** comes up with a classic Dylan bewilderment as Bob bemoans the treatment in the populist press of the Jewish people from time immemorial. Or was it a return to roots of a Jewish-born born-again Christian? Surely the tiny synagogue on a side residential street in Hibbing where Bob grew up learning Hebrew and attending summer camps was still ensconced in the recesses of his sub-conscious.

It was somewhere around this time that Bob was known to show up without fanfare or notice in "that little Minnesota town" he sang about in **Went To See The Gypsy** on *New Morning*, pull up in front of sites like his childhood home on 7th Avenue and the reformed temple that was now an apartment building, and sit momentarily in a darkened-windowed limo just before disappearing from sight unseen by man or beast. In any case, hidden clues tracing back to the Mesabi Iron Range minutes north of Hibbing, in **Neighborhood Bully** and elsewhere, litter his song lexicon.

1980s evangelical skepticism toward the American space program is one of the myriad of talking points suggested in **License To Kill**. Another instance of Dylan at his songwriting best, this gem has been recognized for its brilliant acumen and elementary genius by skillful-in-their-own right Bob buddies such as Tom Petty and Willie Nelson, whose cover versions of this song have categorically killed. Part of the genius of **License To Kill** is its bridging of geopolitical, meta-physical, and romantic themes, which come to think of it, might not be a bad way to characterize all of *Infidels*.

Side two kicks off with a stern warning concerning evil and the glistening packaging of modern-day prophets. **Man of Peace** clearly is a throwback to the so-called Christian phase that Dylan seemingly abandoned on side one of *Infidels*. Chameleon Bob Dylan sheds off one more layer of skin here, much as he cried out in **Jokerman**. Believing in God is apparently not the same animal as trusting in God. Bob seems to be telling somebody not to complain by saying he did not tell them so. If you think some of these sentences and rhetorical questions are indecipherable due to double entendres and triple negatives, my friend, I invite you to attempt to make sense out of *Infidels* without numbing your cerebral cortex with meta-physical intricacies taking you to the mountaintop or the gutter, but without passing go, for there is, as we all know so well, no neutral ground (think **Precious Angel** off *Slow Train Coming*).

Haunting backup vocals from Clydie King help to protest global economic rape in **Union Sundown**, marked by Sly Dunbar's dominating drum beat that (no offense Sly) sounds eerily like that embarrassingly grating 1980s drum kit impersonating an f-ing machine style, fad, or craze (What the hell was going on there and who should be shot for it?) that we have all come to know and hate. Here is a song that rightly needs to exist, but have mercy Bob, not on this album. Here the what-if game can only wonder what **Foot of Pride** and **Blind Willie McTell** would have done to the already-stellar reviews this album got back in the day. Misguided executive decision making at its artistic and tragic worst, if I might be so bold.

I and I gives lead guitarist Knopfler some reggae floor space, and he does not disappoint in this (possible) exploration of the distance between Bob's inner identity and public face. Culminating with a tangent love song as he had on *John Wesley Harding*, material concerns are discarded as **Don't Fall Apart On Me Tonight** adjourns the courtroom, but not without first treating his amorous lady to a searing harmonica for dessert while the millionaire with drum sticks in his pants has trouble planning their wedding dance.

Whaaaat? And why do I love listening to music that I am incapable of comprehending on any logical level?

And that, my good friends, is as good as any way to wind up *Infidels*, an artistic treasure which would sadly prove to usher in a painful mid-80s period of two bottom-of-the-barrel live albums, an astonishing retrospective compilation triple LP, and three rotten-to-the-core studio LPs.

#28

Real Live

In the interest of full disclosure, *Real Live*, which was released November 29, 1984, along with *Live At Budokan* from 1979, are two live albums, which because my commitment to rigorous honesty, I must admit that even while researching for this here book, I point blank refused to listen to again. Well, at first. Only because of this book did I finally allow them into my home, and one agonizing listen confirmed my long-held convictions. If nothing else, I am having too good a day at the moment to risk the sure-fire demoralization, if not psychological vomit, that would unquestionably be guaranteed sleep dream nightmare grist for the mill when my little heady hits the pillow tonight. Life is too short!

So, as the story goes, during the 1984 European tour, on July 7 at Wembley Stadium in London and on July 5 at Newcastle and on July 8 at Slane Castle, Ireland, Bob was backed by Mick Taylor of the Rolling Stones and Faces fame, keyboardist Ian McLagen, and Carlos Santana (in a cameo guest appearance) to make a live album to support sales of *Infidels*. They just commenced to unnecessarily re-work a bunch of war horses. The problem was that Bob's fans worldwide were immediately on to whatever gimmick this was supposed to be, so initial sales naturally achieved career-low levels.

Bob Dylan was flailing onstage and was about to start doing so in the studio, carrying on serial affairs with young women across international borders, marrying and divorcing and purportedly re-marrying one of his backup singers, and needing a band he believed in that likewise trusted him enough to follow him anywhere he ventured.

You are forgiven, Bob Dylan. You forgot that trust is a two way street and starts with being trustworthy. Hmmm, I wonder how come I know that?

#29

Empire Burlesque

*E*mpire Burlesque, when all is said and done, was Bob's 6th puzzling LP in a row that took fans unaware. Plus, it was conspicuously sub-par, and his following two records would get even worse. However, perspective provides wisdom in this case. The worst pizza I have ever had was pretty good. Same goes for ice cream.

Similarly, mediocre Bob Dylan records may not be life-changing, but they are overall still brilliant, always curious, and at sporadic moments, moving, inspiring, and thought-provoking. Furthermore, even when Bob is obviously not at his best as a songwriter, given the pure genius and sagacity he is capable of, he nevertheless engenders a sort of universal compassion and merciful self-pity in the listener, a two-way willingness to cut him some slack, see him for the human being he is, ever-fallible, as his songs point out, especially as he has gotten older.

Having said all that, this record was morose, morbidly dark, witless, and artistically unnecessary in the scheme of things on this planet we call God's green earth. Please be patient, though, because during that dreadful decade known as the 80s, just when the darkest hour before the dawn would rear its ugly head, a black hole of hopeless, helpless, slimy, snotty, worthless nonsense would beacon in the new day. Wait, are we still on Bob Dylan's music or did I just meander into the pasture of that really bad B movie comprising my life at the time? Oooops.

In any case, with the release of *Empire Burlesque* one thing was for sure. Bob Dylan had shed another layer of skin, ridding himself of even a hint of the aura of religiosity in which he had operated for the previous six years. He had become another animal alright. Reptilian, mammalian, two-legged, feathered, gilled, or four-legged, you tell me, pal.

Released June 10, 1985 after an all-time Dylan record of 8 months in the LP recording process, *Empire Burlesque* hit #3 in the U.S. and #11 in the U.K., modest (for Dylan) sales, indeed. Songwriting began prior to Bob's '84 European tour as he began making recording demos in his Malibu home recording studio. The whole process was so casual and laid back that a stable set of musicians was never selected. Dylan chose to produce *Empire Burlesque* himself and did not utilize engineer Arthur Baker much at all until the songs had all been cut, when Baker was relied on to mix everything in order to make it sound like a record in the Dylan tradition of LPs sounding like unique fictional novels. Bob invited into the studio (mostly Cherokee Studios in Hollywood) various musicians ranging from Al Green's band to Ronnie Wood to drummer Anton Fig of David Letterman's world's most dangerous band fame. Wood later stated that Dylan was a slave driver in the musical cutting process but displayed no authority or interest in the mixing process, which seemed to bore him.

During the making of *Empire Burlesque* Dylan got involved in numerous other charity benefits such as *We Are the World* and *Live Aid* to help victims of African famines, *Artists United Against Apartheid*, and *Farm Aid*. These endeavors eventually overshadowed *Empire Burlesque* despite three music videos filmed to market it. In addition, in 1985 Bob carried out his first tour with Tom Petty and the Heartbreakers and released *Biograph*, a 3 volume box set retrospective. Thus, despite the lackluster of *Empire Burlesque*, 1985 was in fact a year of a fairly stunning volume of artistic output from Bob.

The lineup of session players ultimately included three members of Tom Petty's band, Howie Epstein playing bass, Benmont Trench on keyboards, and virtuoso lead guitarist Mike Campbell. Three drummers,

Jim Keltner, Sly Dunbar, and Fig filled in at one time or another. Most notably serving as backup female vocalist was Carolyn Dennis, whose daughter with Dylan, Desiree, is inconspicuously thanked in the lengthy liner notes along with countless others hoodwinked into going down with this stale, disastrous debacle.

A couple dozen outtakes surfaced in the long course of recording, most importantly **New Danville Girl**, ultimately re-titled **Brownsville Girl**, partly inspired and written by playwright Sam Shepard, and **Drifting Too Far From Shore**, both of which were rejected and a year later added to Bob's next album, *Knocked Out Loaded*. These and almost all of the songs making the final set list were distinctly characterized by a 1980s sound aesthetic, which, first, has caused endless debates over the merits of the album, and more auspiciously, has relegated *Empire Burlesque* to the second and minority tier of Bob's work that certainly does not pass the test of time. The almost disco sound on **When The Night Comes Falling From The Sky** nearly singlehandedly explains a prevailing initial urge to puke in response to *Empire Burlesque*, while its at times mechanical, staccato, syncopated drumming resembling the 1980s machine percussion trend smelled too much like an attempt by none other than Bob Dylan himself to try to fit in with contemporary pop mores.

Empire Burlesque starts with the luscious harmonies of three black American female voices in **Tight Connection to My Heart**, followed immediately by a quick snap of a snare drum, vamping of the chorus line, "You've got a tight connection to my heart", a disco musical rhythm arrangement, and finally Dylan's unmistakable nasally voice wondering if anybody has seen his love. Stripped of any religious allusions whatsoever, back in '85 upon first listen this opener begged the question, "WTF is this?" With Robbie Shakespeare on bass and Sly Dunbar supplying a reggae groove riding a lushly produced pop wave, this song is nothing if not forgettable. Bad and forgettable, as we shall soon discover, totally beats bad and impossible to erase from memory.

Seeing The Real You At Last suffers from a horn section held in check by a poor mix and rather lame, confusingly camouflaged references to some Hollywood films of Humphrey Bogart, *Shane,* and *Bronco Billy.* Is Dylan referring to seeing himself crystal clearly finally, or is he addressing somebody else? Who knows, and what difference would it make anyway? Another throwaway. Okay, Bob you are now 0 for two. By the way, don't I have something else to do before I listen to the rest of this garbage?

All of the sudden, a gem driven by Bob's lovely piano power chords and lyrical sentiments that just might rip your heart out. **I'll Remember You**. A song title that is a grammatical sentence. Four chords, a cloud of dust, and an elementary bridge. Pure magic, despite an uninspired studio take, if you ask me. A precious, obscure treasure in the catalogue of Bob Dylan from the mid 1980s. Lost in the shuffle of the reduction of Bob's fan base, look no further for the song of this album. And try to listen to it, or better yet sing it, without dry tears. Ain't gonna happen, dude. The universal, sweeping sentimental sensibility of **I'll Remember You** is a throwback to **Bob Dylan's Dream** on *Freewheelin'* and a mourning of all the long-gone but not long-forgotten people who have come into our lives at some point, touched our hearts, and quietly disappeared after leaving indelible impressions on our sub-conscious psyches. Nice job, Bob.

A leftover from *Infidels* is next up, **Clean Cut Kid**, which tells the tragic tale of a Vietnam veteran radically and permanently altered by the horrors of war. The lead guitars are too low in the mix and Bob's vocal is virtually inaudible, rendering the meaning of the song undetectable. To Bob's credit, he attempted to write one of the toughest Vietnam vet songs up to that point in time, but this comprises another effort that merely falls short of its mark. This is becoming a pattern, man.

Never Gonna Be The Same Again bounces back with a lovely R and B romantic ballad highlighted by well-mixed synthesizers, sweet backup vocals, and slick lead guitar. Taken out by a gospel jam vamp that calls for and rightly receives a low mix, this run-of-the-mill composition is at least well recorded.

Trust Yourself sounds like Bob and his backing band have returned to Muscle Shoals as they propel a tribal groove and soulfully vamp out 8 beat measures in the same chord, switching to the 5 chord briefly prior to a two-chord bridge that totally works. This is a hip-grinding blues essentially, one that could seemingly have been improved upon in live shows with Tom Petty's band. Alas, no such luck, however.

Emotionally Yours is another undercover pearl from the 80s. Bob's impassioned vocals are expertly backed by a tasteful string section providing power chord fills that enhance the heartfelt, naked lyrics. It has often been said that one either loves or hates Bob Dylan's singing, and the essence of this quandary may just be at the core of this recording. Give it a listen or re-listen, and tell me what you think. I say big thumbs up.

Next, we have the one, only, and singular song that unquestionably epitomizes *Empire Burlesque*, **When The Night Comes Falling From The Sky**. An evocative, apocalyptic, upbeat, pile-driving rocker when first recorded with Springsteen's E Street Band's Steve Van Zandt on lead guitar, Dylan inexplicably and tragically re-recorded it to sound like a contemporary dance track because he thought it sounded too much like a Bruce Springsteen song. Fortunately, we have the much more palatable version on the *Bootleg Series 1-3*. This cop out is a prime example of wrong turns made by Bob Dylan in the 1980s. I mean, dude, you're Bob Dylan! Who cares who thinks what about anything whatsoever anyway?

Rightly or wrongly, when Dylan fans who even possess educated opinions on the matter, since so many draw utter blanks when it comes to the 1980s, conjure up a mental image when the words Bob Dylan and 1980s are thrown out, it is this precise song, **When The Night Comes Falling From The Sky**, that hauntingly, hideously, horridly, horribly, and harshly pops from their repressed sub-conscious minds and snaps a hellish, nightmarish still-life photograph capable of inducing panic attacks unless immediately filed in "de nile", which ain't a river in Egypt. With no apology at all, I say Bob Dylan has only himself to blame for the 1980s vitriolic backlash that this song singlehandedly brought on. Of all the not-up-to-snuff songs Dylan recorded in his down days of the 80s, **When The Night Comes Falling From The Sky** is one of his most embarrassing. When attributes of a song include bad as well as memorable, it is not pretty.

I'm glad that's over, but somebody's had to do it.

Something's Burning, Baby is arguably the strongest track on *Empire Burlesque*, which, granted, is not saying much. Yet, I'm not buying; my money is on **I'll Remember You**. Others say the consensus choice is **Emotionally Yours**. The question is, in any case, one of trivia, for what difference would it make what the best song is unless the album weren't so monotonously ho hum. Nevertheless, **Something's Burning, Baby** is almost enough to forgive Bob for **When The Night Comes Falling From The Sky**. The key word is almost. It paints an ominous portrait of a feminine archetype set to a slow march beat accented by a haunting synthesizer that builds and builds prior to surrendering to fabulously blended horns, feminine shrieking, and eerie, fuzzy electric guitar.

Engineer Arthur Baker can be thanked for the wonderful closing tune, **Dark Eyes**, which truly completes the forgive-but-not-quite-forget process on **When The Night Comes Falling From The Sky**. Dylan pretty much wrote this one on demand when Baker suggested the album was begging for something simple to conclude it. Its stark acoustic guitar and harmonica arrangement contrasts sharply with the heavy production of the rest of *Empire Burlesque*. A silly melody structured sort of like a children's nursery rhyme, the song's muse came from a split-second encounter Bob had walking back to his hotel room one night in L.A. A dark-eyed blonde with blue circles around her eyes holding a wine glass full of purple wine told Bob she was dying for a drink. Apparently, Bob took this for a way to fulfill Baker's request for a closing song that would provide some semblance of tonal balance on an album that otherwise contains two-bit, over-produced, tired throwaways. However comma, the acoustic masterpiece **Dark Eyes**, admittedly, rescues *Empire Burlesque* just at the right and its best moment, which is its end. Thank God it is finally over.

The only remaining problem is, 20/20 hindsight being what it is, we are about to go from pissing in the wind to descending down the toilet. Where's the bleach?

Here was Bob Dylan's music, like my life, seeming to bottom out, but things would only get worse and worse. It all seemed like my life, either this one or the last.

#30

Biograph

However comma, hold the phone, and before flushing the toilet, a little thing called *Biograph*, a non-chronological retrospective compilation, had a little inventing to do. Introducing, for the first time in retail record sales history, the concept of the box set, which went on to be commonplace, if not expectable from pop music icons who survive decades and decades. Once again, and this speaks volumes about Dylan as a cultural force transcending commercial success, we find ever-the-visionary and trend-setting Bob Dylan ahead of the times, even at arguably the lowest bottoming out in his career. Another case in point in the who-can-claim-to-have-done-that (?) department.

So, on November 7, 1985 (oooh, that was a rough time for this Bobcat) an interlude in the 1980s Dylan shit storm arrived. Take a deep breath – while you can!

A key feature of the package was a 42-page booklet containing some amazing photos and even more amazing rare commentary from Dylan himself, who sat through track-by-53-track interviewing by Cameron Crowe, whose engaging liner notes are to be saluted. Given that *Biograph* merely scratches the surface of the tip of the iceberg of the trajectory of Dylan's career from 1962 to 1981, several volumes could be written on it alone, yet in keeping with the focus on Bob's original music on studio albums, here goes the perhaps futile endeavor to keep this brief without selling a masterpiece short.

Most noteworthy are the 18 previously unreleased songs, 9 of which are either new studio or live versions of songs we knew about, and 9 more of which are just plain compositions that we did not know existed, way beyond previously unreleased. In addition, there are 4 rather rare and hard to find singles, and the rest of *Biograph* is comprised of a well-selected and wisely sequenced bunch of both familiar and more obscure albums tracks.

Even the inclusion of 9 of the 10 war horses on *Greatest Hits Volume 1* could not smother the oozing ingenuity found on this record, enough so that untold numbers of new Dylan fans came to the party right at the outset of Dylan's 80s shit storm, all due to *Biograph*. Who would have thunk?

This was true of the lovely Lori C., a good Catholic girl who accompanied me to my first of 57 live Dylan concerts at Poplar Creek Music Theater in the suburbs of Chicago in the summer of '86. I recall Lori's cherishing of *Biograph* in the confines of her Lincoln Park studio apartment as well as her experience of sitting on a steep-sloped lawn, lying down with me on a blanket and gazing up into the evening stars, and hearing Tom Petty and the Heartbreakers back up what I now know to have been a pretty lame concert and tour in general. Nonetheless, wherever you are Lori, I have no doubt that you are still a Bob fan, and for that, *Biograph* is to be thanked. The ties that tie which bind together global networks of Dylan fans are close and deep.

Rarities standing out on *Biograph* include, but are not limited to the following treasures dug up from the resplendent Dylan vaults at Columbia. First, from the real early *Freewheelin'* days there were **Baby, I'm In The Mood For You** and **Lay Down Your Weary Tune**, which both represent stellar instances of Bob's early vocal virtuosity and wildly stunning harmonica skills, and **Percy's Song**, an incredible folk tune right in the wheelhouse of Joan Baez if you ask me, which wouldn't stop me anyway. Also from this early period is Bob's first collaboration with an electric band on record, **Mixed Up Confusion**, which seems like it could have been resurrected for *Bringing It All Back Home*, *Highway 61 Revisited*, or even *Blonde On Blonde*, but what do I know? Hindsight sometimes ain't what it's cracked up to be. Bob probably thought it sounded too much like a Johnny Cash production. Oh, who knows? Actually, if you do, please clue me in.

From the indescribably prolific summer of 1965 and *Highway 61 Revisited*, for starters we got treated to **Can You Please Crawl Out Your Window**, a briefly-released single almost unobtainable unless you were in the right place at the right time. The abbreviated rockabilly remnant **Jet Pilot** is a similarly hot 1965 riff that simply suffers a crash ending and was never heard from again. Oh well, there goes another sure #1 single, but who's counting? Finally, there is a live **I Wanna Be Your Lover**, yet another sensational rocker that gave us our first official glimpse into the wild spring '66 world tour with the Hawks. You get the feeling, and rightly so, that there just was nothing, as in nada, stopping, a hyped up on uppers Bob Dylan in 1965. After all, in just under 12 months, he released 3 albums that changed music history, which we now know to be a drop in the bucket of master songwriting and crack recording that was going on at all hours of the day and night. Believe it or not, this was pretty much the 24/7 case from early '62 to early '66. Sometimes I marvel at the world's good fortune that Dylan did not precede the ways of Brian Jones, Janis Joplin, Jim Morrison, Jimi Hendrix, and numerous well and lesser known others during this time period.

Two mid-70s secrets and a late Christian era enigmatic gem on *Biograph* also revealed further evidence of the true trajectory of Dylan's career and plethora of influences on his back catalogue. **Up To Me** is a fascinating mirror of **Shelter From The Storm** on *Blood On The Tracks*, **Abandoned Love** has got to be Bob's all-time best rocking Johnny Cash impersonation up there with **Mixed Up Confusion**, and 1981's genuinely hot **Caribbean Wind** is a revealing glimpse into the strength of Bob's songwriting in an era during which he had supposedly lost it, or at least had begun to lose it. I say listen to **Every Grain Of Sand** and tell me that.

Rounding out the tracks worthy of distinction on *Biograph*, we have an awesome though crude demo of **Forever Young** and a handful of previously unreleased live versions of **It's All Over Now Baby Blue**,

I Don't Believe You, and **Visions of Johanna** from the spring '66 psychedelic escapade. A '75 Rolling Thunder **Romance In Durango** even before *Desire* came out, **Isis**, and 1981 live **Heart Of Mine** complete a random list of remaining standouts on *Biograph*.

Much more can be said, but will not. We shall stay committed to primarily focusing on unreleased original material. *Biograph* was a commercial goldmine that got re-issued on CD in 1997, and to this day this clever sequence of the familiar and rare continues to sell well, merit praise for being quite well thought out, hold its own when compared to the official bootleg series, and even earn Bob Dylan devotion from new waves of fans, some of whom are just 1/5 his age.

What can, at the bare minimum, never be taken away is *Biograph's* rightful title to being the first box set in the history of the music industry. Even more impressively and pertinently, it passes the artistic test of time litmus exam with brilliant, complimentary, and flying colors.

#31

Knocked Out Loaded

Ladies and gentlemen, the toilet has been flushed. But somebody stuffed it full of tampons. How low can Bob go without relying on dipping into his back catalogue?

The answer to this maddening riddle was discovered when the absolute, bleakest bottom of Dylan's barrel found its destination in record stores with the release of *Knocked Out Loaded* on July 14, 1986. Employing roughly 50 musicians in a disjointed project repeatedly winding down roads to dead ends, at best Bob's *Knocked Out Loaded* aim is too scattershot and roams down too many detours to be consistently compelling. Or, and I may be stretching a bit too far here, it is one of Dylan's least understood works, and it has gained an oddball cult following over time, but critical consensus persists to be apathetically negative. Having stated these overly kind half truths, for one brief moment in time, in fact, *Knocked Out Loaded* was a career killer knockout blow.

To start with, the album was a conceptual mess. It is truly not as bad as it is pointless. If artistic vision is present, would it please stand and account for itself? Don't hold your breath. *Knocked Out Loaded* does quite definitely manage to stand as the worst selling record in Dylan's 54 year professional career. Just the facts, folks. Its one and only credible achievement was coming within a hair of eternally shutting down Dylan's 1980s declining career via a momentary botched suicide attempt on it while appearing to but never actually delivering the music industry's version of the Grim Reaper. *Knocked Out Loaded* was

Dylan's scariest sleight of hand and most spellbinding black magic ever from which he appeared to suffer a certain death drop. Surely Dylan's hat was out of rabbits. Or was it?

Knocked Out Loaded contains 3 covers songs, 3 collaborations with other songwriters, and 2 solo compositions. The fiasco all began in early 1986 in between the Australian and American legs of Bob's tour with Tom Petty and the Heartbreakers and the resurrection of some instrumental tracks leftover from *Empire Burlesque* with which Bob started experimenting. This genesis can be blamed for what ended up as a slipshod patchwork which, once again, caused an ultimately depressing affair. Somewhere along the line *Knocked Out Loaded* was impetuously released simply in order to cash in on Bob's 1986 American tour. Everything was done in a hurry. Too unbearable apparently was the notion of performing the songs live, for the 8 songs lasting a mere 36 minutes on *Knocked Out Loaded* were only played live a handful of times in the year or two after its release. History has all but forgotten them, and for good reason.

The opening track, **You Wanna Ramble**, composed by little-known bluesman Little Junior Parker, was recorded with talents such as T Bone Burnett (on lead slide guitar), Al Kooper on keyboards, and Bob's then wife, Carolyn Dennis, anchoring the vocal backup trio, all of whom should have known better. Why did Dylan insist on relying on choral backup singing on this specific song, and, for that matter, in general in the 1980s, is a cosmic rhetorical question. Did he not trust his own singing to carry tunes great and small? **You Wanna Ramble** is no doubt a great song, but Bob's lyrics cannot be deciphered, and a blues tavern been-there-and-done-that echo renders this catchy riff pathetically pedestrian. Would somebody pllleeeeeease call for take two?

On song two Bob confounds the issue even further by covering a Kris Kristofferson haunting, endlessly-repeating, hypnotic melody, **They Killed Him**. The primary problem is that Kristofferson's intention for the song is both never achieved and fails to prevent the charade to which Dylan subjects his faithful. Should not in a perfect world Kris be covering Bob and not vice versa? "Surely this will be the worst song on this album," I recall thinking while standing in Dusty Grooves (a record store that really was dusty) on Morse Avenue on the far north side of Chicago on a sweltering July day in 1986. Little did I know. Although Kristofferson's version is marginally better, Dylan's mawkish, melodramatic treatment of the theme of lamentation of the murders of martyrs like Ghandhi, Dr. King, and Jesus serves to, ironically, murder any merit this tune had in the first place. The noble theme of **They Killed Him** is hackneyed and most regrettably becomes banal, trite, and void of any shred of credibility.

My trust in Dylan was all but shattered. "Come on, Bob," I thought, "You can do better than this!" Which Bob was I talking to? Surely things would not get worse. Truth is, I personally still had another 18 months of pathetic, controlled (i.e. out of control) drinking and drugging to do. Talk about not having a clue, man.

Shockingly, we are then treated to what constitutes the song that gets my vote for Dylan's worst song on his worst album, **Driftin' Too Far From Shore**. A few questions are begged. What could explain the resurrection of this best-forgotten *Empire Burlesque* outtake? Could not Bob have delved into *Infidels* tapes for **Blind Willie McTell**? Did I hear fingernails on the blackboard? Shameless schlock. What is Bob saying? This is the longest 3 minutes and 42 seconds of a life that deserves better. If there is such a thing as musical abuse, this is it. Artistic perpetration of insulting, unjust, offensive debasement at the depths of **Driftin' Too Far From Shore** is only forgivable if relegated to the privacy of the cutting room floor, in which case, we are all human. Full of trite idioms and insufferable, irritating banging of steel drums, **Driftin' Too Far From Shore** discovers Bob really reaching artistically, disastrously staining his reputation as the greatest songwriter and musical artist of the 20th century. Did he actually think that, if he released such racket, that other (dim-witted) two-leggeds would not recall this deed into perpetuity?

Keep in mind that, when a man bottoms out, if he manages to come back to life, and that is an enormous if, it does not happen overnight.

Precious Memories, at least, brings to a halt to the bothersome, obnoxious cacophony of **Driftin' Too Far From Shore** to finally give the listener a chance to come up for air. Bob's vocal is delivered with great heart, raising this country gospel standard to the celestial heights it deserves. Bob takes this lightweight material, with its plain and uncomplicated arrangement, and reworks it into a lilting reggae ballad, much in the bold, legendary Bob Dylan mythical tradition that we know and love. Bewilderingly, however, in 1986 praiseworthy sophisticated nuances such as this were largely lost in the disillusionment of most Dylan followers, what few were even left. Others lacked the music knowledge base to even realize that Bob did not write **Precious Memories**, a fitting example of the sort of pre-rock and roll musical heritage that surely inspired Bob to pen the touching, sentimental lyrics of songs like **Bob Dylan's Dream** and **I'll Remember You**.

On that note (incoming tangent), one ought to ever be conscious that Bob grew up in a Midwestern town of 20,000 or so, the kind of place where nostalgia is a nutrient tapping the roots of all forms of life in which we live in relationships. It is this endearing, charming part of Bob Dylan, the guy with the wide open, sentimental heart of gold, beyond his predictably unpredictable, outrageous, angry, oxymoronic, brazen personas, that forms the base foundation of his lasting charisma and counteracts any, justifiable or not, doubts of his greatness. In the interest of full disclosure, this is just me, and I admit to sharing the Midwestern roots of Robert Allen Zimmerman. I neither believe that all others agree nor that they ought to or have any reason to. I remain, on the other hand, quite curious how others either are or have been impacted by not only Bob Dylan but life in general.

Maybe Someday brings side one to an exceeding-the-speed-limit termination. Thematic betrayal, bitterness, and finger-pointing is regrettably lost in the shuffle of garbled lyrics in a song that somehow works but is usually overlooked because this album sucks. The riff of **Maybe**

Someday sounds unmistakably like that of **Dignity**, which three years later was left off of *Oh Mercy* very likely for this very reason. There is no doubting that Bob ought to have kept to the 40 m.p.h. speed limit instead of obstinately insisting on 60 as his bullheaded velocity. Both **Maybe Someday** and **Driftin' Too Far From Shore** come off as self-made demos, not studio album soundtracks. Dylan admitted so much in 1980s interviews. For instance, after breaking his all-time record for taking his time to record an album and *Empire Burlesque* tanked in record stores, he pondered, "If my records aren't selling real well, why should I invest much of my time recording them?"

And on THAT note, it should be pointed out that such uncharacteristic disrespect exhibited towards his 1980s listeners will justifiably but deservedly accompany Bob Dylan to and haunt his grave. Fortunately for Bob, on the other hand, the healing powers of time will probably by then render this unfortunate verdict to be past the statute of limitations in the court of public opinion, not to mention the incredibly short memories of human beings, particularly rock and roll fans, and thus, excluded from his obituary. Hence, to be fair, Bob Dylan's 1980s brazen conduct not befitting a rock star genius is regretfully documented in the publication you are now reading. Forgiveness does not mean forgetting. It means remembering, letting it go, and getting oneself out of jail. Nobody's perfect.

Knocked Out Loaded is frequently depicted as one excellent track surrounded by mediocrity, or some variation thereof, a critique that surely can be chalked up to **Brownsville Girl**, a superbly mixed, wonderful, innovative major work, both subtle and innovative. Here Dylan is witnessed in command of his incomparable vocal resources and impressive use of language. Centered around Bob's viewing of a 1950 Gregory Peck western, *The Gunfighter*, **Brownsville Girl** ridiculously narrates one his greatest ridiculous epics, though it is incapable of grabbing one's attention by the throat as does **Desolation Row**. Bob at his best in the 80s was not still capable of transcribing on the wings of the universal, intuitive channel to which he and pretty much he alone had crystal clear reception in the 60s. Still, **Brownsville Girl** comes razor sharp close to doing so, requiring momentary patience here and there only when listening to it for a time numbering in the triple digits, which, believe me, I have. It was nothing short of a stunning achievement, though, upon virgin placement of the needle on vinyl in the summer of '86. On the other hand, this otherwise loyal listener still refused to waste any of the little money I had on the worst of the worst in a Dylan era in which Bob seemed tunnel-vision focused on music quantity, not quality.

Got My Mind Made Up was written in collaboration with Tom Petty and was recorded abruptly on a one-day tour break, with his heart-breakers doing the session work. A prelude to some of the written-by-numbers stuff the Traveling Wilburys came up with 3 years later, this uninspired little rocker is another of the seemingly countless Dylan songs in the 80s that do not conjure up adjectives like memorable or clever. Lackluster, tired, amateurish, however, fit the proverbial bill. In the end, and in short, shamelessly disconcerting.

Even though this is one of Dylan's shortest albums ever time-wise (except for *Pat Garret and Billy The Kid* and *Shadows In The Night*, which clock in at one minute less – 35 minutes), the forbearance, endurance, and Zen-like composure required to give it an uninterrupted listen is a pathetic paradox. Eventually, however, relief is on the horizon when Bob starts giving us a more-than-decent vocal on **Under Your Spell**, which mercifully ends *Knocked Out Loaded*. Another songwriting collaboration, this one with Carole Bayer Sager, who claims Bob only allowed her to title the song, but Bob insists that Sager's input was needed. Whatever. Malnourished, miserable rubbish, period.

Knocked Out Loaded was, is, and always will be rightly, justly, and aptly ripped by weirdo critics who even bother to do so, but it nevertheless ironically possesses a warmth and charm lacking on *Empire Burlesque*, which repels closer inspection as opposed to attracting it, even though *Empire Burlesque* is a far better record. Moreover, it leaves a trail of alluring breadcrumbs sufficient to navigate to calm waters of loose-limbed blues jam fervor on **Maybe Someday**, and **You Wanna Ramble**, and Bob's 1960s singing gusto is retrieved on **Brownsville Girl** in particular.

If none of this makes any sense, all I can say is, "You had to be there at the time." And, for better or worse, make that worse, I was. The bewildering pain of it all.

When the time comes for the fat lady to sing, *Knocked Out Loaded* is evidence enough to justify the sad, wrong-headed, post-1960s rejection of Bob Dylan by plenty of his pee brain so-called fans. That's how bad it is. To non-Dylan freaks who went on living their lives and never looked back after *Blonde On Blonde*, granted slack can be cut on a purely intellectual, logical, linear, rational level. All sarcasm intended, I would never suggest executing, at least through lethal injection, such pathetic excuses for musical fandom. Yet, isn't it a pity that a few shreds of circumstantial confirming data like the album *Knocked Out Loaded* are capable of ruining the reputations of even human beings who have been cast in bronze on pedestals, despite the sheer idiocy of blanket accusations that do not, for they cannot, stand up in the court of overall historical truth and nothing but the truth. *Knocked Out Loaded's* lasting legacy is its illustration of the human frailty of Robert Zimmerman, the Ukrainian-American Jewish son of Beatrice and Abraham, and it passes go without stopping on the topic of Bob Dylan.

As lame as Dylan's next record would turn out to be, it did manage to turn the corner from the toilet to the sewer, which is no doubt progress. Just ask any plumber.

To Bob's credit, at least he had the courtesy to flush the pisser one more time. It still stinks in here!

Strike two.

#32

Down In The Groove

Strike three, and you're out, unless you're Bob Dylan.

Now, granted I have been trashing our friend Bob for 15 of the last 18 pages, but hang in there for 8 more pages of imperative, wholly merited, tortuous negative reviewing, and trust me, we'll be free and clear and out of the woods. This ain't easy on yours truly, either.

After the disaster that *Knocked Out Loaded* epitomized, Bob went back on tour with Tom Petty and the Heartbreakers, which reaped an entertaining Australian concert film, *Hard To Handle*, he played a reclusive rock star named Billy Parker in *Hearts of Fire*, a film that did so poorly at the box office in England that is was never even released into American theaters (but do NOT let that stop you from watching the best awful film ever), and he got involved in the infamous, underwhelming Grateful Dead tour in the summer of 1987 prior to the release of his next 1980s boondoggle, *Down In The Groove*, on May 30, 1988. Every bit the disastrous concept *Knocked Out Loaded* was from its inception, this (once again) highly collaborative mess of a project haphazardly dumped together indiscriminate studio blurbs executed over a six year span from 1982 to 1988. Yikes!

Utilizing 5 different sound engineering assistants and roughly 40 studio musicians, the commercial release of *Down In The Groove* was repeatedly delayed but unfortunately never nixed. On the heels of *Empire Burlesque* and *Knocked Out Loaded*, *Down In The Groove* went virtually unnoticed by all but diehards, essentially pounding a few final nails into the coffin of Bob Dylan's reputation and giving birth to a prevailing perception of him as a has-been rock star in the process of aging without a hint of grace.

Almost unanimous negative reviews were the rotten fruit reaped. The record reached #61 in the U.S. and #32 on the billboards in the U.K. *Down In The Groove* can be blamed for what became known as the Dylanizing of songs, for no matter what conglomeration of backups artists Bob cast behind him, in the mid-80s there seemed to incessantly be this sort of meaningless one-take sound that parodied Bob himself, a pathetic, lifeless, intellectually vacant horror of reverberating racket.

The song selection on *Down In The Groove* repeated the bland recipe cooked up on *Knocked Out Loaded*, resulting in two self-composed tunes, two songs written in collaboration with Robert Hunter, and no less than 6 cover songs. On some level this was a most sensible step given that Bob's creative writing ability had pitifully sailed into the doldrums, hampering his competence to come up with any new material. Still, it failed miserably due to what cannot be denied was an undeniable lull in anything approaching the pure genius mankind had come to yearn, if not expect from Bob.

Historically, Dylan's 26 year and counting never-ending tour commenced right after *Down In The Groove* came out in the summer of 1988. However, not with any fanfare to speak of. Bob's stage presence appeared distracted and unconcerned with delivering an artistic product with any degree of quality. In his 2004 memoir *Chronicles Volume One* Bob wrote that for concerts goers it must have been like being in a deserted orchard with dead grass, and that there was a missing person inside him he needed to find. From 1985 to 1988, uncannily, those words could easily have described my own personal life. Go figure. To Bob's credit as well as my own, and not without divine assistance, neither of us were down for the count, which very well might have been the case.

Backed by a garage rock band featuring Saturday Night Live bandleader G.E. Smith on lead guitar, Kenny Aaronson on bass, Christopher Parker on drums, and occasional cameo appearances by other struggling artists none other than Neil Young, the set lists were nothing if not adventurous, punctuated by three distinct sets of full band electric stuff, solo acoustic songs, and acoustic arrangements with Smith accompaniment. Despite somewhat generous praise that the press gave of these concerts, I was there, and I wish, I wish, oh how I wish in vain I could look you in the eye and tell you that I did not want my money back after the disaster I witnessed at Alpine Valley near East Troy, Wisconsin in the summer of '88. I will without hesitation grant that the never-ending tour started out with a passionate determination on Bob's part to rework his song lexicon up to that point in time. Succeeding in this endeavor, though, required years, quite a few backup band adjustments, and more patience than most live concerts fans were willing to financially invest. For neither the first or last time in Dylan's career, fans were fed up and literally swearing they would never be duped by Bob again.

This confusing, zigzagging, frustrating, yet intermittently fabulous period in Dylan history has forever driven Dylanologists bananas. Amid the chaos of *Down In The Groove*, as well as *Knocked Out Loaded* for that matter, there existed real possibility. Nonetheless, Bob was seemingly not to be bothered by caring what he put out in the studio or on stage.

This led to a prevailing consensus that Bob Dylan was doomed to be remembered only for what he had done in the past and where he had taken American music and fans. To this day, this accusation cast in bronze persists amongst a few one-time Dylan fans who cannot find it in their hearts to give him another chance, let alone forgive him for being human. Hmmmm, do I smell any projections here. Better not go there, man.

Down In The Groove's first song is a wonderful and really hot R and B classic written by Wilbert Harrison, **Let's Stick Together**, featuring an aggressive vocal and fairly cool stuttering tremolo guitars, but the problem is it ultimately paints the blues by numbers. This effort needs at least a couple more takes, perhaps after Bob and the boys have had a good night's sleep and wake in the morning ready to give a crap.

The indifferent parade marches forward with **When Did You Leave Heaven**, a fine gospel dirge composed by Walter Bullock and Richard

Whiting. The tempo regrettably drags quite badly and Bob's voice meanders on the verge of being outright out-of-tune. Incomprehensible is the only explanation of why this was not re-recorded after a strong cup of java and some mandatory artistic commitment. Madelyn Quebec's background vocal is indispensible, yet inaudible. The end product is insulting. What is a good man supposed to do? Grin and bear it, I reckon.

Sally Sue Brown is a good example of a concept with promise that went unfulfilled. Written by Arthur Alexander of **Anna** fame on the Beatles first American album, Dylan commissioned the services of Clash bassist Paul Simonen and Sex Pistol Steve Jones, but to no special punk rock effect. An actually decent garage boogie, this version of **Sally Sue Brown** ventures down a dead end alley, going well out of its way to pour salt into the wound of artistic insult. Where is the Bob Dylan who not only assumes but respects the intelligence of his audience, and would he please stand up, present and accounted for?

The next song, **Death Is Not The End,** is a striking understated spiritual from the *Infidels* sessions with Mark Knopfler on guitar. Highly anticipated was the contribution of Brooklyn-based hip-hop ensemble Full Force's to this number, but to no avail. The song lags, straddles, and dawdles on and on for about 2 or 3 minutes too long, and Dylan starts to sound no better than a high school kid with promise. His opening harmonica verse is unnecessary and tasteless, Clydie King's vocal help is insufficient at best, and the certain promise held by this melancholy riff remains unrealized.

Side one closes with Dylan's **Had A Dream About You Baby**, a gritty rocker highlighted by Bob's spirited vocal, the authority of Ronnie Wood and Eric Clapton on guitars, and Mitchell Froom's blistering hot organ. The whole shebang comes off as mixed a hair too low, especially Froom's organ. Another disappointment when all is said and done.

Side two kicks off with **Ugliest Girl In The World**, an early rock and roll throwback collaboration with Grateful Dead lyricist Robert Hunter. The song itself, and particularly this version of it, comes off as a promising high school band effort, so embarrassing for an artist of Dylan's stature that even the listener is inclined to feel ashamed both for and of Bob. Sort of like that icky feeling disco music used to illicit in my very bones, at least until I had had enough to drink that I became so void of shame, which I have come to learn has its place, that I would dance to anything.

This is followed by **Silvio**, another Hunter co-write, which despite being the best song on *Down In The Groove*, suffers from a recording that pales in comparison to what Bob eventually was doing with this tune in the mid to late 90s in live shows. The Bob Weir and Jerry Garcia background vocals stamped this FM radio hit with a distinctive Grateful Dead aura. Bob's unmistakable nasally singing, however, make clear this is a Bob Dylan record with Grateful Dead support, not vice versa.

A cover version of **Ninety Miles An Hour**, a Hal Blair gospel spiritual, is next, and its eerie morbidity is anchored by the bass background vocals of Willie Green and Bobby King. Perhaps this song would have served well as a mood enhancer in between up tempo tunes in live shows, but its delivery on this studio version is at long last insufficient and, again, falls short of its promise.

Unlike in the 90s when he respectfully, and even reverentially resur-rected oldie traditionals, standards, spirituals, and lovers' laments on two consecutive cover LPs, in the 80s, because Bob's own songwrit-ing skills had become so stale, superficial, sub-par, strained, stiff, void of spirit, shortsighted, schlock-filled, sterile, spotty, spineless, slipshod, senseless, self-defeating, second rate, scattered, unsavory, sorry, insuf-ferable, and sloppy, it was as if he could not bear to, nor was capable of releasing even modestly mixed mediocre original material of his own, so he reverted to gifting us with what we got from 1985 to 1988. Life is difficult, AND that is NOT a problem if we accept that simple fact and move on, moving downstream, not up. Whew!

On that nice nugget of neither here nor there (for which I appreciate your indulgence, for it may well be the most cathartic of the many divergent, tangential remarks in this here book), Bob then cranks into **Shenandoah**, a fine, albeit a bit corny, traditional folk ballad, and although he seems emotionally invested in his vocal, the G major key chosen ought to have been brought up to at least A flat for Bob's vocal to shine. In the end, sadly forgettable. When easy pickins like **Shenandoah** are massacred, we have a problem, Houston.

Closing out Bob's third 1980s disaster album in a row, **Rank Strangers To Me**, written by Albert Brumley and popularized by the Stanley Brothers, suffers from yet another rhythm that drags and an arrangement that at the very least needs some work. This apocalyptic country anthem remained a Dylan favorite into the mid and late 90s, when his live set lists fortunately contained much improved versions delighting the gospel bluegrass faithful amongst Dylanites.

Thus ends *Down In The Groove* in a most unceremonious manner, an album that lingers with the stench of Dylan's Christian era, particularly on **When Did You Leave Heaven**, **Death Is Not The End**, and **Ninety Miles An Hour**. Perhaps Bob Dylan's capacity to glue songs together into a novel on albums like *John Wesley Harding* and *Blood On The Tracks* is what *Knocked Out Loaded* and *Down in the Groove* fail to achieve when all is said and done. Come to think of it, that is the nicest thing, most woefully understated aside, that can be said about these two 80s debacles.

Intellectually, these two terribly lousy records would probably not have been comprehensible even if they had been well recorded. Dylan seemed to be flailing as an artist, begging for direction, and willing to stoop to the lowest common denominator to find it.

Most interestingly, it was exactly one month before the release of *Down In The Groove* that Bob joined up with Jeff Lynne, Tom Petty, Roy Orbison, and George Harrison to cut *Traveling Wilburys Volume 1*, an endeavor that more than proved that Dylan still held great promise, while also indicating that he required an infusion of creative help to live up to it and that he was, at that juncture on his path, unable to go it alone.

What are friends for? With a little help from them, we get by!

#33

Dylan and The Dead

Okay, here is another live album not worth wasting breath on. Yes, ending a sentence with a preposition was a passive aggressive sideways shot. But, come on, dude. We are talking about four either rather or extraordinarily lame live albums in a row going back 12 years.

On February 6, 1989 only 7 songs appeared on *Dylan and the Dead*, a sad, disheartening money maker anyway. I just pity those who sat through entire concerts of this crap. Like *Real Live* and *Live at Budokan*, *Dylan and the Dead* is worth one good listen, enough to surmise that it is nothing more than a ruse to get some mullah off a bunch of weed heads in dreadlocks. It was in the summer of '87, my last summer still using, that the Grateful Dead hooked up with Dylan for a rather brief, but commercially profitable concert tour which turned out did not at all merit the hype it logically generated.

Bob Wier, Jerry Garcia, Phil Lesh, and Dylan might have done well to write a song entitled **The Magic Is Gone**, for it just wasn't happening. Conspicuously, however, the magic reappeared instantly when Roy, Jeff, Tom, and George hooked up with Bob in 1988 and formed the Traveling Wilburys, who strangely never traveled outside the studio at all. Now that would have been a live album, but, alas, it was not in the cards.

The two astonishing records the Wilburys put out are nothing but fun and games and rock and roll at its best, and they did wonders for

Bob Dylan personally and professionally. Check out the CD re-issue and DVD that came out in 2007. It'll help almost make you forget completely about the sewer that Bob's buddies pulled him out of. A big however, though, is that Dylan's superb contribution to *Traveling Wilburys Volume 1* raised a lot of hopes that got deflated when *Dylan and the Dead* came out a few months later.

Interesting. I get sober. Dylan puts out another pretty much shit album (*Down In The Groove*). Hope resurfaces with *Traveling Wilbury's Volume 1*. Then, *Dylan And The Dead* is depressingly disappointing. Next, *Oh Mercy* in '89 transports us back to the mountaintops. It all mirrored the why do I feel worse if my life is supposedly getting better merry-go-round that addiction recovery, at first, was for me. Is my life lost, or is it found? I wish one of these Bobs would make up his mind.

Isn't it fortunate and grand that rock and roll fans have such short memories? Or, more pointedly, that intellectually they are actually idiots? Hey! I'm starting to really resemble some these uninvited, rude, uncalled-for comments!

More to the point (which isn't saying much), my favorite, loveliest, and safest assumption when I wake up in the morning is, "I don't know anything." Or shall we say, "Not everything." This humbling point was proven beyond any reasonable doubt by Dylan's next album.

Welcome back, Bob, and thanks for the air freshener! Don't you love it when you're tickled pink that you're wrong?!

And, wrong about the world's penultimate maestro at proving his critics fallible, no less.

#34

Oh Mercy

Lack of faith in Bob Dylan as a captivating artist reached one more final pinnacle in the years preceding *Oh Mercy* in 1989. Having resorted to touring with the Grateful Dead as a way to unsuccessfully ignite his creative genius and fledgling career which *Down In The Groove* and *Knocked Out Loaded* had essentially buried in a stream of pure mediocrity, Dylan resembled Willie Mays in his last season as a New York Met, only unlike Willie, Bob somehow stepped up to the plate and proceeded to not only rally himself and his flair for music, but (think John McGlaughlin on PBS television) prove all his naysayers wrong, wrong, WRONG! He doubled in the winning runs with the bases loaded and two outs in the 9th inning.

What explains this? How could Willie Mays' knees suddenly go from age 42 to age 20 again? Wasn't Bob supposedly lost? Did he not entertain thoughts of cashing in his music career? Well, all that is true. So, first let me preface what I'm about to say with, "Who knows?"

Yet, in addition to the jolt of inspiration Bob got from the Traveling Wilburys, he claims that in the summer of '87 he took a walk in San Raphael, California one day while rehearsing with the Grateful Dead, and he ended up having a gin and tonic in a bar where some cats were playing jazz. The guy singing reminded him of the iconic bebop and Grammy hall of fame vocalist Billy Eckstine, which in turn reminded Bob of something inside of him that he had lost. Subsequently, while standing onstage with Tom Petty's band in Locarno, Switzerland on

October 5, 1987, Bob found himself completely lost and making up, or resurrecting, on the spot a way to deliver his music which seemed to exorcise some sort of devil in him that perhaps was at the root of his 1980s artistic doldrums. Looking back, it seems that somewhere in this time period Bob got to the bottom of whatever it was he needed to face inside himself. Hmmm. The summer and fall of 1987. The last 6 months of my active career in the circus of drug and alcohol abuse.

The next thing you know, Bob conspired with Elliot Roberts, one of his tour organizers, to find him a steady band with which he could do an American tour in 1988. This, in June 1988, right on the heels of Bob's collaboration on *Traveling Wilburys Volume One*, started what has turned out to be a 27-year never-ending tour (well, let's say 100 plus shows a year) as of this writing in 2015.

On *Oh Mercy* rock's foremost lyricist rediscovered his flair for words, teaming up with Daniel Lanois in a New Orleans corner mansion posing as a homemade recording studio designed as half bordello, half tidewater swamp to fashion a record the likes of which neither Dylan or any other artist has achieved before or since. Featuring mostly mid-tempo ballads that again and again conjure up **Man In The Long Black Coat's** images of a moonlit Louisiana backwater swamp, *Oh Mercy* is stamped with Lanois' sonic vision and Dylan's once familiar accessibility to the right word, phrase, and/or idiom at just the right time. A classic example of a Bob Dylan album with a one-of-a-kind sound and vocal quality, *Oh Mercy* furthermore exhibits some of Bob's "A" game songwriting, unquestionably reviving his image as a formidable, if not master composer and musical interpreter who could do it all on his own without the likes of the Traveling Wilburys.

Side one, towering over the mid-tempo-ballad-heavy side two in terms of quality, embarks into an unredeemable reality of men who commit crimes without faces. A catchy, driving riff shoves the stark lyrics into your face with the one and only known recorded take, to this day, of **Political World**. The just plain lovely **Where Teardrops Fall** steps toward romantic metaphysics as John Hart punctuates this lovely ballad with a sweet closing tenor sax.

House in New Orleans where *Oh Mercy* was recorded in 1989. Photo by unknown photographer.

The jumpin' rhythm section on **Everything Is Broken**, spearheaded by Willie Green's drumming and Tony Halls thumping bass, shuffles this little boogie into a deadly harmonica that takes us out on a 12-bar limb. Something's definitely gone wrong in this broken world, a theme continued with the solemnity of **Ring Them Bells**, perhaps the best song of the bunch, theologically warning of the perils of ignoring the pain of innocent human beings lost on mountainsides like lost sheep. Bob pleads with St. Peter and St. Catherine to intervene in a world plagued by ethical dilemmas. How very and uncharacteristically Catholic of him.

A midnight wade into murky waters in **Man In The Long Black Coat,** with background crickets chirping, meanders face-to-face with a character that is either a biblical prophet or dangerous outlaw in a land where there truly are no mistakes if you care to see it that way. **Man In The Long Black Coat** has always seemed to me more like a painting than a song and an early peek into the doorway of Dylan's late era of songwriting, which began, let's say, in roughly 1997. **Most Of The Time** contains a series of sub-conscious portraits of idealized love straddling the fence on the border of fantasy and reality. **Most Of The Time**, like **Not Dark Yet** eight years later on *Time Out Of Mind*, implies the opposite, that is sometimes, whereas if things aren't dark yet, the point is that they will be eventually. Here Dylan has a way of saying something by NOT saying it.

What Good Am I, an ode to self doubt and glance at unadulterated evil, ventures to answer the age-old rhetorical mystery surrounding the possibility that human beings are nothing but worthless scumbags. **Disease Of Conceit** sustains this merry little roll with a walk down the indiscreet killer of conceit lane, lined with delusions of grandeur giving mankind the idea that it's too good to die. These two tunes do not paint a pretty portrait of human nature, but they are such beautiful songs that they are beyond alluring, even seductive. Bob's solo piano encore rendition of **Disease Of Conceit** at the Airie Crown Theater on Halloween in 1989 (an otherwise forgettable concert), dripping with both soul and gospel simultaneously, was one of the highlights of my 57 live Dylan concerts. Too bad security went home that night with my roll of 400 ASA kodachrome camera film with close ups of Bob sitting behind a baby grand. Oh well.

Next, we are invited to ponder our lack of ability to comprehend the needs of others in human relationships with the hypnotic, perplexing, haunting enigmatic inquiry **What Was It You Wanted?** Leaving us on a delightful, chivalrous, charming mirage is **Shooting Star**, a prototype for courtly adventures to the terrain of exalted feminine muses between this galaxy and the next.

Two critically notable outtakes from *Oh Mercy*, **Series of Dreams** and **Dignity**, were incomprehensibly somehow left off the final song roster but later respectively featured on *Bootleg Series 1-3* and *Bob's Greatest Hits*

Volume 3. **Born In Time** and **God Knows** were fortunately given further attention and included on Bob's next studio album, *Under The Red Sky.*

It is worth mentioning that all the *Oh Mercy* songs and outtakes represent stellar instances of Dylan's repertoire which vast majorities of casual music fans have utterly overlooked. Chalk this up to what amounts to a pathetic abandonment of Bob Dylan by the commercial music industry and its under-critical, cynical, undiscerning, unreflective, intellectually lightweight fan base drowning in the sedatives of late-70s disco and unimaginative, overly mechanized, heartless, mindless, shameless pandering to the lowest common denominator at the core of what otherwise substituted for musical entertainment during the 1980s. The entire *Oh Mercy* catalogue finds Dylan at the top of his poetry game, and with Lanois' production assistance, capturing a sound in an eerie mansion down in New Orleans that can and will never be duplicated.

A, if not the, persistent puzzle of Dylan's six-and-counting decade career seems to be: How many times will Mr. Jokerman himself inadvertently point out the folly of making snap artistic judgments based on limited data? Is this not perhaps a life lesson worth its weight in gold?

Does it not rival Bob's greatest insights up there with **Precious Angel's** "My so-called friends have fallen under a spell, They look me squarely in the eye and say, 'All is well.' Can they imagine the darkness that will fall from on high when men beg God to kill them and they won't be able to die?" I mean, I'm juuuust asking...!!!

Of all of our friend's transformations, so-called comebacks, and rabbits in his hat, *Oh Mercy* has to take the cake. It was as though Willie Mays in 1973 had suddenly been able to once again throw out base runners from deep center, steal bases, and hit for average as well as power. Our melodious mystic had never been closer to his last breath. Therefore, *Oh Mercy* is my most beloved Bob Dylan dressing room costume adjustment.

Foxhole prayer answered. Life, and Dylan, were getting better. What more can you ask for?

#35

Under The Red Sky

Exactly one year after *Oh Mercy*, Bob Dylan released *Under The Red Sky* on September 10, 1990 to mixed reviews ranging from attacks that it was a strange, disappointing follow up to the mostly highly acclaimed *Oh Mercy* to (comeback) comparisons to *New Morning* that hailed its understated genius for being so much better than it sounded on the surface. Of these two camps, I find myself placed smack dab in the middle of neither. It's an f***-ing great album about once every couple years. Although it initially sounded rather rushed and mediocre at best, it somehow most miraculously stands the test of time. Don't ask me.

Another way to say it is to quote **Mississippi**, written about six years after *Oh Mercy* and *Under The Red Sky* brought Dylan back to life. "You can always come back, but you can't come back all the way." Perhaps keep this in mind as we proceed here.

Bob dedicated this entire album to Desiree, his then four-year-old daughter with Carolyn Dennis, and four of the ten songs on the album are essentially children's nursery rhymes put to some gorgeous chord, rock and roll, and instrumental arrangements. Slick sound producer Don Was is rightly credited for pulling together disparate compositions, hurried and unfocused recording sessions, and some rather forced songwriting by Mr. Bob. How did Was synthesize it all into what comes off as a relatively cohesive outcome? Well, depending on what kind of mood I'm in, he DIDN'T.

Comparing and contrasting *Under The Red Sky* with *Oh Mercy* is only natural due to the fact that they are two excellent records recorded within a year of each other, for one, and they represent the only truly great self-written music that Dylan came up with over the twelve long years between 1985 and 1997. Don Was did not at all achieve the sonic certainty that Daniel Lanois did on *Oh Mercy*, yet *Under The Red Sky's* seemingly deliberately lightweight material somehow contains an appealing lack of substance in comparison to *Oh Mercy*. *Under The Red Sky* intentionally recoils from *Oh Mercy's* depth, atmosphere, and shadowy thought provocation. While *Oh Mercy* is written for middle aged adults, who tend to hibernate in pensive places of not knowing, *Under The Red Sky* is a triumph aimed at innocent pre-adolescents open to the persuasively charming and alluring powers of playful suggestion.

It bears repeating that both *Oh Mercy* and *Under The Red Sky* came out on the heels of Bob's contribution to the Traveling Wilburys, for which he was justifiably hailed as a still-potent artist with much to contribute. It was surely this invigorating experience, and not the grand commercial success of the Wilburys which, at least for a couple years, re-ignited Dylan as a songwriter and recording artist. Furthermore, Bob's successful collaborations with the Wilburys led him to seek out unanimously successful cameo appearances on *Under The Red Sky* by rock stars the likes of Elton John, Stevie Ray Vaughan and his brother Jimmy, Al Kooper, David Crosby, Bruce Hornsby, and George Harrison.

These supportive studio performances came in most handy by rescuing sloppily-written songs like **T.V. Talkin' Song** and **Two By Two** and sprucing up spontaneous, if not rushed, efforts like **10,000 Men** and **God Knows**, which Bob admitted had been hastened as a result of his busy schedule cramped with his never-ending tour and recording his own album while simultaneously not letting down his buddies in the Traveling Wilburys.

The album jumps right off with **Wiggle Wiggle**, which comes off resembling a trite rock and roll T.V. theme song or something. The lead guitar by Slash and drumming of Kenny Aranoff play wonderfully off Bob's vocal that builds into a crescendo and commits like he used to in the 60s on anthems such as **Like A Rolling Stone**. In live European concerts Bob claimed the song was a big hit back in the states and further pulled the wool over his audience's eyes by suggesting it was about going fishing, which upon further analysis does actually appear plausible. **Wiggle Wiggle** is a classic example of two rock chords, a cloud of dust, and an absolute lack of relevance, necessity, and/or any other earthly pertinence. Sort of in the tradition of **Tutti Frutti**. **Wiggle, Wiggle** ain't no **Gates Of Eden**, let's face it, and it constitutes a bit of a stretch, I'll grant you, but I personally have no trouble going to its childlike galaxy and certain grease for hip grinding at the very least every couple years or so.

Next is the sublime title track nursery rhyme, **Under The Red Sky**, an instance of superb, under-praised songwriting in the Dylan catalogue. The tender, fatherly vocal is virtually unrecognizable, especially in the wake of **Wiggle Wiggle**. Elongating the vowels at the end of lines and embracing the listener in a cocoon of love, Bob croons a bedtime melody and dreamlike lyric prior to George Harrison's **My Sweet Lord**-esque solo, which George nailed on only his second pass and eventually takes the song out on a puffy white cloud floating on delta waves.

Unbelievable rockets off with a jangly **Honey Don't** Beatles cover intro by Waddy Wachtal and drives into rock and rollville complete with honky tonk piano and classic Dylan rage expressed in lines like, "They said it was the land of milk and honey, now they say it's the land of money." Bob's vocal, again, comes off as powerful, this time in the form of his signature decisive, nuanced, and subtly exquisite phrasing.

The crown jewel of this LP, **Born In Time**, is next. Re-worked from an earlier, less sentimental and bluesy outtake on *Oh Mercy*, Bob's thin vocal sparkles with Was' heavy reverb on the record. Bruce Hornsby's lovely piano carries the melody as Bob competently debuts on an accordion. Bob came into the studio with dozens of verses for the songs on *Under The Red Sky* and at times sounds like he is reading the lyrics while spontaneously deciding which lines to include and which to disregard. This detracts from **Born In Time** and causes this version to lose its power at moments, oddly not fitting what this songwriting gem calls for.

Rambling into the slightly forced **T.V. Talkin' Song**, which simply vamps on an A7#9 chord for 3 minutes and 2 seconds, Bob's bitter wit is given a soap box to drone on and on about the evils of boob tubes as he complains, "Sometimes you gotta do what Elvis did and shoot the damn thing out." The main problem with the studio version is that piano and guitars ought to lead the vibes, not drums. Furthermore, Bob gives the impression he is reading lyrics from the scraps of paper on which he had painstakingly written verse after verse, so verses chronologically got randomly interspersed in the spur of the moment. Kudos to Was as well as Dylan for making a fairly horrible song sound almost listenable. *T.V. Talkin' Song* just might take the cake for the Dylan recording that most motivates the listener to cut Zimmy some slack when he's clearly not at his best.

10,000 Men suffers from another thin vocal performance too low in the mix, not to mention slide guitar by Stevie Ray Vaughan and Dave Lindley that sounds like it is suffocating from tired guitar amp syndrome. **10,000 Men** is a terrific rock song poorly recorded that still manages to sound hot 24 years later. **2 by 2** is another children's rhyming verse on which Elton John contributes a piano solo that sympathetically responds to Bob's groove, which rises each rung of the number-by-number ladder before Elton's electric 88s come in and provide his signature virtuosity.

The last three songs on *Under The Red Sky* close out the album with some of Dylan's most under-praised stuff ever. **God Knows** is full bore Dylan soul-baring candor at its penultimate best. This long-forgotten pearl is nothing less than a potential rock anthem that never was. On the other hand, it is an audio rocket to behold in concert with Charlie Sexton or Larry Campbell doing lead guitar.

Handy Dandy is a hoot of a Dylan studio performance that went on for a thirty-four minute jam, and Was edited it down to the 4:03 we ended up with. Al Kooper shines on an organ posing as an accordion as the killer bridge throws us back to a chord groove reminiscent of that on **Like A Rolling Stone**.

Appropriately, another tune catered to kids, **Cat's In The Well,** takes us out with Stevie Ray Vaughan picking a fluid, funky, perfectly-timed lead slide, proving that Stevie did not just play guitar, but psychically channeled something besides guitar playing coming right through him. **Cat's In The Well** notably held more than its own in its role as a concert closing encore for a several month run in the 2001 to 2002 era of Larry Campbell and Charlie Sexton dueling guitars with Bob Dylan night after night. How can human beings make three guitars sound like seven?

Incidentally, expanding on that tangential note, look to concert bootlegs from Charlie's fall farewell of 2002 for instances of this phenomenon on **Summer Days** in Chicago, Indianapolis, or Columbus. Bob even gleefully tolerated Charlie shaking his legs in the air while lying on his back (while still ripping out fabulous lead licks, mind you) as Tony Ganier twirled his double bass like a spinning top, somehow not missing a beat in his own right. During **Summer Days** they all acted like bad little boys who couldn't wait to go on summer vacation, but it netted live Dylan highlights that rank with **I Don't Believe You** and **Tell Me, Momma** from the spring '66 world tour.

Under The Red Sky will be remembered for its tough, trash can production, not having much of heady substance to say, workmanlike perfunctory recording, stylized and simple songwriting, and narration by a character with the air of Rumplestiltskin. It was followed a month later by *Traveling Wilburys Volume 3* (really 2, but who's counting), which did not exactly hurt Dylan's stature as an artist still with something to contribute, both establishing 1990 as a solidly positive year in Dylan history and, most importantly, constituting the fourth out of Dylan's five most recent commercial releases (if you count the

Traveling Wilburys stuff) that indicated nothing at all was wrong in Bob Dylanland.

Of all the under-rated and/or unheard of Bob Dylan albums, *Under The Red Sky* just might make your day if given the tolerance, patience, and the imperative slack-cutting it requires. In researching this here book, it is the particular album that rekindled my affection(s) the most, and that's speaking volumes, let me tell ya. Put together on the fly between Wilbury collaborations and Bob's new-found passion for the art of live performing (the never-ending-tour was now in full swing), *Red Sky* was Bob's last album of original songs for the ensuing 7 in terminable years. One gets the sense that this album taught Bob to respect his human limitations as an aging and mere mortal. Though *Under The Red Sky* and *Oh Mercy* marked an abrupt yet clear end to the haunting nightmares of his 80s shit storm and were plain evidence that Bob's songwriting skills were still in full force, juggling a lifestyle practically constantly on the road with composing and recording well-produced music had to be done with prudence and mindfulness. So, he just didn't do it for about 7 years. But what a wise choice – in retrospect.

In 1990, ever so slowly, Bob Dylan was incontestably, though imperceptively in the eyes of pop culture, turning a corner, and two years clean, in my own merry way, so was I.

Way to go dude, even if you weren't really trying.

#36

Bootleg Series Volumes 1-3

On March 26, 1991 Columbia Records, in response to enormous demand, finally opened its vaults to its abundance of unissued, backlogged, and much-bootlegged (unofficially on the black market, if you will) Dylan material spanning the 60s, 70s, and 80s. Another box set in the tradition of *Biograph* and expertly compiled and produced by Jeff Rosen, a close Dylan confidante and really professional handy man over the years, *Bootleg Series Volumes 1-3* gave us quite the hodgepodge of 58 tracks overwhelmingly comprised of chronologically sequenced studio outtakes, but peppered with previously unreleased live recordings, demo takes, alternate versions, and even a couple *Basement Tapes* that surfaced for the first time.

Rosen would go on to team up with Steve Berkowitz to produce an entire series of 11 and counting official bootleg releases that has proved to be not only commercially quite profitable, but artistically praised by critics and fans alike. The first volume encompassed 1961 to 1963, volume 2 spans 1963 to 1974, and volume 3 covers 1974 to 1989. What jumps out of these recordings is the shocking number of distinguished compositions in Dylan's back catalogue that at various times had provided litter for the recording room floor. Without detailing the literally dozens of previously released stellar outtakes on *Bootleg Series Volumes 1-3*, what is mostly in order here is just a sketching of the remarkable songs never heard of up until this time.

The first volume revolved almost entirely around the era of *The Freewheelin' Bob Dylan*, a period of enormous creativity for Bob, to say the least. Two original volume 1 compositions previously unreleased stand out, namely **Ramblin' Gamblin' Willie** and **Walls of Red Wing**. These melodies reaffirm, in hindsight, the latent songwriting virtuosity that was surfacing in between Bob's first album and *Freewheelin'*.

Furthermore, given what we now know, in no small part due to volume 1, roughly 3 albums worth of commercially very viable material could conceivably been released at the time of *Freewheelin'*. Even more astounding is the self-confidence Bob displayed by not reverting back to these unreleased recordings on future records. Ever the artistic visionary, he not only forged onward by writing a whole new batch of songs for *The Times They Are A-Changin'* and *Another Side of Bob Dylan*, but he evolved his craft in a direction away from social commentary and toward intellectually surreal poetry with beat literary overtones on his three electric earthquake albums in 1965-66.

Also noteworthy on the first volume were Bob's outstanding, old bluesman rendition of the traditional **Moonshiner**, hard to imagine being sung by a 21 year old, and **Last Thoughts On Woody Guthrie**, a 5 page rambling poem he read orally to close his April 12, 1963 New York City Town Hall performance 6 weeks before the release of *Freewheelin'*.

For a sublimely stellar portal entering the elegant epoch of 1961 to 1963, look no further than volume 1 of the official bootleg series. One of my personal dirty little secrets, and honey let's keep it between us, is that this captivating collection has been a comforting companion, in audio cassette form no less, in the small but pretty decent ghetto blaster on my kitchen counter for the past 12 years. And I am talkin' 24/7 ladies and gentlemen. Shhhhhh.

The second volume covered the years 1963 to 1974 and is highlighted by five eclectic masterpieces that indicate the wide range of musical genres in which Dylan can operate. First, we hear, from 1963, **Seven**

Curses, a dramatic ballad clearly in the folk tradition musically, which narrates a tense Shakespearean tragic tale of a father-daughter bond ripped apart by an unjust criminal justice system. Second, **Farewell Angelina** is a captivating, splendid *Bringing It All Back Home* reject still in the folk department that was mostly popularized by Joan Baez. Third, yet another killer rocker from the *Highway 61 Revisited* sessions, **She's Your Lover Now**, which was tossed out back in '65 and disappeared until this first official bootleg. Fourth, we were treated to **Santa Fe**, a tremendous vocal and melody from Big Pink in '67.

And last, but not least, **Wallflower** is a sweet country classic that Bob threw into some of the sessions to complete his second greatest hits collection in 1971 and which was later covered by numerous Nashville cats, perhaps most notably David Bromberg on one of his solo LPs in 1974. Bromberg, incidentally, to this day slips this one into his live act as he did, most energetically to say the least, at Space in Evanston, Illinois in 2013, illustrating how this crowd-pleasing gem stands the test of time.

Volume 3 spans a mystifyingly misunderstood 16 year time frame from 1975 to 1991 marked by various aforementioned periodic artistic wastelands, doldrums, and triumphant exploits. Like on volumes 1 and 2, all tracks are fascinatingly fun, but sprinkled in are five previously unreleased Dylan originals standing out from the rest.

First, **Seven Days** is a real treasure unearthed from the 1976 2nd leg of the Rolling Thunder Revue. As good as this track is, the one Ronnie Wood pulled off one year later at the 30th anniversary concert celebration (we'll get to that live LP) takes the cake.

Furthermore, four over-the-top outtake overtures are finally served up on a silver platter, for the taking. And, for the 3rd class misdemeanor of excluding these ditties from studio album song lists, please, put each of these in that confoundingly confusing Dylan category of what on earth, or the hell, take your pick, were you possibly thinking, Bob?

First, **Angelina**, from the days of *Shot of Love*. Speaking personally, and I mean extremely personally, I would gladly without hesitation, donate my left and/or right testicle to medical research to compose a song the likes of this, capable of excavating an opening of the ole heart chakra wider than the upper Mississippi valley, broader than the Grand Canyon, deeper than the bluest ocean, and more bottomless than the depths of the Pacific Ocean's Marianna Trench, the deepest, darkest subterranean spot on planet Earth. However comma, with the gorgeous, alluring **Angelina** once again Bob Dylan is witnessed discarding an otherwise verifiable musical gem.

Next, there are two *Infidels* outtakes, **Foot Of Pride** and **Blind Willie McTell**. **Foot of Pride** is one of those *Infidels* era songs that still imparts an air of Christian bias, as do **Neighborhood Bully**, **Man of Peace**, and even the apocalyptic **Union Sundown**. Thus, did Dylan's so-called Christian phase ever really have a beginning, a middle, and end, or was it simply part and parcel of 5.5 and counting decade long lexicon of music that has always had a divine connection on its speed dial? Regardless, **Foot Of Pride** was also nailed most spectacularly at the 30th anniversary Bob Fest by none other than Velvet Underground Mr. Cool, Lou Reed. Lou treats it with reverence without abandoning his unmistakable gruff vocal delivery, which, not so incidentally, might have been commercially unthinkable, unviable, and tossed off had it not been preceded by Dylan's head-scratching authoritative 1960s stamp of approval granted to pop singers who lack conventional singing ability.

As for **Blind Willie McTell**, first please excuse me, as I always have to wipe away a few tears while listening to this *Infidels* outcast, which I am doing at this very moment. Let's start with a safe assumption. It is a more-than-fine song, landing somewhere in the top 20% drawer in Dylan's illustrious catalog. However, throw in this particular jaw-dropping take, with Bob handling solo vocal and piano duties and Mark Knopfler leading from one step behind on acoustic guitar, and what comes out of the oven is one of the top 5 Dylan studio recordings ever. **Blind Willie McTell** instantly became a never-ending-tour audience request that was not bequeathed for years until the late 90s, when it eventually became a somewhat consistent live performance treat that played host to numerous re-interpretations, each one better than the last. Having said all that, this Dylan fan remains a sucker for the original **Blind Willie McTell** studio rendition due to its patient, soulful, melancholy mojo capable of stopping a heartbeat on a dime, grabbing one by the throat and not letting go, and conducting of mouth-to-mouth resuscitation on the walking dead.

Last, and certainly not least, there is **Series of Dreams**, driven by a hypnotic rolling thunder drum serenade by the unheralded Roddy Colonna. What the heck was in your coffee that day, Roddy? I'll have a double shot of what he's having. **Series of Dreams**, most unfortunately, has never found its way onto any live set lists over the years, although this possibility persists in the fantasy department of my own series of dreams, be they sleep or day. It does, on the other hand, bring to a close the first, and to this day still the most remarkable volume of Columbia's eleven volumes of official bootlegs. Given that the other ten ain't too shabby, especially *Tell Tale Times (Volume 8)*, you might reckon I just stepped out of line, but sometimes a man has just got to go out on a limb.

Bootleg Series Volumes 1-3! Spanning eras, epochs, genres, and decades. Absolutely stunning, revelatory, and good company while making morning smoothies. Since 2004!

#37

Good As I Been To You

And

#38

World Gone Wrong

So, in 1992 and 1993 how in the heck did Bob Dylan come to re-cord two consecutive fascinating solo acoustic albums of entirely old-timey cover songs? *Good As I Been To You* and *World Gone Wrong* ought to be clearly put into the context of yet another Bob Dylan skin shedding. This time he surprisingly stepped back from precisely what he is most revered for, songwriting, but unflinchingly continued to relentlessly pursue his inner muse in new directions.

Bob's late 80s shit storm may have been imperceptibly interrupted by *Oh Mercy* and *Under The Red Sky*, yet his artistic attention had focused away from the studio and onto performance art. As a matter of fact, I hereby challenge any and all takers out there to draft a thoughtful historiography on that very Bob Dylan sub-topic (Dylan live!), which is actually a heretofore under-explored, massive subject matter monster. All I can say (think **Bob Dylan's 115th Dream**) is, "Good luck."

Anyhoo, entering his fifties, Bob had long since embraced his decreased though still considerable skills as a songwriter, and a cowboy touring band anchored by Tony Ganier (bass), Winston Watson (drums), John Jackson (guitarist who took over when the no-doubt-talented, mugging-for-the-crowd show off G.E. Smith exited the scene), and Bucky Baxter (Steve Earle's pedal steel and mandolin man) organically evolved into a roving tour de force, sustaining what then-emerging Dylan expert Clinton Heylin has described as a monumental-for-a-man-of-any-age schedule of 90-some concerts a year.

In addition, offstage, not enough can be said for the Dylan and Columbia's creation of *The Bootleg Series* concept for digging into the treasure trove of unreleased Dylan recordings going back to the early 60s. Again, the 1991 first version/volume, was chocked full of some superlative and some not-so outtakes, demos, live gems, and various and sundry pearls ranging from 1961 to 1989, but more importantly, here began a grand unfolding of pure gold that lay in the secret alcoves of Columbia's vaults. The official bootleg series is a revelation that not only continues to this day, but which will unquestionably persevere and escalate long after our favorite prolific bard has gone to his maker.

Add to this an early 90s legendary tour with Carlos Santana's Latin rock groove on which Bob started coming up with completely random goofy comedic gimmicks like introducing songs by asking the audience if they'd ever heard of U2 and diving straight into the lyrics of **Rainy Day Woman #12 and 35** while the band thinks they are to be playing **Watching The River Flow.**

Between legs on this storied roaming caravan, in early 1992 trusted conspirator David Bromberg was pulled out of his self-imposed violin-making woodwork to serve as producer, bandleader, and handyman to lay down an album's worth of songs in Chicago's Acme Studios on Belmont Avenue. However comma, as David was left to mix what constituted a contractual filler for a ten album deal with Columbia in 1988, Bob ventured off on an eleven show European jaunt and re-turned to his Malibu garage studio to log a few solo acoustic fillers between the Bromberg stuff already in the can.

As Bob pursued his inner muse all by his lonesome, the Bromberg Chicago sessions were pulled from what became Bob's next album, *Good As I Been To You*, a compilation of traditional covers that began to be featured in his increasingly prioritized live performances. What became of the Bromberg recordings or why has never been explained by either Bob or David, although I had to bite my tongue in order to not inquire when I chanced to meet and chat for 20 minutes with the ever-in-stellar-form Bromberg at his 2013 appearance at Space in Evanston, Illinois. As an aside, one can only wonder aghast in awe and powerlessly hope that the day will come when such potential pearls will be rescued from their proverbial graves.

So, with a minimum of fuss and without notes or lyric sheets during studio takes, on November 3, 1992 Bob came out with *Good As I Been To You*, which can be described as a minor high point in his discography during an age of music industry hysteria over unplugged forays into the past to find something relevant and timeless in the present. To say or bellyache that Dylan jumped on this bandwagon is a bit of a misnomer, considering that he can be justly credited with having drawn up the blueprints for the wagon in the first place. So much for cheap shots.

Using the words of others to relocate his true voice, on *Good As I Been To You* Dylan takes the listener on a fascinating exploration of folk music roots. As for musicologists, the record may appear somewhat a diversion at first glance, but it is absolutely more than that. Although no instrumental virtuoso in the traditional sense, in this case Bob's wonderfully idiosyncratic guitar and harmonica playing is genuinely inspired and primitive in a good way. The unadorned setting in Bob's home studio in Malibu furnished ideal surroundings for Bob's reverent takes on well-known and forgotten ballads of Ireland, England, Appalachia, and the American South.

Given the modest ambitions of what Bob and hands-off producer Debbie Gold undertook, surprisingly positive reactions resulted, and Bob's interpretive skills were duly praised. Ghostly, but a powerful ghost at that, his physically ravaged rasp focuses on phrasing in the mold of none other than Frank Sinatra, with whom Bob shared a membership in a mutual admiration society as well as the Musical Lyric Phrasing Hall of Fame. Not in the least parenthetically, with Sinatra's death in May of 1998, surely, to Dylan, an age had come to an end. Be that as it may, Bob has done wonders since Sinatra's death to keep that pre-rock age of classical American songwriting alive and well.

Arresting and amusing is Dylan's invitation to and performance of **Restless Farewell** at Frank's 80th birthday party at Madison Square Garden Theater in '95, where Frank's speechless gaze in the front row during Bob's stupendous rendition is, to say the least, priceless. If you held a gun to my head and told me I could only keep one item in my Dylan audio and video library, I would keep this one (on VHS no less), on which Bob directly serenades "Mr. Frank" and after which he joined Bruce Springsteen at a most intimate private after-party bash in Sinatra's Manhattan condo.

As for *Good As I Been To You*, first, a precious Mississippi John Hurt country romp, **Frankie and Albert**, is given brilliant flat-picking run-downs meandering through quickly circling chords, in contrast to Hurt's complex blues finger picking. Dylan's chilling take on this mur-der ballad is delivered in a satisfied, fearless, faint hush as though he recognizes the outstanding commencement his new album is about to take. Ladies and gentlemen, let the master interpreter begin…

Jim Jones, a song legally credited to Australian folksinger Mick Slocum and that would go on to get regular inclusion in mid-90s live set lists, received no liner note arrangement credit whatsoever. After this tech-nically illegal deed had been done, Dylan's music publisher sheepishly conceded the flagrant error, a little episode which Bob apparently took to heart when his self-written liner notes on his subsequent cover album, *World Gone Wrong*, would prove to be not only exhaustive, but wordy, tongue-in-cheek, weird, subtly vengeful, and notwithstanding all this, an unrivaled self-written literary companion to any of his albums ever.

The British/Irish folksy roots tunes, **Blackjack Davey** and **Canadee-i-o**, escort us to mythological lands of alarming minor key romantic esca-pades gone tragic and heroines who cross dress to strike deals with sailors to sail the seven seas to avoid the fate of grief-stricken separation from mythical true-love beloveds. No joke my dear reader, this stuff has to be heard to be fathomed. Suffice it to say, both these narratives find Dylan at his most patient, magnificently rough around the edges and willing to descend deep within without coming off as nostalgic in any way.

Subsequently, we navigate back across the pond to a rousing take on Howlin' Wolf's **Sitting On Top Of The World**, a folk/blues standard not heard much ever since the British John Mayall and the Bluesbreakers ironically exposed it to American audiences on their 1960s debut masterpiece LP. Here we witness Dylan quite at home, literally, while figuratively digging below the surface of the southern AM radio programs he meticulously tuned into late at night in the Hibbing days of his youth.

Side two takes center stage and won't stop with a bluegrass standard, **Little Maggie**, on which Bob tolerantly allows his measure-ending guitar strums to ring out prior to re-engaging a completely committed haunting vocal detailing alcohol-induced ventures into the pre-destined hand of fate. Then, 19th century composer, perhaps America's first, Stephen Foster, is suitably saluted in an emotionally wide open, rigorously honest rendition of **Hard Times**. The song, once again, takes its time, slicing through to get to Dylan's genuinely open heart and illustrating none of Bob's shape-shifting persona we have come to know and love.

Blind Boy Fuller's **Step It Up and Go** finds Dylan effortlessly moving over frets as if he were trying to break a land speed world record. This breathtaking little romp makes you wonder if Bob himself is ever going to come up for air. Well, he certainly does, eventually, by cozying into a lazy intro harmonica break on Lonnie Johnson's 1947 hit, **Tomorrow Night**, a romantic croon, Dylan's warmest in years, which would surely have made Elvis, who recorded a version of his own in 1965, proud. Original composers Sam Coslow and Will Grosz's ultra-sexy ballad is taken where even they could never have imagined, completely brake-pedaled and aching from Bob Dylan's signature disarming sincerity.

Arthur McBride, originally arranged by Irishman Paul Brady, who ironically discovered the song while touring the U.S. in 1972 and added and altered a number of verses, gets the Brady treatment of a 17th century melody that came to life in Ireland's 19th century fight for freedom from its British invaders. In it, brave Irish lads end up turning their swords on British military recruiters in an anti-war protest anthem right in Dylan's wheelhouse.

You're Gonna Quit Me is simply ripped off of Mance Lipscomb, a thievery target of Dylan's going back to the 1963 Newport Folk Festival, where Bob purportedly appeared on stage doing Lipscomb's backstage stuff and claiming it as his own. You get the feeling that at some point Dylan's early-found penchant for pulling the wool over the eyes of fellow musicians, audiences, the press, and himself alike eventually led to his inability to recall his own lies, which ones required defense ammunition, and whether, at any given moment, he was telling the truth or not, for habitual liars (take it from me) are wont to lie even when the truth will suffice. Was the inclusion of this composition by Mance on *Good As I Been To You* an amends long in the making? Even Bob himself is quite likely not sure.

Diamond Joe is a number Bob picked up from folk revivalist and ole buddy Ramblin' Jack Elliot of Bob's Greenwich Village Days. Bob's first cover album in 19 years closes with **Froggie Went A- Courtin'**, another folk classic from the British Isles that hearkens back to Bob's penchant for children's nursery rhymes, which stood out so on *Under The Red Sky*, on which his vocals intermittently and frustratingly lacked the punch they have on *Good As I Been To You*.

While Bob continued to relentlessly pound the pavement on his never-ending tour to the tune of over 100 shows a year, the success with ease which he pulled off on *Good As I Been To You* warranted a cover album sequel, to which we now shall seamlessly segue.

Even more impressive execution than *Good As I Been To You* is the calling card of *World Gone Wrong*, which hit record stores a year later on

October 26, 1993. This album comes off sort of like the following image, which as an artist on a healing path of life myself, I have personally experienced hundreds of times over the years.

Bob, Dylan or Shiel, take your pick, wakes up in the morning and walks into his garage studio or third bedroom medicine room, depending on whether he is in Malibu or Chicago. Picks up his acoustic axe. First cup of coffee is not even a thought yet. Sleep dreams still a little foggy, but they find themselves plainly on the first twelve frets. Out comes something from another realm, but the tapes weren't rolling. Gone forever into the land of that great audio cemetery in the sky.

Only, on *World Gone Wrong*, magically, it is as if the tapes WERE rolling, and the tide of the backwash made its way to Columbia records. Hallelujah, this was saved for the sake of mankind's prosperity. *World Gone Wrong* stands alone as THE Bob Dylan album that demonstrates inimitably the notion that Bob Dylan, were he to choose to do so, could on an annual basis readily release an album of restorative, reinvigorating, whimsical dips into the medicine cabinet of pre-rock and roll roots tapping into planet earth herself. Both *World Gone Wrong* and *Good As I Been To You* suggest that Dylan at times adheres to that ole adage, "Heal thyself, healer!" Especially on *World Gone Wrong*, you get the feeling Bob is singing to as well as resuscitating himself and we get to eavesdrop!

Reminds me of a non-fictional (or fictional, who know?) anecdote reporting a 1970s late night hotel room pass-the-gee-tar-around-the-circle episode involving none other than guys like Roger McGuinn, David Bromberg, and our hymnal hybrid ham from Hibbing. So, Jimmy McGuinn, an early banjo/pioneering student at Chicago's famed Old Town School of Folk Music, delivers a colorful, drunken rendition of something right out of the storied Old Town songbook, let's just say **Barbara Allen**. Bromberg, likewise, takes his turn, after the appropriate applause for Roger/Jimmy subsides, and he launches into a Hank Williams number that is so obscure he has to identify it upon completing his whimsical ditty. Finally, Bob takes HIS turn. Jaws commence to drop, eyes glow ablaze in awe, and the night becomes morning before Dylan shrugs his shoulders and, yawning, says, "I better get to bed, man!" Even walking jukeboxes like McGuinn and Bromberg, when push comes to shove, are no match for the matchbox, I mean jukebox, itself. His name is Bob Dylan, and *World Gone Wrong* tells his tale.

Compared to *Good As I Been To You*, on *World Gone Wrong* darker and more tragic themes are the order of the day. Like on *Good As I Been To You* we find primitive-by-modern-standards sound quality marked by slight but tasteful distortion, casual microphone placement, little attention given to exact tuning of steel strings, and obvious consequences of the documented fact that, in the course of 14 master takes, not a single change in guitar strings was made. An eerie, enticing expression that illustrates as much about the art of Bob Dylan as any collection of compelling originals ever could, *World Gone Wrong* features music more obscure than that on *Good As I Been To You*, yet terrific song choices steeped in deceit, treachery, venality, and despair.

And those surrealistic liner notes! Personally written by Dylan himself, a rarity in itself, Bob playfully credits, in order to cover his adversarial ass, the sources that he brought into the set list mix. Berserk annotations, grammar off the radar, and horrible punctuation like this have not been served up since, dare I say it, *Tarantula* in the 60s. Can you say *Ulysses*? This stuff has got to be seen to be believed. Hard to get through, but what fun, fun, fun till Daddy takes the T-bird away, which, in case you have forgotten, is what *61 Highways Revisited* is really, really, really all about. A little reality orientation never hurts.

Lest I digress, which, I know, I know, I am wont to do, let us embark on a short and sweet journey into the heart of these choice, choice songs. The indecipherable, though not-to-be-missed, liners notes, I must say, leave me all alone, left to my own devices, but I'll give it a shot.

The title track, **World Gone Wrong**, instantly finds Bob at his most ruminative amidst a downbeat number extolling the gobbledygook of evil charlatans masquerading in pullover vests and talking tuxedos. I am not making this stuff up, folks. Check it out yourself. Slightly altering the title of a song the Mississippi Sheiks and the great Bo Carter left to posterity back in the 1920s, Dylan treats us to some gorgeous level 1 guitar strumming that camouflages distinctly nuanced and subtly intricate blues runs and completely credible and throaty warbling.

Fine minstrel barring none, Bob gifts we the lucky with his most stupefying vocal on the album, quite the mouthful, on **Love Henry**. Scottish folklore origins are to be thanked for these themes of duplicity and deceit corroborating the witnessing of murder by a parrot couched in a veiled threat. Again, I'm not making this stuff up!

Ragged and Dirty, if I might be so bold, might be a classic scenario of self-identifying derelict male wanting the unobtainable in his feminine heroine. Did Dylan, or did he not, credit somebody named Willie Brown in the liner notes? All I can say is, "Don't EVEN go there."

Blood In My Eyes uncovers all shrouds hiding all-out lust, as in raw-to-the-bone sex, with an entirely cheerless, melancholy audio track which accompanied a commercial video shot in the rundown Camden vicinity of London. In it Bob is found wondering the streets appearing in a self-cameo as passersby acknowledge what appears to be Bob Dylan himself ending up in a coffee shop that just might be the café in **Highlands** where he runs into the streetwise waitress with lip and long shiny white legs. That's just me, though.

Willie McTell's up tempo **Broke Down Engine**, despite liner note claims to the contrary, is not about trains. Well, a train metaphor surfaces and resurfaces, but it is really about the human condition, complete with its pains and miseries, as we walk spiritual paths trapped in human bodies. How many ways are trains and human beings similar? Sounds like a worthwhile comparison/contrast essay to me.

Delia is one of those songs, like the Appalachian standard **Life Is Like A Mountain Railroad**, that has morphed into all kinds of different forms melodically and lyrically, but this one is as sweetly devastating as folk songs get. Bob's empathy for the killer of a 14 year old bleeds bloody compassion flowing out of Tennessee tributaries into the mighty Mississippi. "99 in the big house, Delia in the graveyard, and all the friends I ever had are gone." Ouch…this one smarts like a big dog!

Stack and Lee reverts back once again to an oft-modified melody by Frank Hutchinson regarding the theft of a hat, a John B. Stetson to be exact, after which a miscreant gets his just deserve. Be true to the straight and narrow appears to be the point, so don't get too high and mighty no matter HOW good you masquerade as one of the good guys and WHAT color your hat is.

Two Soldiers had shown up sporadically on live sets going back to 1988, when Jerry Garcia shared it somewhere along the line of the Dylan/Dead debacle smack dab in the middle of Bob's unceremonious 80s shit storm. Relax, we're not going back there. In it the tale is told of a December 1862 American Civil War incident in which two rebels promise to deliver news home after the war, but both tragically die at Fredericksburg. Rattling phlegm, passion, and tenderness of heart evoke classic impersonality, which the true traditionalist eternally seeks.

Jack-A-Roe is a lovely New Lost City Rambler Tom Paley portrayal of daughter defying father if she doesn't abandon her sailor beau, which leads to hasty nuptials implying a deathbed marriage after said daughter inexplicitly finds said sailor among the dying.

A Benjamin Franklin White/Adger Pace traditional fairy tale narrating serene, placid scenes and graveyard streams of consciousness, **Lone Pilgrim**, sublimely brings to a conclusion an album befitting a tranquil note on which to end. It furthermore is a most appropriate adjournment to Dylan's most revealing costume change ever, another mouthful man, or were these two unheralded acoustic solo endeavors in the early 90s Dylan's most convincing sleight of hand ever? Surely the former is the case. **Lone Pilgrim**, which traces back to the tradition of sacred harp music originating in the American South and New England in the 18th and 19th centuries, places an exclamation point on Bob's willingness to bare his soul by tenderly paying tribute to deep roots of American music that precede even the concept of songwriting (as we know it) itself.

Doubters of Dylan's lack of phoniness are advised to see for themselves by literally, as in actually, experimenting with the first thing in the morning metaphor, before coffee and after bladder relief. I dare you to start your day with these two albums and tell me Bob is not trustworthy on them both. The truth is the truth, man, no matter how you slice and dice it and what label you call it or what box you put it in.

A number of interesting tidbits took place in the wake of *World Gone Wrong*. To start with, Columbia and Bob inked another contract for 10 more albums in '93, and a month after its release, *World Gone Wrong* songs were fairly featured in filmed live performances at New York City's Supper Club. But alas, an acoustic television special and live album in the works were apparently not meant to be and scrapped for unknown reasons. They were instantly, nevertheless, and remain treasured bootlegs in international Dylan networks circling the seven seas. Furthermore, on Bob's November '93 Letterman/NBC 10th anniversary appearance, a potentially suitable showcase indeed, he ignored *Good As I Been To You* as well as *World Gone Wrong* and instead chose reliable standby, **Forever Young**. I'm a grave digger in a doggie litter this beer's a bitter old lady babysitter home run hitter pipe fitter my canoe's an outrigger child's a getting' bigger so why, why, why Bob Dylan, go figure…Oh, sorry man, sorry. Yet, this characteristically inexplicable song choice on national television did wonders in deepening the ignorance of, for lack of a better word, the general public's awareness of what the heck Bob Dylan was artistically up to in the early 90s, let alone that fact that he was up to anything whatsoever. I mean, as good as the first official bootleg series was, a lot of folks figured Bob was a past relic who was not up to anything anymore. Did our favorite bard give a hoot? Obviously, apparently, and regrettably (in the Letterman case) in my meaningless humble opinion, not.

Anyhoo, before, during, and after *World Gone Wrong* the point remains that Dylan retreated into the paradoxical seclusion of live performing, a perfect locale to alchemize in front of an audience new takes on old warhorses and a newfound rapture with bluegrass spirituals, traditional throwbacks, and healing hymnals for the heart. Meanwhile, not that many were noticing, despite these two killer cover albums, Dylan was in the longest dry spell between albums of new material in his, at the point of this writing, 53 year stint as a professional troubadour. To say that doubts Dylan would ever return to original songwriting and recording form haunted this writer during this interminable mid-90s dry spell would be an unbelievable, undue, ungainly, and unquestionable understatement. I for one concluded Dylan was done, and I am not too proud to admit I was royally wrong. Of course, I also gave up hope on myself back in the 80s and had that wrong, too.

Little did we know, though (and thank the almighty above), that Bob's life as an elder was about to reveal a fundamental, long-lasting metamorphosis that would meander its way well into the 21st century. As relentless touring sharpened the cutting edge concerts going on in the early to mid 90s, lurking underneath was a guy soon about to age gracefully into his own sovereign kingdom of chief minister of musical Americana.

Who knew?

#39

30th Anniversary Concert Celebration

Actually two months before *World Gone Wrong* chronologically, August 24, 1993 Columbia released Bob Dylan's *30th Anniversary Concert Celebration*, which took place October 16, 1992. Dubbed Bob Fest by Neil Young, upwards of more than thirty big name guest artists joined together to pay tribute to Dylan's legacy dating back to his first album in 1962. Musical director G.E. Smith, Bob's trusted lead guitarist on tour from '88 to '90, returned to coordinate an all-star house band made up of Stax Records trio Booker T. Jones, Duck Dunn, and Steve Cropper, along with drummers Anton Fig and Jim Keltner. Both DVD and CD releases were well received by critics and fans alike, thanks in no small part to sound production by Don DeVito and Jeff Rosen. Bonus rehearsal tracks and backstage interviews were later added to a 2014 two-DVD, blue-ray, and double CD re-release.

Dylan himself only appears on the last three songs of the soundtrack, but the list of headliners who showed up to pay homage seems to go on endlessly. Virtually all performances are worthwhile at the least, and a few just kill. Such instances include Stevie Wonder doing a gospel train **Blowin' In The Wind**, Lou Reed doing a sort of Velvet Underground **Foot Of Pride**, Ronnie Wood doing the Bootleg Volume 1-3 **Seven Days**, Richie Havens doing his open tuning **Just Like A Woman** like no one else can, Neil Young doing Neil Young's screaming one-note lead guitar version of **All Along The Watchtower**, and Eric Clapton doing his signature version of **Don't Think Twice, It's Alright**.

Other performers rounding out this historically huge gala were George Thorogood, John Mellencamp, Kris Kristofferson, Eddie Vedder and Mike McCready of Pearl Jam, Tracy Chapman, Johnny and June Carter Cash, Willie Nelson, Johnny Winter, the Clancy Brothers, Mary Chapin Carpenter, Shawn Colvin, Roseanne Cash, Chrissie Hyne, the O'Jays, Levon Helm, Garth Hudson, Rich Danko, George Harrison, Tom Petty and his Heartbreakers, Sinead O'Conner, and Roger McGuinn.

At the very least, the *30ᵗʰ Anniversary Concert Celebration* was a step up from Bob's four previous live album flops, but then it was not really a Bob Dylan album in the true sense of the word. Still, some of this stuff absolutely stands the test of time and merits repeated listening. In terms of live albums, at least things seemed to be going in the right direction, even though this event and album reflect virtually nothing on the artist Bob Dylan had evolved into in 1993.

Friends, even a bit drunk and stoned, are the best.

40

Bob Dylan's Greatest Hits Volume 3

About *Bob Dylan's Greatest Hits Volume 3*, released November 15, 1994, there is not a whole lot to say, other than it represents mid-Dylan era material from each of the 14 Dylan albums, except *Saved* and *Empire Burlesque*, from '73 to '91. Artistically, a fine enough compilation, I guess. Commercially, it didn't do crap, though. Proof that all that 1980s bull**** did some lasting damage.

Like *Greatest Hits Volumes 1 and 2, Volume 3* hit record stores while Dylan was in the doldrums as far as any original new material is concerned. Great stuff, no doubt, with merely one unheard mystery and *Oh Mercy* outtake, **Dignity**, confounding us all again by being called a greatest hit, but by this time, we have come to expect such endearing arrogance on greatest hits volumes from Bob Dylan. That might be a good place to leave it.

On the other hand, here we have, in historically chronological order, the remaining ingredients of how-could-it-not-be-a-treasure *Volume 3*: **Knockin' On Heaven's Door, Forever Young, Tangled Up In Blue, Hurricane, Changing of the Guards, Gotta Serve Somebody, Jokerman, The Groom's Still Waiting At The Altar, Brownsville Girl, Silvio, Series of Dreams** (from **Bootleg Series Vol. 1-3**), **Ring Them Bells**, and, finally, **Under The Red Sky**.

Period.

Except, with all due respect and for the sake of historical accuracy, in October 2007, in between *Modern Times* and *Tell Tale Times* (volume 8 of the official bootleg series), a greatest hits volume 4, in a sense, was released. Simply titled *Dylan*, a 3 disc deluxe edition contained 51 (previously released) songs in a box set presented in replica-vinyl packaging along with 10 postcards (with historical photos of Dylan going back to his childhood in Hibbing) and an extensive booklet. A one disc edition was also made available. The song list actually includes more than a handful of recordings which also appeared on the first three volumes of greatest hits albums. Primarily for this reason (can you say redundancy?) but also because its fancy packaging was just sort of a sales gimmick, it is not included as an album entry in this here book. Originally overpriced, it is characterized by a stale stench of capitalizing on and milking too many war horses, commercial profit conceptualization, and an overall lack of originality. Having said that, for Dylan novices wishing to possess a fine sample of the wide spectrum of music Bob Dylan had written and recorded up to 2007, this album is no doubt one of many logical places to start. Furthermore, unlike the first 3 greatest hits volumes, it contains a few songs off *Time Out Of Mind, Love and Theft*, and *Modern Times*. So much for imagination, ingeniousness, and artistic distinction. Yeehaw for mullah.

#41

Bob Dylan MTV Unplugged

Jumping on the bandwagon of unplugged acoustic releases spearhead-ed probably the most by Eric Clapton's trend setting work, on May 2, 1995 Columbia came out with *Bob Dylan MTV Unplugged* as part of the television program series by the same name. Recorded in front of a live audience November 17 and 18, 1994 in New York City at Sony Music Studios, the eleven songs selected for inclusion are mostly Dylan classics. Bob originally thought he would feature songs off *Good As I Been To You* and *World Gone Wrong*, but at Sony's behest he stuck to more familiar war horses to attempt to bring MTV youngsters into the fold. Whatever.

The core of Bob's never-ending tour band appears for the first time on record, with the unmistakable-in-a-good-way Winston Watson on drums, Tony Ganier on bass, John Jackson on lead and rhythm guitar, and Bucky Baxter on mandolin and steel guitar. Producer and Bob Dylan overall jack of all trades Jeff Rosen is to be thanked for nice au-dio balancing, mixing, and leveling.

Baxter and Ganier would go on to long term roles on the never-ending tour, but this ensemble with Jackson and Watson more than held its own with, albeit intermittently, some outstanding concerts for a few years there in the early to mid-90s. Watson, from what I witnessed, was a one man inferno behind a drum kit with an animated fan club in the front row on a pretty much nightly basis. Tony Ganier, of course, is another biography altogether waiting to be written, for he broke the record for most appearances on stage with Bob Dylan in history back in the mid 90s, and since then has supported in the neighborhood of 2,000 more shows and counting. His family lines go back to Preservation Hall in the French Quarter of New Orleans, and he has quietly served as Bob's band leader on the road from 1989 to the present. You never hear as much as a peep out of Tony in public, and this both likely and largely explains his longevity with our friend Bob. After some 2,600 appearances on stage with said friend, I reckon there exist more than a few peeps that Tony may or may not someday utter.

As for *Bob Dylan MTV Unplugged*, Bob's third mid-90s retro compilation. Essential album? Hardly. Not even close to the best stuff this entourage of characters came up with in the mid-90s. Great album? Well, sure, as long as you're asking.

#42

Time Out Of Mind

It had been seven years since any new original material. *Time Out of Mind*, designed mostly at Bob's Minnesota farmhouse in 1996, was recorded in south Florida under the tutelage once again of Canadian producer Daniel Lanois of *Oh Mercy* fame. It was Dylan's best work, album concept, and indications pointing back towards genius since *Blonde On Blonde* thirty one years prior. Yes, I said that. It also raised Bob Dylan not only from the MIA list, but almost literally from the dead. More on that momentarily.

Laced with 12-bar blues instinctively emerging from a sultry midnight swamp, Bob sings his way out of a grave buried in reverb as if he is making it up as he goes. Hazy and ominous, yet grounded on a gritty foundation, the songs are given bitter, resigned, anguished performances of sleepy post-junk funk. Live reinterpretations, countless and each one more novel than the next, underscore the merit, essence, and brilliance of this three-time victorious cream of the crop at the 1998 Grammys. Having said all this, perhaps the proverbial gun has been jumped, for there survives, lives in infamy, and exists for the historical record a most contorted, though pretty pertinent back story.

After putting a wrap on the recording process in May 1997 and just prior to embarking on a June European tour, Bob was diagnosed in Great Britain with histoplasmosis, or caver's disease, a fungal infection in the sac surrounding the heart, a strictly mortal malady if not detected early and properly treated. News of this deeply dismayed fans worldwide, including this writer, who got drift of Bob holed up in a British hospital suffering from this potentially lethal condition, unable to carry out already sold out concerts, while driving north on Sheridan Road in the East Rogers Park community of Chicago listening to WXRT on FM radio. Yelling at and pounding on the dashboard of my 1990 burgundy Chevy Cavalier, I proceeded to pull over and turn up the radio full blast while furiously weeping and struggling to pray myself out of a foxhole of grave clinical panic, fury, and despondency which persisted for the subsequent three or four days.

Par for my personal pre-Internet course (the Internet was just about to daily plug me into all things Dylan at this point in '97), scoop on *Time Out Of Mind* already being in the can when Bob's illness hit the wires was not at all common knowledge. Thus, here we have our friend Bob purportedly lying dying, not having released anything actually noteworthy, at least in the original song department, for roughly eight years, unable to tour, and his legacy in preeminent, unrivaled jeopardy. Thinking back and playing the what if game, one can only wonder where Bob Dylan would reside in the annals of recorded history if he had faded into the afterlife, met his maker, and kicked the idiomatic bucket at that particular juncture in the scheme of things. Indeed, a sobering, humbling, tangible hypothetical. We are NOT going THERE.

However comma, as Bob recuperated from what he reckons was caused by breezes carrying fungal matter air-born emanating from a stream near his Malibu estate, Columbia reassured heaven and earth that Bob's new album was due for release in September and that his autumn American tour was a go. To say that I felt relieved would be like saying Dylan has influenced American music. Quite the understatement that goes without saying. Then, the next thing we all knew was that *Time Out Of Mind* was entertaining us daily on our car stereos and Bob was once again on the cover of *Newsweek* looking and sounding as fit as a fiddle.

To top it off, ridiculously improbably, in October Bob was invited by the Vatican to appear and perform onstage with Pope John Paul deuce at a Catholic youth convention in Bologna, Italy. Shockingly, Bob not only accepted, but showed up with his touring band, which just so happened to be evolving into arguably the finest backing ensemble in Dylan's whole professional tenure. Bootleg videos of this unlikely papal rendezvous are, understandably, a sensationally humorous must.

If that were not enough, the first week of December the Kennedy Center, quite likely due to sheer shock over just the possibility of Bob Dylan going the way of all flesh, awarded Bob one of its coveted awards, and again the out of the ordinary manifested its astounding head when Bob graciously accepted the honor, attended in black tie threads, was magnificently introduced by none other than Gregory Peck, and untrue to form, conspicuously included his aging mother, Beatrice, who reverently, approvingly, and nobly sat with Bob in the front row of the VIP section on the night of the big gala. Could things get any more bizarre, or touching, for that matter?

From my vantage point, the cherry on top of this completely remarkable combination of chains of events culminated, came to a head, climaxed, peaked, and reached its zenith at Chicago's Metro at 7:30 p.m. CST December 13, 1997 when Bob ambled onto stage, wearing the same black and white two-tone shiny shoes he wore at the Kennedy Center a week before. He subsequently delivered a Hollywood performance and guitar attack with Bucky Baxter and Larry Campbell which covered a few re-worked favorites from *Time Out Of Mind* as well as surprises from the dark ages like **Cocaine** and **Thomas I Am The Man**.

This spectacle was much to the delight of the adoring fans in the balcony and the entire electrified front row of fans, which somehow included this writer, who lucked into a last minute general admission ticket at face value on the street. I also encountered a gang of Internetera Dylan network friends, not to mention a stellar spot in a line that wound around the block on a fu**ing nippy-as-a-witch's-titty Chicago afternoon and evening. Furthermore, the following night I was again in the front row with another unobstructed view of Dylan from a distance of about eight feet. Bob and the band seemed to get a charge from my tuxedo and black cowboy hat (which I was only wearing co-incidentally due to a pre-concert ballroom dancing event), which made me the only formal western wear-adorned audience member overtly outdoing them all! The one single problem I noticed with being in the front row was needing to dodge the spit from David Bromberg's mouth when he opened December 14, backed by Bob's dapper cowboys, do-ing his trademark, slapstick do-NOT-"F"- with-me-dude delivery on **It Takes A Lot To Laugh, A Train To Cry**.

Bob Dylan, Bucky Baxter on pedal steel guitar, and Tony Ganier on bass guitar at the Chicago Metro on December 14, 1997. South Bend Gary in backwards white cap in front row next to his bride Michelle and Janet Fleming of Chicago. Photo by Paul B.

Navigating back to *Time Out Of Mind*, my humble opinion is this. The Chicago Metro shows December 13 and 14 of '97 stand above the other 55 Dylan concerts I have witnessed, which, had *Time Out Of Mind* not happened, would not be the case. This LP lit quite the fire in, under, and in between not only Bob Dylan, but his entire touring entourage.

So, not to further digress, on to the sensational songs on *Time Out Of Mind*. First, credit Lanois and Dylan for assembling an eclectic ensemble of 13 musicians, each carefully selected, to support the very creative, downright spooky at times, heavy-on-pyrotechnics, atypical, and successful sound production achieved on *Time Out Of Mind*. Of particular note were the following. Lanois brought in slide guitarist Cindy Cashdollar and drummer Brian Blade, whereas Dylan invited a whole bunch of folks that turned out to be just what the doctor ordered. There were his touring band bassist, Tony Ganier, and drummer, David Kemper. Also brought in for very particular drumming duties was the ever-reliable Jim Keltner from the '79 to '81 gospel days. Memphis pianist Jim Dickinson, Tex-Mex organist Augie Meyers, and Nashville guitarists Duke Robillard and Bob Britt greatly helped round out the backup cast. Kudos to each and every one. Magic, as they say, was caught in a bottle.

Proceedings kick off with Bob's harmonica-like voice overdriven into a small guitar amp on **Love Sick**, which immediately seizes the consciously aspired to understated, subtly sizzling vibe just before this ambiance is destroyed by **Dirt Road Blues**, a fairly mediocre rendition of a simply killer rockabilly riff which features Dylan's touring drummer, Winston Watson, in his only contribution to the album. This is just me, but I was still on **Love Sick**, which might be Bob's best broken relationship song ever. Furthermore, countless wondrous live concert renditions of it over the years have etched it into stone as a signature doorway into Dylan's late era renaissance. **Dirt Road Blues**, on the other hand, neither belongs on *Time Out Of Mind* nor was given the respect, expertise, and straightforward treatment it deserves.

Standing In The Doorway captures the hopelessness of the album and hints of the return to form that Bob had not achieved for, well, let's not even venture to guess how long. **Million Miles** renders a 12-bar blues in straightforward fashion, all the while underscoring apocalyptic futility. All good stuff, to put it lightly. Four songs in and all doubt has been removed. We are in the Dylan department of holy crap in a good way.

Trying To Get To Heaven was born out of a studio parking lot discussion on the back fender of a pickup truck between Bob and Lanois in which Lanois suggested that they intentionally steal the feel of **Sad Eyed Lady of the Lowlands**, to which Bob replied, "Can we get away with that?" Goes to show how Bob needed Lanois in '97. **Till I Fell In Love With You,** in all earnestness, evolved from tweaking the outtake **Marching To The City,** highlighted by Bob's only harmonica playing on the entire record. In both cases, Bob is found discovering his own signature variation(s) of the blues. **Not Dark Yet**, universally regarded as the best of the *Time Out Of Mind* bunch, takes John Keats' winter metaphor in *Ode To A Nightingale* and turns it into a murky ally of darkness not quite actualized. Impending peril never seemed so sublime.

Portending doom continues to simmer with the ricocheting electric steel strings, rockabilly percussion, distorted organ, and Bob's voice floating on a rainbow of its own reverb highlight on **Cold Irons Bound**, reminding one and all that songwriting rivaling **Visions of Johanna** was still entirely within the capacity of Bob's arsenal, here in his mid-fifties. This one, which got the Grammy for best rock vocal in '98, has been redone any number of fascinating ways in live shows over the ensuing years.

Make You Feel My Love once again shatters the album's mystic spell with a musical and lyrical interlude into greeting card lyrics with the right song on the wrong album. Don't get me wrong – this is a sweet, versatile song that deservedly has been covered by numerous musicians of various walks who recognize it as one of Dylan's most beautiful compositions ever. Yet, it just shouldn't be on this particular album, and neither should the piping-hot **Dirt Road Blues**, which at the very least was wrongly sequenced.

Then, Bob's inner chivalrous knight on **Make You Feel My Love** turns into a foreboding voodoo wizard, making one of his most outlandishly bad-ass song sequences in a good way ever. **Can't Wait**, despite the setback of its predecessor, delights just when things cannot get any better, disguising its 12-bar structure with various studio and chord change gimmicks that black magically work, period.

Dylan's longest song ever, the 16-minute, hypnotic **Highlands**, royally rounds out the melodic parade, or death march if you will, consummated in the recording studio with Bob's tip of the hat to a 1790 Robert Burns poem mentioning the Scottish highlands, after which one of the studio techies inquired, "Do you have a short version of that song?", to which Bob replied, "That WAS the short version!"

As if the superlative-laced *Time Out Of Mind* had not done enough to restore Dylan's reputation as an assassin in Americana artistry, there is the little tidbit concerning its cool-as-hell outtakes. Eleven years after the fact **Red River Shore**, **Dreamin' Of You**, and **Marchin' To The City** discovered the light of day on *Tell Tale Signs* in 2008. **Mississippi** showed up on a Cheryl Crowe record prior to its inclusion by Dylan on *Love and Theft* the day the World Trade Center went down. Four richly and deeply moving compositions and fine recording takes to boot. Thus, when one thinks of the concept of 'on fire' and Bob Dylan, think spring of '97, spring of '97, spring of '97, a pertinent point worth mentioning only because it went over many if not most (Dylan)heads. In fact, I would almost but not quite go so far as to put the spring of 1997 up there with the spring of '61 as the most magical, if not downright miraculous phases in Dylan's artistic development.

Comeback is such a worn out term when describing Dylan albums. Call *Time Out Of Mind* what you want, but perhaps its most lasting significance is that it either ignited or re-fueled, depending on which train you're riding, the greatest stretch of live concerts in Dylan's never-ending tour going back to 1988. If there was even a single dud concert from 1997 to 2002, this Dylan freak has not heard it. Having been in the front row for live shows during this period for precisely 15 of the 25 concerts I personally attended, plus possessing around 25 full concert audio CD bootlegs from this period, not to mention having heard or read hundreds of firsthand verbal and written concert reviews in this time period compliments of other Bobcats and music writers alike, I can fairly safely conclude that Bob and his dapper outlaw backup cats were nothing less than on fire each and every f-ing night for a five year run. That's upwards of well over 500 shows. Sure, signs were there before *Time Out Of Mind*, but what this album did for Bob as a fifty-six year old artist can never be underestimated. It sparked a 17-and-counting year run without any all-out dips back into the toilet, in or out of the recording studio. You can't get any more auspicious than that, dude.

Therefore, Bob, if I may get personal, for we became quite well-acquainted via our 15 front row/stage encounters from 1997 to 2002, despite your own assessment to the contrary on **Mississippi**, on *Time Out Of Mind* you came back all the way and have yet to leave. It marked the birth of the old man in you, who has been busy being born ever since.

Ten songs. No duds. All returns to form. Way to go, old man. I would temper all this by once again saying, "But that's just me," but few were then or are now eager to debate the issue. So I ain't qualifyin' nothin', amigo.

Still, there are more than a few folks out there who not only missed out on *Time Out Of Mind*, but ALL SIX of Bob's late era masterworks because they wrote him off in the 80s, got old and stopped following the arts, and/or assumed Dylan was dead (or whatever). Hmmmm. Sounds like somebody's dead alright.

Actually, judging from dozens of Bob's live shows after (and due to) *Time Out Of Mind* all the way to the present, he without question possesses legions of new and younger (even teenage) fans who know the real musical deal when they see/hear it. At 56, Bob Dylan, with indispensable assistance from Daniel Lanois, had given birth to his unstoppable elder statesman era and the voice of his mad minister of Americana within.

#43

Bootleg Series Volume 4 Live 1966 The "Royal Albert Hall" Concert

So, more than synchronously, while Bob and his dapper string band cowboys were lighting up audiences nightly on the heels of a long-awaited masterpiece and conceivably greatest return to form ever (*Time Out Of Mind*), quite the mouthful, but I said it anyway, on October 12, 1998 Columbia finally decided to let go of another official bootleg. Turned out, and we will get more into this in the next little vignette in this here book, finally not only did some worthy live Dylan material come out, but lo and behold (pun intended, of course), this would occur in back-to-back-to-back-to-back-to-back-to-back fashion!

It may have taken Columbia seven f-ing years to dole out another volume in the official bootleg series, but believe it or not, it was well worth the wait. *Bootleg Series Volume 4: Live 1966* may not have been, and in fact was absolutely not, recorded at Royal Albert Hall (hence the quotations marks in the album title), where, according to erroneous legend, Bob yelled, "Playing f-ing loud!", before launching into a scorching version of **Like A Rolling Stone** much to the chagrin of a jeering audience that felt betrayed by their folk music guru. On the other hand comma, contrary to legend, what in actuality took place on the evening of May 17, 1966 at Manchester Trade Hall was nothing out of the ordinary on the whirlwind world tour Bob undertook with the Hawks in the fall of 1965 and spring of '66.

Each show consisted of a solo acoustic set, a short intermission, and a crazed electric act aided and abetted by that Canadian quartet, this time minus their heralded hillbilly, percussionist, best-of-the-bunch vocalist, and original headliner, Levon Helm. The Hawks, after changing their name to The Band a couple years later, would go on to modify the face of popular music in their own right in the ensuing 10 years and punctuate their curtain call with the filming of *The Last Waltz*, Martin Scorsese's magnum opus and pretty much still today the finest straight rock concert full-length feature movie ever. Perhaps fittingly, Scorsese in 2005 would eventually compile and direct the blockbuster documentary *No Direction Home*, a documentary on Dylan's early career up to the motorcycle accident, which leaned heavily on story lines and footage from the spring '66 manically-wired Dylan-has-gone-electric global caravan.

Live 1966 is blessed with excellent sound quality that far surpasses what at the time seemed elegant on the renowned late 1970 and '71 initial vinyl bootlegs from the spring '66 world tour. Kudos to producer Jeff Rosen, but also to Dylan himself, who, though long, lean and frail-appearing in the onstage footage in *No Direction Home*, nonetheless delivers unbelievably complex lyrics on unfathomably long songs without ever faltering, even once. Yes, the audience claps at wrong times throughout the electric set, either to throw Dylan off timing or else because the music they are hearing is so foreign to them that they lack rhythmic intelligence and/or fluency. Nonetheless, the whole thing is f***-ing and dramatically gripping!

For the unconventional, ahead-of-its-time drumming on the electric sets on *Live 1966*, we have the unrecognized, long-forgotten, and pretty much never-heard-from-again Mickey Jones to thank. The Hawks took this legendary journey without their heart-and-soul Arkansian, Levon Helm, whose displeasure over being constantly booed while backing a mere folk musician led him to exit the music entertainment business stage left for greener pastures for what turned out to be two years while he toiled on oil rigs in the Gulf of Mexico and turned his back on the whole Big Pink scene. Not to be overlooked are Rich Danko's deft contributions to the rhythm section and Robbie Robertson's always superb, subtle support of some of the most outrageous in a good way vocals that we have ever heard from the throat of Bob Dylan.

Direct comparisons of *Live 1966* with music standards of the day, such as the Beatles' *Rubber Soul* and *Revolver*, for instance, are simply preposterous cases in point of the ole apples and oranges metaphor. *Live 1966* aptly captures the deed being done of Bob Dylan pushing the musical limits of what was hitherto considered out of bounds lyrically and melodically. There was no comparing Dylan in 1966 really. All were left to just appreciate, admire, emulate, and last but most importantly, defer to. That's just how it was. And don't shoot me please, just ask the surviving Beatles or check the documented John Lennon and George Harrison historical records.

Of particular interest on *Live 1966* are countless nuances, certainly too many to enumerate in this brief synopsis (a whole book on the matter would be more appropriate). Nevertheless, during the acoustic set we got versions of **Visions of Johanna** (the only tune on *Live 1966* that truly WAS from Royal Albert Hall) and an **It's All Over Now, Baby Blue** that had previously surfaced on *Biograph* in late 1985. Moreover, the Egyptian ring in **She Belongs To Me** was now for some reason suddenly red in color, and Bob's right hand syncopation change during his **Desolation Row** harmonica showcases his adroit adaptation ability while improvising and re-interpreting in real time.

Worth pointing out on the electric disc are Bob's "Don't clap so hard" audience admonishment during a psychotic intro to **One Too Many Mornings,** to which the crowd surrealistically responds by cheering or jeering, I'm not quite sure, with great enthusiasm. Finally, there is Bob's celebrated "I don't believe you, you're a liar" accusation in the wake of the eminent "Judas" indictment which precedes, "Play f-ing loud," on **Like A Rolling Stone** and the eventual audience eruption into frenetic applause at the end of the song before Dylan's lampooning sneer, "Thank you." Topping everything on *Live 1966* has got to be **Tell Me, Momma's** vocal, on which Dylan's voice sounds likes it's doing a high wire balancing act and risking a death drop onto a roller coaster about to veer off the tracks at any moment (which can also be said particularly about how he sings **Just Like Tom Thumb's Blues**).

If it all seems a little too far-fetched to digest, it surely was in '66 and is now on *Live 1966*. Remember that we are hearing Dylan at the very end of a five plus year stint in the scope of public view, frenzied creative combustion, alcohol, amphetamine, narcotic, barbiturate and God knows what dependence, plus the existence of what was just dawning on him to be the puppet-string manipulation of his professional and personal affairs by the ingenious yet rapacious, parsimonious, and exploitative Albert Grossman.

Hence, how 'bout a little commiseration, compassion, and mercy for how this all went down in Bob's world in '66. We got some of the most amazing cutting-edge musical entertainment of the twentieth century.

Bob Dylan, or better yet, Robert Allen Zimmerman, nearly lost his life.

#44

Bob Dylan Live 1961-2000 Thirty Nine Years
Of Great Concert Performances

This international release out of Japan on February 28, 2001 is such an entertaining potpourri, wonderfully weird cross-section, and eclectic compilation that it cannot be ignored. *Bob Dylan Live 1961-2000: 39 Years of Great Concert Performances* (released only in Japan by Sony Music Entertainment but thank the Lordy available internationally via online ordering) constitutes quite the 65-minute conglomeration of 16 live recordings in England and the U.S. Six of these songs had never been released before, period. Five had never appeared on Dylan albums. One was an audio cassette only B side single, and one was only an album promotion. As for further particulars, we will get back to that later.

As an aside, as part of Columbia's essential series, *The Essential Bob Dylan* was released in 2000, containing 2 discs and 30 previously released tracks. Note that superfluous releases such as this are repeatedly omitted in this here book because they ought to be. Ain't more to say other than some folks made some mullah. Besides, it's ALL essential if you ask me, which you can do at your own risk.

Because *Bob Dylan Live 1961-2000: 39 Years of Great Concert Performances* is all live material and it came out when it did, it gives me the perfect excuse to do what I am going to do next, which is go slightly off topic, because I can.

Please allow for a not-so-brief, yet contextually obligatory side bar discussion with two main points. Both require that we detour away from Dylan's commercial albums for an instant (as in 20 fleeting paragraphs) and explore what it was like to periodically and faithfully, no, make that religiously, witness Dylan in concert, as I did on 26 occasions, during the most consistent, night in, night out live performance phase of his life (from roughly the fall of 1997 to 2002). We're talkin' spiritual experiences, as in, "Woo-woo, dude."

First, context. In early 2001, when this fabulous *Live 1961-2000* disc became available online only in the states, it came on the heels of the killer *Live 1966*, albeit 2.5 years later, making it the second live Dylan release in a row. Most auspiciously, these two live compilations became available simultaneously with the most sizzling, hands down, live performance period in Bob Dylan's storied resume as a performing artist. It was THE phase when the topic is Bob Dylan the live performer. Unlike the eminent and so-called best-ever Dylan world tour with the Hawks in the 60s, which lasted a matter of a couple months added together, Dylan ended the 20th century and began the new millennium with a five-year 550-gig live concert run that, to my knowledge, has never been equaled by any artist at any time in history. I welcome anyone caring to refute this proposition with reliable evidence. As a matter of fact, being wrong is one of my hobbies.

Not-so-parenthetically, not to minimize the topics of Bob Dylan the songwriter and recording artist, getting to the bottom of his performing artist output is unquestionably indispensible, fundamental, and imperative to get a handle on Dylan's legendary artistic myth and cultural impact. That, my friends, is another surely staggering book waiting to be written, and don't you dare look at me!

It is impossible to be exact, but we are talking roughly about the years 1997 to 2002, essentially between *Time Out Of Mind* and just after *Love and Theft*. During these hallowed years Dylan's peak live performance mojo clearly reached its pinnacle, although I own this as my subjective, but firm belief and bow to those who feel otherwise. After all, at the age of nine in 1965, I was not there to see Bob and the Hawks rip through **Tell Me, Momma**. I was probably watching *The Andy Griffith Show, Gunsmoke,* or *The Flintstones*. However comma, I was up close and personal enough times from 1997 to 2002 that Bob, his touring band, and I were well acquainted. More on that forthcoming.

As of this writing in early 2015, Bob's touring band has become more solidified in recent years, but it is fair to say that it is always in some stage of dynamic evolution. For one thing, artists, especially the good ones, like to move on from time to time. Back in the late 90s, drummer David Kemper (replaced by George Recile in December 2001), multi-instrumentalist Bucky Baxter (replaced by guitarist Charlie Sexton after the spring 1999 European tour), bassist Tony Ganier, and all-purpose lead guitarist extraordinaire Larry Campbell, first of all, looked really cool on stage. Having said that, they also provided Dylan with the finest string band effect he has ever assembled, making 3 guitars, at times, sound like 5 to 7 competing tommy guns on electric numbers like **Silvio**, **Maggie's Farm**, **I Can't Wait**, and **Cold Irons Bound**.

Second, speaking of the infinite topic of the live concerts of Bob Dylan, the following firsthand drama ought to be shared at some point in this here book, and, by God, I deem that point has been reached.

During this 1997 to 2002 great live show streak, on October 26, 1999 I personally was engaged in conversation by Dylan four times during the 10:00 show at the Park West in Chicago. How tripped out is that? I found it most remarkable since Bob normally is notoriously close-mouthed and/or mum (sometimes not even bothering to introduce his band) when it comes to onstage interactions with audience members. If you'll just indulge me for a moment, it went down like this.

In the fall of 1999 Phil Lesh and Friends joined up with Dylan's rolling caravan after Bob's acclaimed tour with Paul Simon in the summer of 1999. The official opening date was October 27 at the Assembly Hall in Champaign, Illinois, but at the last minute, about three days before show time, it was announced that Dylan's band (without Phil Lesh and Friends) would play 7:00 and 10:00 shows at the cozy Park West in Chicago the night before the fall tour was to begin. The word was that Dylan merely wanted to do a quick nightclub show in order to ready the band for the huge arenas on the tour schedule in the upcoming six weeks.

Due to these most unusual circumstances, I arrived at the Park West about 5:00 guaranteed only of a ticket for the early show, thanks to a friendly concert compadre connection. However, I quickly was able to buy a ticket at face value for the late show from a guy in front of the theater in a line formed on the sidewalk winding around the corner. Both shows, mind you, were general admission only and outstanding performances in an intimate nightclub, complete with a diminutive dance floor, cabaret tables, and a meager balcony with a capacity to hold a maximum of about 300 two-leggeds as long as they are packed in like sardines. You can perhaps imagine how such a dramatic setting set the stage for what I experienced at that fateful concert.

Having been second row center for the early show, thanks to friendly buddies in line, when I landed front row center three feet away from the microphone Dylan was singing into for the late show, thanks to Ed and Michelle of South Bend, he and I had already had direct eye contact several times that evening. Thus, when the 10:00 show commenced, Dylan promptly made it apparent that he appreciated my front row dancing, singing, and obvious familiarity with his repertoire. So far, nothing new, as Bob had on numerous previous occasions non-verbally expressed to me a sense that he got that I got his music. It is as if he intuitively picks up on audience members who are musicians themselves and possess an apparent familiarity with his songs, which I certainly am and innately do. I guess another way of saying it is that musicians feel each other, and language is not at all how they communicate.

In any case, for some reason that night's encounter turned out to be extraordinarily different. After **Tombstone Blues**, the eighth song in the late show, Dylan started tapping me on the shoulder as I was writing down the set list up to that point in the show on a small notepad I had brought with me for that very purpose. He asked me if I was writing him a check! Then, he started laughing hysterically and repeated this question into his microphone for all to hear, although I don't think the audience had any idea what he was talking about.

In the ensuing 30 seconds or so before the band broke into song 9, **Make You Feel My Love**, I swiftly pulled out a wad of cash, which I had brought along, knowing that purchasing tickets on the street required exact dollar amounts. I told Bob that I had not brought my checkbook to the concert but that he could have all my cash, which amused him and the rest of the band to no end. Bob's response was to absurdly ask me how much I was making the check out for, as if he had no interest in my cash. The band immediately broke into **Make You Feel My Love**, and I was left to wonder if this incident had really happened. Little did I know that things were just getting started.

During the final four songs of the set, **Make You Feel My Love**, **Everything Is Broken**, **Like A Rolling Stone**, and **Blowin' In The Wind**, Bob kept giving me the eye, sometimes squinting his baby blues at me and at others raising his eyebrows like a clown. In between these songs he repeatedly pointed both his index fingers at me in a rooty-toot pistol fashion while dipping his knees down practically to the floor of the stage. I got the feeling at this bizarre, surreal point that he was recalling me from previous concerts at which I had been standing in the first three rows and well within his close range eyesight. I also got the feeling that this would be the closest I would ever get to a private performance from Bob Dylan. Of course, all the while, the folks standing in my vicinity kept asking me what the hell was going on and why Dylan was paying me so much attention. I felt like Ralph Cramdon on *The Honeymooners*, "Humany humany humany humany!"

Fast forward to the crescendo of the last song, **Blowin' In The Wind**, after which the crowd erupted in wild cheering, screaming, hooting, and whistling. Thus, nobody but Dylan and I myself were privy to his last verbal foray with me of the evening.

I only half-jokingly pulled out my cash one last time and offered it to him. My intention and hope, by the way, was that Bob would, in jest, actually pocket my cash, which might merit an invitation backstage to retrieve it after the show. Alas, no such fortune.

Instead, Bob momentarily grabbed the cash out of my left hand and laughingly thanked me for it, but then grunted (well, whatever that is when Bob Dylan talks), "No man, that's YOUR cash, you keep it!" Knowing that my ploy to get backstage was not coming to fruition, my next split second decision is one about which I now feel embarrassed, but only slightly so.

With my right hand I abruptly grabbed the back of Dylan's right hand and pulled it to my lips and gave it a brisk peck. Bob was seemingly totally cool with this gesture of affection and was actually still barreling over in howling laughter from his ripping-off-my-cash pretense.

Then, as he reverted back to center stage and, in stitches, stood in single file formation with the band and acknowledged the audience applause, Bob beamed at me as if to say, "That was fun, thanks dude."

As the band chuckled their way to the dressing room in what I would describe as silly hysterics, for they all knew darn well how oddly and comically Bob Dylan had just broken character on stage, Charlie Sexton bent over and told me in all sincerity that I was lucky that Bob hadn't taken my cash.

I was then surrounded by dozens of other fans who wanted to know what Bob had been saying to me during the last four songs. This included some really attractive young ladies who ignored the men they were with in favor of yours truly. Can you say, "Ego trip?" The cherry on top of this astonishing experience was being given Dylan's water cup by John, one of his long term roadies at the time, as he broke down the stage.

I vividly recall after the concert walking to my car parked over by Lincoln Park Zoo. Although I had not smoked marijuana in twelve years, it felt precisely like the first time I got high in Campion Hall at Loyola University in 1975. My cowboy boots felt like they were on a conveyor belt about six inches off the ground. Bob Dylan had talked to me.

Five nights later, on Halloween night at the University of Illinois Pavilion I was again in the front row and given Dylan's gleeful, charming index-fingers-revolvers-howdy-do gesture. Bob understandably, on the other hand, got a little distracted when four security guards hauled off an LSD-tripping lady trying to climb her way onto the stage. Her idea for a Halloween costume was getting naked. The look on Bob's face was, naturally, priceless. On the other hand, as well as more importantly (ha, ha ha), the best Halloween costume had to be the guy who came as **Tangled Up In Blue**. When Phil Lesh and Friends are in the mix and you sprinkle in Halloween night, it brings out the looniest in Deadheads.

Even two years later in Bob's first Chicago visit after *Love and Theft*, he again relentlessly gave me the ole bent-knee, index fingers revolver salute as I danced away in the front row at the United Center. As this was a good fifteen to twenty feet away, you gotta figure Bob's eyesight wasn't too shabby for a guy in his early 60s. Nice to be remembered, too!

Alrighty then, end of requisite tangent.

Does anybody even recall that the album topic at hand is *Bob Dylan Live 1961-2000 Thirty Nine Years Of Great Concert Performances*? Well, it is. And even though it was an international release, it is such a wonderful and inventive compilation that excluding it from this here book just ain't gonna happen. And as good as it sounded on a car stereo, I will state one final time, seeing Dylan live and in the flesh at the time this album came out was, simply, a sight to see.

Although the songs are sequenced chronologically, the one exception is that the first song is really last, a 2000 rendition of **Somebody**

Touched Me, a bluegrass spiritual that Bob was fond of opening with in the heydays of his aforementioned cowboy string band with Charlie and Larry on dueling gee-tars (accent on the first syllable), Kemper of Jerry Garcia Band fame on drums, and Ganier doing the honor of performing percussion on bass. Now that was THE band, man. Not that Canadian quartet and a hillbilly back in the day. It in actuality only lasted a couple years, but the two years preceding (with Bucky Baxter in the mix) and subsequent to it (when George Recile joined the "long strange trip") were right up there, too.

Anyway, after **Somebody Touched Me** the song sequence jolts back to 1961 and follows a straightforward chronological order. Other highlights on **Live 1961-2000** are **Wade In The Water** from the 1961 Minnesota tapes, **Handsome Molly** from the Gaslight in 1962, **Grand Coulee Dam** from the Woody Guthrie tribute concert in 1968, **It Ain't Me Babe** from *Renaldo and Clara*, **Dead Man, Dead Man** from New Orleans in 1981, **Cold Irons Bound** from the El Rey Theater shows in L.A. in December 1997, **Born In Time** from 1998, and **Country Pie** and **Things Have Changed** from Portsmouth in 2000.

For casual fans, this collection is absolutely superfluous. For avid students it is not only mandatory, but strikingly impressive and a whole lot of fun, as in the hoot Bob Dylan had with me one night back in the day.

#45

Love and Theft

*L*ove and Theft hit record stores with quite the vengeance on the morning of September 11, 2001, the exact day and time of day of the historical attacks on the World Trade Center, Pentagon, and Flight 93, which was deliberately crashed to the ground in rural Pennsylvania.

Please pause a moment in remembrance of all those who suffered then and still suffer from those tragic events. With that reality in perspective, let us carry on. My attempts at humor and entertainingly narrating events of that day surely mean no harm.

For those of us who were avid concerts attendees, the stage for this record had been set by the unparalleled incredible run in Bob's never-ending tour that had been going on ever since *Time Out Of Mind* a full four years before. Keep in mind that pretty much as early as 1997 and here and there in '95 and '96 Bob's live performances had hit an all-time high, with no duds to speak of.

Thus, the fever of new material expectations was running high, and Bob did not at all disappoint. Yet, the drama that unfolded on the very day of *Love and Theft's* release could not have been any more bizarre, horrific, violent, or profound. A personal anecdote perhaps best illustrates.

That morning at about 8:45 AM, as I was getting dressed to leave home for work 2 hours ahead of my normal routine in order to buy Bob's new album and listen to it before showing up for the 12:45 class I was to teach that fateful day, my now beloved ex-wife, Mary, answered the phone and was urged by her daughter/my stepdaughter Rita (think **Motorpsycho Nitemare**) to turn on the television. Within seconds we were witnessing video replays of the first airliner exploding into the south tower of the World Trade Center, and several minutes later we caught a live broadcast of the north tower being hit. Then, the subsequent building collapses ensued, sending chills down the spines of anybody with a pulse.

My mission to get to Tower Records before school was now in doubt, as I wondered whether or not the community college 18 miles away on Chicago's north side where I was employed would even be open when I got there. All telephone reports indicated that it would be, so off I drove, rigidly sticking to my original mission for the day, which was, obviously, to get the new Dylan record the day it came out and listen to it BEFORE showing up for my 12:45 class. This task had been on my to-do list calendar for September 11, 2001 for several months, and NOTHING was going to stop me.

Mission accomplished, but not before witnessing a steady stream of outgoing traffic from downtown Chicago at 10:30 on a Tuesday morning. With the new Dylan CD in hand, I made my way to scenic Montrose Harbor, where I parked with a picturesque view, ironically, of the skyline of downtown Chicago. I stared at all those skyscrapers, recalling the collapse of the twin towers in Manhattan earlier that morning. I could not help but notice the eerie of absence of aircraft in the absolutely empty airspace above in the cloudless, blue, silent sky.

Next to me, as I turned up the volume full blast on my audio cassette player in my burgundy 1990 Chevy Cavalier and enjoyed *Love and Theft* for the first time, two lovers perched on the hood of the early 1960s vintage vehicle parked next to me and engaged in lovers' games in the morning sun, seemingly oblivious of two auspicious historical events, the 9-11 attacks and Bob's new record release, that were simultaneously playing out as they fondled each other's private parts and played kissy poo in apparent romantic bliss.

Somehow, the 91-word sentence I just wrote aside, the drama of it all hit me with a thud, and I realized that this was one of those moments, odd for sure, but actually a melodramatic tragicomedy, that would engrave itself in the part of my psyche that is sometimes wonderfully entertained, tickled pink, and delighted by weirdo surrealism. Here the country was being attacked, paralyzed, and brought to its knees, and these two airhead lovers on the hood of the car next to me were carrying on as if all were normal.

On the other hand, I suddenly realized that by bull-headedly buying the new Dylan CD and being so passionately intent on hearing it on a day when America had come to a standstill, I was doing the exact same thing they were. Talk about having a personal agenda – regardless whether or not America is under attack! What I saw in those public exhibitionist lovers the morning of 9-11, 2001, I was guilty of myself! If you got it you spot it, or if you spot it you got it, or however that works.

In any case, in all honesty, I felt extraordinarily torn between my sadness, anger, and fear about 9-11 and my exhilaration over *Love and Theft*. I guess we all were deeply emotional and can recall idiosyncratic details of our personal lives on that momentous occasion.

Nevertheless, I am once again engaging in that nasty, though whimsical, habit of mine called digressing. Or perhaps not.

Love and Theft, by all accounts, cannot be entirely understood without grasping the backdrop of Sept. 11, 2001. I mean, the first time I heard it was less than two hours after both towers went down. I think it also ironic that I bought *Love and Theft* at **Tower** Records. Does anything ever happen by accident? Such weirdo surrealism. With that said, let's move on.

Love and Theft took off where *Time Out of Mind* left off by treating one and all to the sage Bob Dylan we know and love, who this time greeted the new millennium with predictably unpredictable poetry wrapped in a trifecta of jazz, folk, and blues, nothing short of an instant classic that can quite arguably be portrayed as one of the finest roots rock albums ever made, if I might borrow the words of the Chicago Tribune's rock critic Greg Kot. In short, it kills, dude.

Produced by the soon-to-be familiar Jack Frost, Bob's alias this century whenever he produces himself, and gone for the time being were the reverb echoes and guitar amplifier gimmickry which Lanois used so effectively on *Time Out of Mind*. Still firmly in place were Bob's return to grab-you-by-the-throat songwriting and his old bluesman sneering snarl.

Unveiled on *Time Out of Mind* are a swagger to Bob's performance absent since he fronted for the Band on the '74 world tour and a dip into the myths, mysteries, and folklore of the American South as a backdrop for a sprawling tapestry of jump and slow blues, Tin Pan Alley ballads, rockabilly, country swing, and instinctive, unforced syntheses of all of the above. The album alternately harkens back to the ultra-dry humor of Groucho Marx and the pre-rock voices of Johnny Ray, Charley Patton, and Hank Williams, not to mention (well, I just did) Harry Smith's *Anthology of American Music*.

The lineup of studio musicians was comprised of Texas keyboardist Augie Meyers, back again after his exquisite work on *Time Out Of Mind*, and the well-dressed cowboy outlaws of Bob's touring band, namely drummer David Kemper of Jerry Garcia Band fame, Louisiana bassist Tony Ganier, Texas guitarist Charlie Sexton, and multi-instrumentalist Larry Campbell. Individually and collectively, this ensemble readily lobbed sucker pitches squarely into Bob's pre-meditated wheelhouse, spawning a welcome, resonant, uncluttered sound production given sufficient elbow room to breathe deeply and fully enough to even notice the spaces between the breaths, or in this case the notes of music. That Bob's best backup live band ever, and I mean ever, made it into a studio to record original and unreleased material with him is one of world history's karmic mannas from heaven.

Twiddly Dee and Twiddly Dum cranks up the album's march into immortality, as opposed to death on *Time Out of Mind*, with a venture winding in and out of nursery rhymes and down home country parables punctuated by a hook of Larry Campbell guitar doodling punctuating each verse reminiscent of Mike Bloomfield's iconic contribution to **Like A Rolling Stone**. Next is a *Time Out Of Mind* outtake, **Mississippi**, already debuted on a Cheryl Crowe CD and live performances of the Dixie Chicks, perhaps the only song on the album with much popular sensibility per se.

Summer Days speeds up the velocity as Charlie and Larry trade tasteful, understated lead guitar licks in the studio that conceal evidence of the dormant but mighty dueling gee-tar (accent on first syllable goes without saying) rockets to the moon that would eventually be uncorked in live versions of this outright country swing and some of the most rampant rockabilly in Bob's repertoire prior to Charlie's unfortunate exit from the never-ending tour in the fall of 2003. Hmmm. A 78-word sentence befits **Summer Days** most aptly.

Bye and Bye, the first of no less than four wades into the milieu of pre-rock and roll jazz on *Love and Theft*, suddenly, romantically, and breezily swings around the corner into a hotel lounge act containing lilting guitar leads interspersed with a carnival organ and a rock solid snare drum holding down the low end. The figuratively screaming and literally screamed **Lonesome Day Blues**, for starters, touchingly tips a hat to Beatrice Zimmerman, Bob's mother who had died shortly before *Love and Theft* came out, in a grinding blues rocking the house. Ohhh, the tears which burst forth upon my cheeks the first time I heard this verse, for between *Time Out Of Mind* and *Love And Theft* I had mourned the transition to the afterlife of my own precious mother, Josephine (Jody) Pauline Welch Shiel.

Floater (Too Much To Ask) utilizes Larry's virtuosity on Tennessee swing fiddle, returning to the jazz lounge and sounding like it could have been written in the 1920s. Much was made of no fewer than 8 lines in **Floater** and 4 other song lines on *Love And Theft* which were clearly lifted verbatim from *Confessions Of Yakuza*, an obscure biography by Japanese writer Junichi Saga. Confusing term paper ethics with the time-honored, perfunctory practice of doing fellow artists the honor of emulation, personification, and/or imitation sure makes for a lot of hyperbolic hooey. In this light, a debate over whether or not Bob Dylan is at a loss for words just wouldn't be a fair fight. In the end, Mr. Saga politely thanked Dylan for the salute and subsequent increase in his book sales.

High Water (For Charlie Patton) opens with a perty banjo claw by Campbell and proceeds to seemingly launch itself into a spooky march into a river swamp buried in the recesses of a Faulkner novel. In live shows **High Water** has been a fairly consistent inclusion over the years, and Bob's re-workings of it have been numerous and spine-tingling.

Moonlight peeks back into that now-familiar jazz lounge with a rising bass line culminating in some of Bob's best crooning of all time, no little feat at the age of 60, not to mention some appropriate sweet lead guitar licks rendered by either Charlie or Larry (I'll put my money on Larry). Detouring to the back alley blues band unleashed on **Lonesome Day Blues**, **Honest With Me** declares that this little sojourn includes some deep-seated anger at Him, Her, or It, whatever your name is for that divine force running the universe that ain't you, which reminds Bob that the parental ooze of Abraham and Beatrice is still flowing out of his thick skull.

Just when we thought we had bid farewell to the jazz lounge, back we go in **Po Boy,** which dangles dissonant jazz chords at the end of each bridge, letting the band punctuate Bob's trail of verbosity squeezed into the phrasing in each line, resulting in a soft-shoe shuffle, both charming and reluctant. The well-beaten trail back and forth between the jazz lounge and roadhouse tavern veers into **Cry Awhile** as Bob and the boys finally seem to get the sweet revenge sought after in **Honest With Me**.

The epic, reflective closer **Sugar Baby** travels to neither the lounge nor the roadhouse. This tender, empathetic, sober meditation laced with chasms of empty streams of consciousness aptly embraces an open-minded humility characterizing a slew of eccentric personalities that seem to already have been introduced via the eleven preceding songs. **Sugar Baby** furnishes a brilliant conclusion to Bob Dylan's most impressive album of the 21st century (with all due respect to *Tempest*) and deepest excavation into the mines of Americana of his illustrious career.

Love and Theft is one of those desert isle records that no musician or music fan ought to fail to investigate, lest he/she remain ignorant of the heights that Americana is capable of soaring amidst the turkey vultures, great blue herons, black crows, red-tailed hawks, and pelicans of rebel rivers, sultry swamps, and midnight oases in a resurrected age not-so-gone-by after all. Think William Faulkner not at a loss for words.

Although it would be five interminable years prior to Bob's next release of original studio recordings, Dylanland, in the meantime, was about to be treated to a flurry of creative output unthinkable for a man half his age. This would include a soundtrack to a movie for which Bob co-authored the screenplay and played the lead role, 2 early 60s live concert releases, 3 more official bootlegs, and volume 1 of Bob Dylan's well-written autobiography, *Chronicles*.

All the while, the never-ending tour trudged ever onward toward happy destiny, leaving concert goers guessing as to why, gradually starting in the fall of 2002, Bob abandoned his string band motif and commenced playing jazzy and R and B keyboards more and more and more to the point of abdicating the guitar entirely. Did he have arthritis, or did he just prefer experimenting with circus-like bouncy jazzy fills on the 88s? He certainly was not preserving energy in his old age, for he was still **standing** behind his electric piano.

For answers to these and other Dylan riddles, don't hold your breath, dude. Bob Dylan does what he wants.

In **Tangled Up In Blue** Bob said we always did agree – we just saw it from a different point of view. In that vein, even though an unsafe generalization is that the quality of Dylan's live concerts began to pre-cipitously, or bit by bit, depending on your outlook, dip in the years following *Love and Theft* (partly evidenced by Bob's rather annoying, overdone newfound penchant for "up-singing" the tail end of lines in verses), we were about to go on quite the creative ride of commercial releases without ever stepping foot into a recording studio.

Now how many musical artists can claim to have done that?

#46

Bootleg Series Volume 5/Rolling Thunder Revue

Four years after *Live 1966* and over a year after *Love and Theft*, an extremely gratifying compilation from late 1975, *Bootleg Series 5: Rolling Thunder Revue*, hit records stores October 26, 2002. 1976's *Hard Rain* had not fulfilled the mission of capturing a suitable audio version of the live theater roller coaster of the Rolling Thunder Revue. Fortunately, *Bootleg Series 5* does, and in spades to boot. For those counting, Bob was, in the process, now 3 for 3 on his last 3 live albums.

Oddly, the genesis for the concept of this traveling 57 concert caravan can be traced to the 1972 Rolling Stones American tour, which somehow re-ignited Dylan's imaginative appetite for another concert circuit, or circus. Trouble is, in 1974 *Before The Flood* never did rise to the artistic standard Bob had in mind, and he knew it.

However, after the acclaimed success of *Blood On The Tracks* in 1975, Bob realized that, timing being everything, he ought to start acting on his dream. In other words, get while the gettin's good. Consequently, he went on to spend quite a bit of time in The Other End, a New York City nightclub where he met and collaborated with a number of prospective passengers on a concert caravan that would be the opposite of the much-hyped and anticipated world tour with the Band in '74. Bob was thinking unscripted, spontaneous theater, mixing and matching minstrels, a musical potpourri, and pushing the envelope in all manners possible. He just needed to pull together the appropriate cast of unhinged, wacky characters with whom to conspire. Fortunately, he just so happened to discover the requisite mojo with the same parade of musicians that wondered in and out of the recording studio while he laid down *Desire*.

Thus, right on the heels of the final *Desire* recording sessions, in October '75 rehearsals promptly began for what would organically turn into a showcase for unique vocal precision by Bob Dylan the likes of which we neither had nor have ever encountered. Snapping words off with machete-like cold-blooded deliberation one moment and stretching words to cajole nuanced meanings the next, each of the 22 tracks on *Bootleg Series 5* lacks any of the traditionalism found on *Before The Flood*. Bob sounds more like he's liberated from the shackles of the Band, notwithstanding the four distinct, ingenious, and magical musical genres they had come up with from 1966 to 1974 (i.e. the '66 world tour, *The Basement Tapes*, *Planet Waves*, and *Before The Flood*).

Praise for the supporting cast behind Dylan cannot be overstated. Starting with the *Desire* killer rhythm section of Howie Wyeth on drums and Rob Stoner on bass and on to Bob's personal wheelhouse gypsy fiddler, Scarlet Rivera, the soundboard cuts we are privy to are, for the most part, dead-on spontaneous masterpieces.

About the only failure of the Rolling Thunder spectacle was *Renaldo and Clara*, our masquerading minstrel's marathon in-a-bad-way plotless video version of backstage unscripted dialogues which at best is an opportunity to gaze for hours at the photogenic Bob Dylan and Sara Lownds and at worst an amateurish attempt that at moments devolves into a pathetic unpardonable soft porn production. If this film is any sort of representation whatsoever of the real-life state of Sara/Bob wedlock, you gotta reckon that on some astral level, their parting of the ways was no tragic misfortune. Included in the packaging of *Bootleg Series 5* is a DVD with excerpts from this big film flop as well as videos of the **Tangled Up In Blue** version on *Bootleg Series 5* and the Bob-in-white-face **Isis** version that had appeared on **Biograph** in 1985 and which makes the *Desire* rendition sound like a greeting card from our friends at, of course, Hallmark.

Point blank, *Bootleg Series 5* is none of the *Renaldo and Clara* disastrous train wreck. Rather, it is an audio masterpiece on which *Renaldo and Clara* juxtaposes a video failure. Kicking off with 3 stunningly re-worked gems, **Tonight I'll Be Staying Here With You** is lyrically completely re-written, **It Ain't Me Babe** features a whole new melodic twist, and **A Hard Rain's A-Gonna Fall** is driven at a velocity and rock and roll pitch that ought to be felonious on folk anthems. From here the album does not look back, pun intended, and takes no prisoners. It truly just kills. All songs are Dylan originals except for the traditional **The Water Is Wide**, on which Joan Baez unequivocally nails her harmony piece, and not one sounds cookie cutter, forced, or flat. More like intentional, fresh, brilliant reckless abandon.

Fortunately, all tracks come from late November early December '75 shows in Boston, Worcester, Cambridge, and Montreal, long before the Rolling Thunder Revue ran out of steam on its second leg in '76. *Bootleg Series 5 Rolling Thunder Revue* accomplishes 36 years later what in 1976 *Hard Rain* failed to achieve, which is a fantastic audio release of the utterly wild circus Dylan and his colleagues created in the fall of '75 and spring of '76.

Unfortunately omitted is the Johnny Ace hit **Never Let Me Go**, but other than that the song list and sequence cannot be argued with. Once again, as on the first four official bootleg volumes, we have producer Jeff Rosen to thank, and this time Steve Berkowitz as well. What they achieve here sonically soars over the Fort Collins show that was featured on the 1976 *Hard Rain* live album. In addition, the '76 performances are simply no comparison to the novelty and freshness hallmarking the late '75 Rolling Thunder extravaganzas.

Dylan introduces **It Takes A Lot To Laugh, A Train To Cry** by claiming it is an autobiographical song. Hmmmm. If you say so, pal. **Oh Sister** at one point brings time to a sublime standstill. Even an audience request for **Just Like A Woman** is graciously granted, without missing a beat no less.

These recordings make the listener feel like he/she was there at these historic shows. Like all honestly good music, this stuff stands the test of time, even though it was pulled off in the moment by a troupe of vaudevillian characters traversing the U.S. and unexpectedly putting on concerts for the ages without much advance warning or hype, while incidentally, at least sub-consciously, sowing the seeds for the concept of never-ending Dylan tours.

Bootleg Series Volume 5: Rolling Thunder Revue is not just a bunch of re-hackings of nostalgic studio album favorites. Captured are virtuosic performances by a bunch of mind-altered stoner thespians in drag clearly having a ball.

It is another feather in the cap of Bob Dylan, duke of the dominion of being the first and frequently emulated, but never duplicated.

#47

Masked and Anonymous Soundtrack

The outset of the new millennium will go down as one of the more artistically creative outbursts of Bob Dylan's life. He was, as usual, doing over 100 live concerts a year, but that had long since turned into a mere given. Add to that the writing of *Chronicles Volume 1*, his best-selling memoir eventually hitting bookstores in 2004. Plus, Bob was painting at a rate that is inconceivable given his busy schedule. Finally, how did he find time to collaborate with Larry Charles (of *Seinfeld* fame) and co-write (under the pseudonym Sergei Petrov) a screenplay for *Masked and Anonymous*? And then star in the film to boot? Leave that for somebody else to comprehend because I just don't get it.

In any case, Larry and Bob procured enough BBC funding to pay for a mere 20 days of film shooting to create this un-categorizable comedy/drama which is pretty much a movie impersonating a Bob Dylan song. Another abridged way to get a grip on this thing perhaps is to liken it to, well, Bob Dylan, in all his enigmatic glory. It's a spoof, people, emotionally, intellectually, and spiritually drawing you into a dramatic parody of itself. If that ain't our dear friend Bob Dylan, or at least one of his gimmicks, I don't know what is. You don't know whether to laugh, cry, roll up in a ball of paranoia, roll your eyes, scratch your head, or pretend you weren't impacted one way or the other and just ignore it. Don't you love multiple choice quandaries, and you get to make a conscious choice and live with it? Regardless, if you haven't seen this thing, I recommend riding its roller coaster and not giving up on it before the miracle, which, of course, you can decide for yourself.

Dylan plays the protagonist, Jack Fate, an aging rock star (not much acting required) bailed out of prison to do a one-man benefit concert to rescue a decaying ambivalent future North American society. Hysterical, loosely-tied sardonic skits are pieced together with meandering themes including, but not limited to political futility, confusing government conspiracies, chaotic anarchy, 1984-like totalitarianism, God's uncertain place on a planet beset with turmoil, the deeper meaning(s) of life, daydreams, sleep dreams, Shakespearean bloodbaths, female bondage, biblical evil represented in the form of serpents, spooky sarcasm swirling around a guy in black face, and powerlessness in the face of it all. I'm not sure that quite covers all the bases, but you get the drift. Somehow, all this surrealism remains compelling enough that even though at points it DOES completely crash into pointless silliness, it DOESN'T, thanks largely to a compelling star-studded cast and the enticing soundtrack.

As for the soundtrack, getting back to the topic, it's pretty much all over the place like the film, but the core is performed by Bob's crack touring band in a makeshift (think cardboard boxes being utilized as percussion instruments) musical studio choreographed on the actual movie set. Dylan originals from 1964 to 2003 are covered by incredibly creative bands from overseas such as Articulo 31 of Milan, Italy doing **Like A Rolling Stone** in Spanish, Italian Francesco De Gregori doing **If You See Her, Say Hello** in Italian, and the Mugakoro Brothers of Japan doing **My Back Pages** in Japanese. In English, Shirley Ceasar does **Gotta Serve Somebody** (as she did at the Kennedy Center Awards in 1997), the Dixie Hummingbirds do **City of Gold**, Jerry Garcia does **Senor**, Sertab (Erener) of Turkey does **One More Cup Of Coffee**, Los Lobos does **On A Night Like This**, Selfi Dolmani of Sweden does **Most Of The Time**, and the Grateful Dead does **It's All Over Now, Baby Blue**. The soundtrack also includes four additional songs by Bob's band, namely **Down In The Flood, Diamond Joe** (cover), **Dixie** (cover), and **Cold Irons Bound**. Like I say, all over the place.

Omitted, strangely, are a handful of songs by Bob's band that momen-tarily appear in the film itself (such as **Blind Willie McTell**). If this makes no sense, neither does the movie, but nonsense in a good way pretty much sums up not only *Masked and Anonymous*, but on some level Bob Dylan, period. Moreover, the cut of **I'll Remember You**, uninterrupted in the film, is an audio and visual superlative and must. Other tunes (unfortunately) cut from the soundtrack were **Drifter's Escape**, **Blowin' In The Wind**, **Watching The River Flow**, **Dirt Road Blues**, and a cover of **Amazing Grace**.

The soundtrack falls into the pretty damn good category, though it does seem to fall short of its potential. Although one of Bob's best bands ever appears on film and backs him musically, the performances are for some reason intentionally understated, but wonderful nonethe-less. Fortunately, filming occurred just in the nick of time to include Charlie Sexton before he left Dylan's never-ending tour in 2002 (only to gloriously return some eight years later). New Orleans native George Recile on drums (who had replaced David Kemper just before filming began), musical virtuoso Larry Campbell on guitar, and the reliably soulful Tony Ganier round out a band (at least in this movie) of misfits answering Bob's beck and call.

Hollywood heavyweights willing to earn union pay or nothing at all in order to do any project whatsoever with you know who included Ed Harris, Cheech Marin, Bruce Dern, Angela Basset, Luke Wilson, Jessica Lange, Mickey O'Rourke, Val Kilmer, Penelope Cruz, Jeff Bridges, and John Goodman. I'm not sure how many Oscar nomi-nations that comprises, but they all respectfully checked their egos at the door. The star of the show, and they all knew it, was Bob, who looks just about as cool in this one not only as he ever has on film, but as anybody, anytime, in any movie, ever. Only if you ask me, which wouldn't stop me anyway. So, if you are any sort of any film lover, maker, student, or fan, check out *Masked and Anonymous*. If only for a few minutes, it will surely help you take yourself less seriously, indeed no little thing, my friend (but that's just me again…man, that little voice keeps popping up!).

Absurd? Yes. Funny? Yes. Mind-bending? Yes. Great music? Yes. Terrific acting? With the list of artists just mentioned, you tell me. Waste of time? No. Watchable repeatedly? F-ing A.

Just bring a some hot popcorn and an open mind, and you're good.

#48

Bootleg Series Volume 6/Bob Dylan Live 1964
Concert At Philharmonic Hall

Nine months went by before 2004 brought us a Simon and Schuster memoir, *Chronicles Volume 1*, and another official bootleg from the vaults at Columbia, *Bootleg Series Volume 6: Live 1964 Concert At Philharmonic Hall*. About the former, not much, but something needs to be said.

Published October 5, 2004, the first of 3 supposed volumes of Bob's only attempt ever at an autobiography spent 19 weeks on the hardcover bestseller list. It haphazardly focuses largely on Bob's very early Greenwich Village days as well as the goings on during the *New Morning* and *Oh Mercy* time periods. Largely ignored are Bob's mid-60s popularity height and his personal affairs in general, especially his two known-about marriages up to the publication date. Incidentally, Dylan had a third, albeit extraordinarily brief, 2012 marriage eight years after *Chronicles*, about which very little is known other than it wasn't pretty and was over before it started. No point in going there.

Praise for *Chronicles* from book critics profoundly touched Bob to, in his words, the point of tears, for he knew they knew more than he does about book writing, unlike most irrelevant music critics, who are not musicians themselves (exceptions exist, and they are plain as day). An entertaining abridged audio book version is well narrated by Sean Penn. Confirmed rumors from 2008 to the present indicate that Bob is unquestionably working on *Chronicles Volume 2* and that the *Blood On The Tracks* era will be addressed in some manner. About a presumed future publishing date Dylan has been clear that nothing is clear. I will go out on a (short) limb and predict it'll be even better than *Chronicles Volume 1*.

However comma, on March 3, 2004 musically we got treated to a wonderful, insightful official bootleg of a Halloween 1964 solo acoustic show in New York's Philharmonic Hall which portrays Bob Dylan right smack dab in the midst of his transition to electric music. As a matter of fact, it provides the last snapshot, historically speaking, we will quite probably ever get of Bob Dylan as a folk artist yet to go electric. Once the fat lady had sung, it was Dylan's fourth consecutive thumbs-up live LP.

Jeff Rosen and Steve Berkowitz, and this is becoming a broken record, deserve great praise once again for their sound production and digital treatment of mid-60s soundboard material. Particularly noteworthy are Bob's inspired takes on four original gems he never bothered to include on studio albums, namely **Talkin' John Birch Paranoid Blues**, **Who Killed Davey Moore**, **If You Gotta Go, Go Now**, and **Mama, You Been On My Mind.** In addition, joining Bob for 3 superb harmony duets is none other than Joan Baez, a caveat which only adds historical significance to this best-of-times and worst-of-times compilation.

Overall, musically this recording has got to be Webster's dictionary definition of a mixed bag. It is essentially a negative watershed mark due to the obvious fact that Bob is stoned and, for the first time on a music stage in public, he appears to be dangerously close to be riding off the rails, as it were. His focus is completely on the new songs in his catalogue, and with anything prior to *Another Side of Bob Dylan*, he seems absolutely bored.

Thus, on **The Times They Are A-Changin'** we get an impetuous strained throwaway, but on **To Ramona** we get a heartfelt masterpiece. **Don't Think Twice, It's Alright** is given a perfunctory, sarcastic, slapstick, tongue-in-cheek treatment despite one of the most skillful, comical, and song-saving harmonica solos in world history. As a result, *Live 1964 Concert At Philharmonic Hall* comes off as utterly brilliant in the sense of the ice cream/pizza metaphor (i.e. that the worst ice cream and pizza I've ever had was pretty good). I am curious how our mercilessly muttering man of miraculous musical mayhem would feel about being likened to a delectable dairy product and an exquisitely appetizing Italian baked dish.

Having said that, still unreleased at the time, all the *Bringing It All Back Home* material on this LP truly takes the proverbial cake. The few shreds of folkie tendencies remaining in Dylan's personage in late 1964 had evolved (think **It's Alright Ma, I'm Only Bleeding** and **Gates Of Eden**) into mind-blowing, tripped out poetic bewilderments bridging Bob into eclectic electric excursions. As a result, on *Live 1964 Concert At Philharmonic Hall* Dylan's former folk fanaticism found itself expressed as one fake, facetious, fainthearted, fallow, fallible, fundamentally f-ing futile, fickle, and forgivable spoof. On the other hand, his new stuff is spellbinding in comparison. Thus, Halloween 1964 marked a milestone as Dylan's first in countless instances over the years, where, both on stage and in recording studios, he has displayed a nonchalant tendency to turn on and off his capacity to appear like a genuine genius one moment and devolve into a mediocre hack the next.

Regardless, **Gates of Eden**, **It's Alright Ma, I'm Only Bleeding**, and **Mr. Tambourine Man** are utterly breathtaking public unveilings of Dylan's (1964) newfound direction on his artistic compass pointing straight at evocative cerebral streams of consciousness. The audience, closely engaged in good-natured banter throughout, seems to undergo mindful transformations into thentofore (don't you love to make up words?) unexplored musical wilderness. God knows what was going through their minds. Here was Bob Dylan in late 1964 passionately pouring out snapshots of peculiar poetic photographic perceptions towering over his previous 1963 social commentary and protest preoccupations. I know, that was a bizarre sentence. Be cool, Dylan preposterously stretched the limits of reason, too.

Some of the choice quotes emanating from Bob's lips at this Halloween hullabaloo, just weeks after he supposedly met the Beatles at the

Delmonico Hotel in New York and turned them on to marijuana: "Don't let this scare you, it's only Halloween. I'm wearing my Bob Dylan mask. I'm masquerading." "I hope I never have to make a living." "**It's Alright Ma, It's Life and Life Only** is a funny song." "This was taken out of the newspaper and nothing has been changed except the words." "This is called **A Sacrilegious Lullaby In D Minor**." Finally, and last, but not least, "Is **Mary Had A Little Lamb** a protest song?"

Speaking of which, at the very least, volume 6 of the official bootlegs brought an end to the incomplete poor dubs of soundboard tapes from Halloween 1964. At most, and most apparent on disc two when Joan Baez joins the pandemonium for **Mama You Been On My Mind**, **With God On Our Side**, and **It Ain't Me Babe** and sings lead on Dylan's buried **Silver Dagger**, *Bootleg Series 6: Live 1964 Concert At Philharmonic Hall* provides one final peek into the last days of Bob Dylan, the Jewish folksinger from Hibbing. Having just become chummy with four charismatic lads from Liverpool themselves, Dylan couldn't wait, on *Bringing It All Back Home*, to start reverting back to his Hibbing High School sweetheart, rock and roll (held in check ever since in his 1959 high school yearbook he revealed that his goal was to join Little Richards' band), where, at least in 1965 and '66, he felt most at home penning and recording, for its time, some of the most glaringly brazen music of the 20th century.

Consequently, on *Bootleg Series Volume 6: Live 1964 Concert At Philharmonic Hall* we are treated to a Bob Dylan who is changing character(s) in front of our eyes. He's just still wearing one of his former and temporary masks, but not for long.

As a matter of fact, his next bootleg series release a year later actually historically exemplified his mid-60s transition from fundamentally freewheeling folkie back to the roots of rock and roll reasonably well chronologically speaking.

#49

Bootleg Series Volume 7/No Direction Home
The Soundtrack

No Direction Home is a four-hour public television documentary directed by the iconic Martin Scorsese focusing on Bob Dylan's life from 1959 to 1966. Production from 2000 to 2004, coinciding with Bob's writing of *Chronicles Volume 1*, commenced with and was highlighted by ten hours of well-filmed interviews with Bob himself conducted by soundman and trustworthy jack of all trades, Jeff Rosen. Assisting Rosen with audio engineering on the film soundtrack were Steve Berkowitz and Scorsese himself, and kudos to them all.

The film itself is a stunning video montage featuring never-seen-before D.A. Pennebaker footage of the spring 1966 world tour with the Hawks, particularly the **Like A Rolling Stone** performance at Manchester Trade Hall, which was miraculously discovered in 2004 in a pile of water-damaged film from the vaults of Dylan himself. In 2001 Scorsese was brought on board to edit and shape the film, which he chose to design in a non-chronological manner, one of the few annoying aspects of the marathon movie memorial to Dylan's pre-motorcycle accident career. Another problem was the over-emphasized and constantly insinuated rejection by Dylan of the royal crown of the political left. Twice would have sufficed. All forgivable small potatoes in the scheme of things, though.

More importantly, a treasure trove of filmed snippets are included from terrific interviews with Suze Rotolo, Alan Ginsburg, and Dave Van Ronk, all of whom have since made their transitions to the afterlife. This is not to mention rare recordings of one of Dylan's high school rock bands and his 1965 screen test for Andy Warhol.

As for the soundtrack, released August 30, 2005, there is no shortage of potentially poignant commentary. First, it cannot rightly even be called a soundtrack because it contains unreleased studio outtakes not even in the film. Thus, it is really a soundtrack and some other stuff. Second, the vast majority of the 28 tracks were highly anticipated previously un-released material, so it immediately went gold. Third, disc one espe-cially, but not exclusively, provides access to extraordinarily early acoustic material that some thought would never see the light of day. However, once Scorsese was on board, all hands were on deck in full cooperation, including Bob's. *No Direction Home* is, academically-speaking, at the very least worthy of being an essential in the library of any film student or Dylan scholar worthy of taking another breath on God's green earth, but artistically, it is undoubtedly worthy of the masterpiece moniker.

In the film we get recordings of Bob in his bedroom in 1959 singing Little Richard cover material, but the soundtrack starts off with a '59 original composition, most likely Dylan's first ever recorded, **When I Got Troubles**. Here we find Bob's songwriting ability light years ahead of his performance skills. Makes you wonder what he could do with this simple gem in his 70s.

For Dylan historians, the rest of disc one is simply one mandatory source after another. It is just the sort of release for which Dylan boot-leggers had been keeping their fingers crossed for forty years. A fall 1960 recording of the traditional **Rambler, Gambler** is a wonderful snapshot of Dylan just prior to his unflinching, fearless, venturesome departure from the Midwest and legendarily inconspicuous arrival in Greenwich Village. We are treated to live renditions of **This Land Is Your Land** and **Blowin' In The Wind** that sound less political anthem-like and more like intimate love songs. This recording of **Blowin' In**

The Wind, its first public performance on a major stage a few weeks prior to the release of *Freewheelin'*, certainly makes it historic, but more curiously, I gotta wonder what the heck was ruminating in the surely-blown minds in that audience at New York's Town Hall.

From the December 1961 Minnesota hotel tapes we get soulful deliveries of **Dink's Song** and **I Was Young When I Left Home**. We also hear Webster's dictionary definition of teetering-on-the-edge harmonica on *Freewheelin'* outtake **Sally Gal**, a Witmark demo of **Don't Think Twice It's Alright**, and a killer **Man Of Constant Sorrow** done for a 1963 TV show called *Folk Songs and More Folk Songs*. Rounding out breathtaking disc one are alternate studio takes of **Mr. Tambourine Man** (with rare vocal harmonies by Ramblin' Jack Elliott!) and **It's All Over Now, Baby Blue** with a slight, lovely melody alteration.

Disc two kicks off with Bruce Langhorne supporting a **She Belongs To Me** outtake with a lovely lilting electric guitar filler. Then, we go right into **Maggie's Farm** at Newport in '65, which we again got two years later in 2007 in Murray Lerner's *The Other Side of the Mirror: Bob Dylan at the Newport Folk Festival*, the best film footage of Bob Dylan in the 1960s, hands down. Since it's not an LP, Lerner's video masterpiece is not included as a distinct entry in this here book, yet his stunning close-up imagery and his, for the time, incredible audio work merit inclusion in any studious Dylan library, discussion, or undertaking.

We also get to hear wild mercurial versions of **It Takes A Lot To Laugh, A Train To Cry** and **Visions of Johanna** that make one question whether the right choices were made on the original studio albums. Furthermore, there are wow-dude renditions of **Tombstone Blues, Tom Thumb's Blues, Desolation Row, Highway 61 Revisited, Leopard Skin Pill Box Hat**, and **Memphis Blues Again** which confirm the proper selections were made back in the day, but that are nonetheless entrancing passers of the ole test of time.

Spring 1966 world tour outrageous recordings of **Ballad of A Thin Man** and **Like A Rolling Stone**, appropriately, end the soundtrack of

No Direction Home, just before Bob's July 29, 1966 Triumph motor-cycle crash that left him with spinal injuries and the opportunity to de-toxify from his substance addictions for a good six months or so while under the care of Dr. Ed Thaler. Prospective future films for which *No Direction Home* wets the appetite are documentaries that chronicle Bob's mid-career of, say 1966 to 1997, and his late career of, say, his '97 histoplasmosis to the present. Will such, or variations of such films ever get made? In my lifetime?

Ahhhh, so much to look forward to in the eternally-springing-forward Dylan department of hope.

Parenthetically, perhaps to cash in on Scorsese's big film, Columbia in 2005, in addition to the *Gaslight* and *Carnegie* recordings, which we are about to get to, released an incredibly original concept album (yeah right) called *The Best of Bob Dylan* with 30 previously released tracks on a single disc. Of course, such a burst of vanguard, pioneering cre-ativity shall be duly ignored in this here book and has got to be legal grounds for somebody needing to be shot.

#50

Live At The Gaslight 1962

August 30, 2005, the same day as the *No Direction Home* soundtrack hit record stores, *Live At The Gaslight 1962* was also released exclusively by Starbucks as part of an 18 month deal, technically separate from the Scorsese film soundtrack, but really as sort of a companion bootleg volume of its own, even though it was not called that. Perhaps due to its mere 10 tracks it was considered unworthy of official bootleg status, yet one never knows what white collar Columbia corporate lackeys are thinking.

In any case, this little live performance tidbit, Dylan's 5th straight outstanding live LP release, manages to equip Dylanologists with a valuable, if not crucial musicology link that begins to account for, however meagerly and inadequately, the inexplicable BIG BANG of the talent of a nobody teenage oddball hailing from Hibbing, Minnesota from mediocrity, to fine in the pedestrian sense of the word, to unparalleled virtuosity in a matter of months. Notwithstanding all this, *Live At The Gaslight* 1962 is really is more of a must for hardcore academics than fans, even devoted ones. My two cents strikes again! I am curious what you think!

Recorded sometime in October 1962 (exact date unknown) on a reel-to-reel tape recorder patched into the house PA system, this long-awaited performance is extraordinarily auspicious, for it was sandwiched in between Dylan's first album and *Freewheelin'*, when Bob was still a virtual unknown outside Greenwich Village. Moreover, this compilation would never have surfaced without the cooperation of Dave Van Ronk's wife, Terri Thal, and the Gaslight owners. In 1973 the first bootlegs of Dylan Gaslight performances commenced to surface, and ever since a growing thirst had persisted for sonically cleaner versions.

Most significantly, *Live At The Gaslight 1962* contains the earliest known public unveilings of '60s folk anthems **A Hard Rain's A-Gonna Fall** and **Don't Think Twice, It's Alright**, not to mention the first known rendition of **John Brown**, unquestionably Dylan's most strident all-out anti-war protest ballad of all time (despite the fact that casual Dylan fans are unfamiliar with it). Pity it is in the case of **A Hard Rain's A-Gonna Fall** that exact recording dates are undocumented. All we know is that the 13-day Cuban missile standoff between John Kennedy and Nikita Krushchev began October 14. Hence, we are left to only imagine what was swirling through the surely-blown minds of the parse Gaslight crowd the night Dylan laid the thought-perturbing **Hard Rain** on them. Like so many other of Dylan's early classics that seemed to have been conceived from and by some immortal entity, **Hard Rain** is delivered on *Live At The Gaslight 1962* in real time, as Americans went to bed on a nightly basis with horrid images of fallout shelters dancing in their heads.

In addition to Dylan's **Rocks and Gravel**, the other 7 numbers on *Live At The Gaslight 1962* are traditional folk covers, 5 of which were previously unreleased and two of which had appeared on earlier official bootleg or live compilations. This includes **The Cuckoo (Is A Pretty Bird)**, **Moonshiner**, **Handsome Molly**, **Cocaine**, **Barbara Allen**, and **West Texas**.

Broadly speaking, more informative and insightfully educational than entertaining, these Gaslight performances portray a more-than-fair insight into the traditional folk repertoire that was influencing a budding genius composer in the midst of his incredible formulation process for *The Freewheelin' Bob Dylan*, as groundbreaking as, if not more so than, any other Dylan release.

Yes, I said that. Again.

#51

Live At Carnegie Hall

November 15, 2005, 10 weeks after the fact, *Live At Carnegie Hall*, completing an array of six widely acclaimed live albums in succession, was released in conjunction with *Bootleg Series 7 No Direction Home The Soundtrack*. The October 26, 1963 concert held at New York City's premier acoustic palace was initially intended to be a live Dylan record entitled *In Concert*. However, after the globally shocking assassination of President Kennedy, seemingly everything changed, and the project was scrapped over Columbia's second thoughts about the inclusion of Dylan's **Last Thoughts On Woody Guthrie** from an earlier 1963 concert at New York's Town Hall.

As with almost all Dylan concerts even back in the early 60s, bootleg recordings from Carnegie have floated around for decades, some complete, some not, and some with better audio quality than others, as was especially and always the case in the pre-digital age. On *Live At Carnegie Hall* we are treated to merely 6 of the 19 songs that got played that night. Four others had previously appeared in either *No Direction Home* or on *Bootleg Series 1-3*. The other nine songs eventually were released in 2013 on the European limited vinyl release, *The 50th Anniversary Collection*, in order to prevent a number of Dylan recordings from legally entering public domain in Europe. Very confusingly and initially available only in Europe to a mere 100 listeners and financially cost prohibitive, this series of discs is omitted from this here book. Although it does contain previously unreleased Dylan recordings, I see it as a slick commercial product and clever legal tactic, not a Dylan work of art or even something on the radar of most fans like yours truly unless one is tenacious and happens to be in the right place at the right time. So, I say forget it.

Previously unreleased highlights of *Live At Carnegie Hall* are killer renditions of **Walls Of Red Ring** and **Lay Down Your Weary Tune**. In addition, from *The Times They Are A-Changin'* there is an extremely rare live version of **North Country Blues**, perhaps one of the most underrated folk ballads in Bob's early folk lexicon. Outstanding takes on **Ballad Of Hollis Brown, The Times They Are A-Changin'**, and **Boots Of Spanish Leather** also grace this short-but-sweet disc. *Live At Carnegie Hall* is yet another glimpse into a live performance of Bob Dylan in his post-*Freewheelin'* solo acoustic folkie prime, complete with the most spellbinding nasally delivery this side of the Appalachians. It, however, suffers from a case of brevity and incompleteness, but in no way incompetence.

Due to their similarly superb concerts venues in the Big Apple, not to mention their resemblance in titles, comparisons are called for of *Live At Carnegie Hall* in October 1963 and *Live 1964 Concert At Philharmonic Hall*. In the latter we find Bob at the very end of his solo acoustic folk days and about to go electric and away from social commentary. As previously pointed out, he sounds bored (and stoned) with his old stuff and sings off the rails at times as if he is enjoying, along with the open-minded, gracious, and I guess hip audience, a stab at self mockery. However, merely one year before, his patrons seem ironically uptight in comparison. *Live At Carnegie Hall* is right between *Freewheelin'* and *The Times They Are A-Changin'*, and Bob reverently treats the reflective folk pilgrims in attendance to two outtakes and four songs from his upcoming third album, which no doubt both found and placed him at the height of his legendary voice of a generation phase that in some people's minds has never ended.

The early Dylan live solo acoustic releases were chronologically released completely out of order with *Concert At Philharmonic Hall* coming out in 2004 and *Live At The Gaslight* and *Live at Carnegie Hall* coming out in 2005 (the actual historical order was Gaslight, Carnegie, and Philharmonic). It all gets more than a little confusing for casual listeners as to how it all makes sense. Especially if one listens deeply and reflectively to this show at Carnegie, Dylan's own mindboggling velocity of change is enough to take on, and when the global tumult of the 1960s is sprinkled into the equation, things can get foggy fast. Nevertheless, to anal students (hey man, I resemble that little sideways insinuation!) of the particularly peculiar topic of Bob Dylan's evolution in the 60s willing to put in the analytical research, the pieces of the puzzle eventually fit together.

Well, as long as one is rationally willing to accept that the wild card variable in the mix is the irrefutable point that we are talking about a genius. This renders a few things inexplicable back there in the 60s. Accept it. Get over it. And move on.

#52

Modern Times

Well, there ain't nothin' like startin' off an album with a 91-word sentence.

After six consecutive non-studio albums without original previously unreleased songwriting, the last four of which focused entirely on the early 60s, *Modern Times*, released August 29, 2006, in some ways was Dylan's least surprising album of new material ever, an out-of-character continuation of the cryptic, tender, snarling, humorous cowboy swing, rockabilly twang, blues ready-mades, and old timey two steps that, lest we forget, graced *Love and Theft* in 2001, a full five agonizing years beforehand for us fans, but five on-fire years for Bob the artist.

Yet, why would Bob entitle an album of musical historical reversions *Modern Times*? Well, I mean, other than the fact that he is Bob Dylan?

First of all, all we know without question is that he coined the ironic title from Charlie Chaplin's 1936 silent film of the same exact title, which was a rare socio-political commentary by the legendary comedian humorously assailing the insidious evils of man's inhumanity to man during the industrial age that was exponentially exacerbated by the Great Depression. Not Dylan's first outright, direct homage to the genius comic whose non-verbal gestures he has mimicked from the beginning (think "mystery tramp" in **Like A Rolling Stone** or his onstage mannerisms at Newport in '63), *Modern Times* is laced with touching sentimental love laments painting a new, weird America on the brink of insane globalism.

Even its iconic cover photo of the *1947 Taxi, New York At Night*, by Ted Croner, aptly reflects the intentional nostalgic nature of what can be characterized as the second in a throwback quadruplet of albums that commenced with *Love and Theft* and would be completed by *Together Through Life* and *Tempest*. Bob starts the 21st century with two straight records warning us to honor American heritage, or else. For the second half of that implied compound sentence, merely peek at the warped way the music industry operates nowadays, squelching creativity in the name of financial profit, and more ominously, just listen to the wayward, carefully marketed, dumb-downed nonsense that passes for professional musicianship these days. Say no more. End of conversation.

Perhaps one way to mentally encapsulate *Modern Times* is to experience it as a musical statement expressing fondness for fellow pilgrims who enter and exit our lives leaving indelible imprints on our psyches and souls. Without overtly uttering Bob's devotion to his diseased musical muses and loved ones as he did in **Bob Dylan's Dream** on *Freewheelin'* and **I'll Remember You** on *Empire Burlesque*, on *Modern Times* the music itself does the talking.

Oxymoronically old fashioned as well as avant-garde (go figure), *Modern Times* marked Bob's third consecutive studio LP with original material that received virtual universal praise from critics and fans alike, despite lame disparaging torpedoes lobbed at his un-credited use, for instance, of choruses and arrangements from older songs from the 1890s and 1930s, the civil war era poetry of Henry Timrod, and even the ancient Roman poet Ovid. This did not prevent *Modern Times* from pocketing two Grammys awards in 2007, one for Best Contemporary Folk Americana Album and another for Best Solo Rock Vocal on the rocka-twangy jump blues **Someday Baby**. For not only do such plagiarism charges confuse the art of American music with standard term paper ethics, but they even more unforgivably overlook the ingenious subtle sarcastic satire displayed by Bob's juxtaposing deference to melodic and lyrical sentiments from bygone epochs with the moniker *Modern Times*.

Bob's weekly hosting of the satellite radio program *Theme Time Radio Hour*, which started up just a few months prior to the release of *Modern Times* and went on to air 100 times over three years, emphasized rock and roll roots popularized primarily in the 30s and 40s. On *Modern Times* Bob utilized what he has referred to as his meditation songwriting strategy, whereby he hears a song from bygone times in his head and commences to switch lyrics, keys, and verse and bridge arrangements until he comes up with what rightly can be claimed to be an original song in its own right. His borrowing from older classics in this manner can be heard clearly on all his later albums going all the way back to *Time Out Of Mind*, which, of course, followed in the old-timey, throwback footsteps of *Good As I Been To You* and *World Gone Wrong*, which were both organic grist for the mill leading to Bob's elder statesman era, during which he has led the music industry, ironically, by traveling backwards in time, pretty much ever since he turned 50.

Achieving a third straight studio masterwork at the age of 65, with *Modern Times* Bob became the oldest musical artist in American history to generate a number 1 album. The record was highly anticipated as a result of the sweeping tributes garnered by *Time Out Of Mind* and *Love and Theft*, the fact that it had been 5 years between albums, and a listening event for record industry VIPs held by Sony far in advance of release. Consequently, *Modern Times* was the first Dylan album to ever rocket to the top of the Billboard 200 in its first week of commercial availability, selling 192,000 copies, which is surely no debut to sneeze at.

It all started during a traditional winter break in the never-ending tour in January of 2006 when Bob arranged for his touring band of veteran Tony Ganier (on bass), George Receli (on drums), Stu Kimball and the jazzy Denny Freeman (on guitars), and Donnie Herron (on pedal steel and mandolin) to rehearse some new songs in Poughkeepsie, New York at the Bardavon 1869 Opera House. Days later the complete LP was recorded and self-produced by Bob under his notorious pseudonym Jack Frost over roughly three weeks in Manhattan at Clinton Studios. Each song reflects the calm of an elder master patiently utilizing his wisdom and knowledge accumulated over the course of a lifetime. Jack Frost

Dylan spontaneously reinvents himself with the aid of a crackerjack backup troupe more than willing to jump at their master's beck and call. In fact, in a 2006 Rolling Stone interview Dylan stated that Tony, George, Stu, Donny, and Denny constituted the best band he had ever been in, that they were individual contributors and not a gang/mob, that they could whip up anything, and that they even surprised HIM sometimes.

Modern Times marks another, yet-again relatively obscure excuse to crown king the one person who can be termed the longest running miracle in rock and roll history. It further unveiled, or piled on, irrefutable evidence that there was no precedent for the pioneering territory that Dylan was now opening. Muddy Waters at 62 was clearly still pushing the boundaries of his unsurpassed eminence, but still within the confines of the blues genre. Here was Dylan cutting, on the fly between gigs, throwback music that seemed to trace the American journey from country to city, crisscrossing musical genres (often from one verse to the next), and sounding one minute like the Texas swing of Hank Williams' Drifting Cowboys and the next like a cross between Chicago street muscle and Stephen Foster in his prime.

The opener, **Thunder On The Mountain,** harkens back to the slick slide guitar of Mike Bloomfield on *Highway 61*, Chuck Berry's **Let It Rock**, and the rocked-out honky-tonk piano of Jerry Lee Lewis. Bob reveals, "I've been sitting down and studying the art of love," directly paying tribute to the ancient Roman Ovid's poem, *The Art of Love*. Sony shrugged off as a non-issue questionings of the inner sleeve claim that all songs were written by Bob Dylan since there existed no legal merit to any law suit threats, considering the age of the source material. Moreover, plagiarism, a term that is born out of the notion of intellectual property, is not the same as humbly and discreetly expressing recognition in a milieu such as songwriting, which is non-rational, as opposed to irrational.

As sure as I'm alive and breathing, none of the poets and composers acknowledged on *Modern Times* (over whom Dylan towers in stature culturally, historically, and artistically, for starters – though Bob would never see it this way) are still alive, or else they would surely express their eternal gratitude for Bob Dylan's salute. *Modern Times* law suit threats to this day remain harmless critical hyperbole. More to the point, on **Thunder On The Mountain**, the album does not delay a nanosecond in alerting all within earshot that this little understated jazzy ensemble is taking no prisoners.

Spirit On The Water yanks us out of the 1950s and hurls us into 1930s romance and innocence. Bob's lovely bouncing piano chords accented by Denny Freeman's Sunday-stroll guitar fills and Donny Herron's stately pedal steel guitar are the first, but absolutely not the last, instance on *Modern Times* of sublime pre-rock and roll sentiments at their best. Hints of this sort of hearkening back to the music of Bob's parents' generation were evident on *Time Out Of Mind* and especially *Love and Theft*, but *Modern Times* picks up this theme and pushes its envelope. Having said that, Bob manages to take the jewel **Spirit On The Water** out with an understated harmonica break as if to declare that, in case anyone has forgotten, this is, after all, a Bob Dylan record, lest we lose sight in the midst of what has begun to sound like a Frank Sinatra cover album.

Rollin' and Tumblin' swipes a riff, opening line, song title, and blues standard credited to Muddy Waters and Hambone Willie Newborne. Bob adds his own lyrics to recreate the traditional blues theme of earthly love and gambling heartache while drawing on ecological images like night shadows, sunrises, glowing landscapes, and vineyard buds. **When The Deal Goes Down** apes the melody of **Where The Blue Night Meets The Gold Of The Day**, a Bing Crosby signature song. Here Bob reverts back to the archaic vibe introduced in **Spirit On The Water**. Mesmerizing, hypnotic, and intuitively channeled right out of the World War II era, **When The Deal Goes Down** is a masterwork that represents some of the best romantic poetry in Dylan's entire massive lexicon.

Someday Baby echoes a song by John Estes made famous by Lightnin' Hopkins and sometimes erroneously credited to Muddy Waters,

Worried Life Blues. Similar to the sensual reflex of **Dirt Road Blues** on *Time Out Of Mine*, this sound recording soars over **Dirt Road Blues** in quintessential merit, packing old rickety blues with an electrically charged wallop.

Workingman Blues #2 is nothing short of a classical Bob Dylan epic, a tip of the hat to June Christy's 1946 **June's Blues**, one of many of June's recordings Bob repeatedly featured on his Sunday satellite radio show. "Meet me at the bottom don't lag behind bring me your boots and shoes" in the chorus line is an example of line lifting for which Dylan ought to be cut some proverbial slack. Plagiarism this is not. Tender, raw, carnal spiritual imagery woven into verses that just won't stop coming sung with a hint of Lonnie Johnson on Bob's cherished **Tomorrow Night** are expertly backed by slippery, sometimes sloppy jazzman's piano. Here Bob embodies a cross between a professional mythmaker and a back alley magician crooning both bawdy joy and restless heartache.

Beyond The Horizon once again reverts to music past its prime, based on the 1935 **Red Sails In The Sunset** by Jimmy Kennedy and Hugh Williams. Denny Freeman steps to the plate with a sweet lead guitar as Bob ricochets 88 chords that steer the enchanting lyrical arrangement onto a full moon suspended on a celestial intersection of earth, sky, and romantic escapade, making this composition sound as old as the hills.

The apocalyptic **Nettie Moore** contains both a melody and lyrics that are unrecognizable from the 1857 **Gentle Nettie Moore** by Marshall Pike and James Lord (the composer of **Jingle Bells**). A stately civil war marching beat bleeds out a prophecy couched in comforting pity for the human condition. Late era Dylan that'll take your breath away.

The Levee's Gonna Break is a creative exploitation of the **When The Levee Breaks** by Kansas Joe McCoy and Memphis Minnie, which had legally entered the realm of public domain two years prior to *Modern Times*. Another audio echo of **Someday Baby** and **Dirt Road Blues**, this interpretation hints at the 1927 Mississippi flood (as did **High Water** on *Love and Theft*), which at one point covered an area engulfing approximately 7,500 square miles of the South, particularly in Arkansas, Mississippi, and Louisiana. **The Levee's Gonna Break** illustrates the end times Dylan has been seeing in store ever since his second album, *Freewheelin'*, in 1963.

With **Ain't Talkin'** Bob brings *Modern Times* to an end with a ghostly gypsy ballad, simmering growl, and wry sense of foreboding in a closer reminiscent of **Desolation Row** and **Highlands**. Here Dylan steals, or borrows, take your pick, chorus lines from the Stanley Brothers' **Highway of Regret** as well as first verse poetry from a traditional Irish ballad, **As I Roved Out**. Bob walks us into a mystic garden that is shrouded in the biblical nursery where Christ was approached unaware by his apostles, who failed to recognize him for who he was. Hard-boiled morality ushers us into the gates of Eden, only here we encounter a godless place. Hand percussion, lonesome fiddle, and piano escort *Modern Times* to the exit doors, ever reminding us that the forgivable Christian pilgrim, fallibly human, with whom we first got acquainted on *Slow Train Coming*, had not met his maker quite yet.

Modern Times is paradoxically peppered with ironic prophecy, creative mischief, a wild sense of humor, bottomless sadness, and front parlor and back porch tunes out of the 1860s, 1890s, 1930s, and 1950s. On it Bob Dylan underscores his stature as one of the greatest blues interpreters and singers ever, adding to his labyrinthian legend, while simultaneously singing the praises of the mortality of life as we know it. *Modern Times* is, in a way, one big catharsis of grief on multiple levels. Writing old fashioned songs is a clever, effective strategy in which to couch pain with which the human mind cannot grapple. Is Dylan a poetic sage, road-worn holy man, untamed artist growing older who sees death as something to accept but not bow to, or an unconcerned genius totally disinterested in his growing super hero status? At 63 minutes 4 seconds, *Modern Times* is far more convincing than it is compelling, which is saying a lot, indeed.

With squinty-eyed disdain and fuck-off detachment, latter day Bob Dylan (i.e. post-*Time Out Of Mind*) heeds the advice of Woody

Guthrie and runs with it: "If you want to learn something, just steal it." Thereby, new songs evolve from old ones, reminding us of who we really are, whose we really are, and that the olden days of yore ain't much different from modern times.

In the end, on *Modern Times* (but really in general), Dylan, like Chaplin, modestly pursues his artistic vision without so much as a nodding glance toward his peers. Moreover, to indicate his shame, remorse, and desire to make amends for committing the crime of plagiarism on *Love and Theft*, on *Modern Times* the deed is repeated repeatedly.

I'm sure Bob is sleeping better at night.

#53

Bootleg Series Volume 8/Tell Tale Signs/Rare and Unreleased 1989-2006

From heaviness personified, how 'bout we segue right into the ole heart of Americana? What the hell?

When *Bootleg Series Volume 8 Tell Tale Signs* came out on October 6, 2008, other than the superbly re-mastered or whatever the heck they did to it re-release of all the Traveling Wilbury material in 2007, which really is a must, we had endured a two-year forever-and-a-day gap between releases, but to say it was worth the wait would be far more the understatement than saying I was surprised that in the '08 Democratic presidential primaries Hillary Clinton had been bested by a skinny guy with a funny name. To be fair, Todd Haynes' *I'm Not There* came out in 2007, which gave Dylan fans an opportunity to see an amazingly complex masterpiece Hollywood production casting six different actors as Bob Dylan at various junctures in his career, not to mention hear quite the double CD soundtrack containing spectacular cover versions of Dylan material. Still, the waiting for something new from Columbia's Bobland was certainly not for naught.

Whereas the first 7 volumes of official bootlegs had entirely addressed Dylan's early and mid-career catalogue, *Tell Tale Signs* finally gave Dylan record buyers, as opposed to concert goers, a fairly authentic glimpse into the rich unreleased lyrical treasures and musical hybrids of Bob's elder statesman era. The album includes 1989 to 2006 studio album outtakes, movie soundtrack contributions, live tracks, a most rare take from the 1992 Bromberg sessions in Chicago, and an awesome duet with Ralph Stanley that, as long as you have a pulse, will give you chills.

If you love Dylan, *Tell Tale Times* is surely a disc you wouldn't leave home on a drive over 500 miles. Or, in some cases, 500 meters. I have not taken a poll, but I would venture to guess that amongst die-hard Dylanheads, and you know who you are, this here has got to be, Dylan or otherwise, the best f-ing road trip disc of the just-dawning 21st century.

As if anything more needed to be said after I get over the mouthful of that previous sentence, I shall, as I am ever wont to do, nonetheless elaborate for both educational and entertainment purposes. My father once exclaimed to me, while he sipped after-dinner burgundy wine, that he only wished that he be buried with a bottle of a beverage characterized by such delicacy. Well, dad, I am totally with you, but I prefer to be buried with *Tell Tale Times*, oh wait, I mean *Highway 61 Revisited*, oh man, I mean *Time Out Of Mine*. Life is multiple choice, and sometimes one must shit or get off the pot. Okay, okay, if you must, I will go with *John Wesley Harding*. Wait, it's Saturday, so my favorite is *Bringing It All Back Home*.

Excuuuuuuse, me, did I just digress? That is sooooo unlike me.! The point is that it is hard to overstate the distinguished nature of *Tell Tale Times*.

It came with a juicy 57 page book by Larry Sloman carefully annotating each of the 27 recordings, but the $129.99 (Did somebody say rip off?) deluxe edition threw in a 150-page volume containing singles artwork spanning Dylan's whole career as well as a bonus disc of 12 additional audio recordings. Furthermore, pre-orders from Dylan's official web site were treated to a 7" vinyl version of the previously unreleased **Dreamin' Of You**, and the first 5,000 such customers were also treated to a cool, colorful twilight urban poster from Bob's extraordinarily popular and well-produced weekly satellite *Theme Time Radio Hour*, which, not so incidentally, generated a two-disc delightful, absolute must on the

Chrome Dreams label, *The Best of Bob Dylan's Theme Time Radio Hour*. Check it out if you ever want to know what makes Bob Dylan tick.

All in all, you got the funny feeling that the historically intermittently well-marketed Bob Dylan had finally stepped into the digital age with a fury, while somehow managing to relentlessly find time to tour the Far East, Europe, and this land is your land itself, from the redwood forests to the Gulf stream waters, not to mention from California to the New York Island. What else does a non-burned out aging rock star do in his late 60s?

There I go digressing again. Man, I gotta watch that.

You want to know what else is on this album. I know. Well, about 15 new versions of studio album songs, either live or studio outtakes, all of which are at the very least listenable and at most breathtaking. However comma, what makes this album pop for casual listeners and critical and gripping historically for earnest pupils of Dylandom are the baker's dozen of inclusions which had hitherto never surfaced on any previous Dylan releases.

Leading this parade of fascinating recordings were three outtakes that simply did not make the cut on *Time Out Of Mind*. **Red River Shore**, **Dreamin' Of You**, and **Marchin' To The City** rank up with the best stuff Dylan has ever written, although the latter two resemble the over-all vibe and specific songs on *Time Out Of Mind* enough to logically justify their rejection.

Tell Ol' Bill from *North Country*, **Huck's Tune** from *Lucky You*, and **Cross The Green Mountain** from *Gods and Generals* were prominently featured in these Hollywood productions, all of which are movies well worth seeing on their own merits. Here again are instances in which Bob commandingly steps to the plate when commissioned to come up with a thematically appropriate musical composition. As when he was given a deadline during the filming of *Pat Garret and Billy the Kid* in his thirties, and again in 1999 when he delivered the

Oscar winner (best original song) **Things Have Changed** for *Wonder Boys*, here we find Bob in his 60s skillfully merging the film and music genres. Quite the official bootleg, come to think of it, would be a Bob Dylan movie soundtrack compilation. No shortage of material there.

For instance, not appearing on any Dylan albums, **Waiting For You** is a lovely track written for *Divine Secrets of Ya Ya Sisterhood* in 2002 and featured in the #5 song list slot during the summer 2014 Australian and fall 2014 U.S. tours. You gotta think that the movie house in Hibbing on 1ˢᵗ Avenue that was in Bob's maternal lineage, now a deli, not only played a role in Dylan's love of motion pictures, but that it has, from the get go, supplied endless streams of inspiration for Bob's entire lexicon of songs, not just those commissioned by film producers.

Another *Time Out Of Mind* previously unreleased Dylan original was the fruit of a sensational 2005 recording that was sort of in no man's land between *Love and Theft* and *Modern Times*, **Can't Escape From You**. In addition, the abandoned 1992 album with David Bromberg was finally unlocked with the inclusion of **Miss The Mississippi**, a stellar enough full-backing-band effort to yank the chains of fans who yearn to know what the hell else went on in Chicago's now long-defunct Acme Recording Studios in early '92. Bob and David remain mysteriously tight-lipped to this day, but this cat-and-mouse prank can't go on forever. Or can it?

A June 30, 1992 Dunkirk, France live rendition of **The Girl On The Greenbriar Shore** and a *World Gone Wrong* outtake, Robert Johnson's **32-20 Blues** throw us back to the obscure early 90s time frame, during which Bob was sowing the seeds for his post-50ᵗʰ birthday bumper crop. Bob's duet and nifty flat-picking with Ralph Stanley on Stanley's **The Lonesome River** finds both vocalizing on that high lonesome plateau Hank Williams brought to the fore of what we now refer to as country music.

Desert isle disc? Keeper? Take it to the grave? They all aptly phrase in English what is beyond words. Reducing, condensing, and/or recapping *Tell Tale Times* with the powerless vehicle of language, an impotent, unnecessary, and distracting obstacle to real communication, unjustly reduces to nonsense what must be heard, preferably at high volume while simultaneously winding through east Tennessee, Carolinian, and Virginian Appalachian switchbacks over Blue Ridge, Smokey, and Allegheny hollows, bluffs, gorges, and groves of backwoods green.

This disc and a country road'll make a true American patriot out of ya.

#54

Together Through Life

In the three years between studio albums with previously unreleased original material that preceded the release of *Together Through Life* on April 28, 2009, ever-the-trooper Bob Dylan relentlessly trudged onward, sustaining his breakneck pace of roughly 100 live performances a year despite a more-than-noticeable-decline in his vocal skills, especially in outdoor concert venues. This album came as somewhat of a last minute surprise with very little fanfare or marketing by Columbia. Its genesis lay in French film director Olivier Dahan's invitation to Bob in the fall of 2008 to compose a song for a film he was working on called *My Own Love Song*. Dahan actually wanted a whole soundtrack worth of songs from the man, but asked for only one, and it turned into an unexpected album. Two months later, unbeknownst to Columbia, the album surprisingly arrived ready for release just six months after the release of the monumental archive project, *Tell Tale Times*.

Together Through Life has a throwback tone like Dylan's three previous studio records with new original material, *Time Out Of Mind*, *Love and Theft*, and *Modern Times*, but it is sonically distinct due to a deliberate Chess and Sun Records timbre about it. Backing Bob are his touring band of Tony Ganier on bass, George Recile on drums, Donnie Herron on pedal steel and mandolin, Los Lobos accordionist David Hidalgo, and Mike Campbell from Tom Petty's Heartbreakers replacing Bob's jazz-inclined lead guitarist on the road, Denny Freeman. Although Freeman was stalwart, resolute, and robust as a lead guitar more-cookie-cutter-than-offhand improviser in the never-ending-tour band from

2005 to 2009, Campbell's rock and blues six-string instincts were certainly more called for than Freeman's jazzy faculties, given the Tex-Mex blues emphasis on *Together Through Life*. Moreover, Freeman's exit from the touring scene brought back to the fold the Texas rockabilly/blues guitar instincts of Charlie Sexton, who has proven to be a key lynchpin in the consolidation of long term firm footing in Bob's touring ensemble.

As a matter of fact, initially upon Charlie's return to Bob's dapper posse in October 2009, he so stole the show that Bob's live concerts could easily have been marketed as *The Charlie Sexton Show With Bob Dylan*. However, it was not long before Bob put Charlie into a cage, which muzzled him more than was necessary (but that's just me), as Bob apparently wanted to explore the expansion of his own maniacally bold jazz and R and B keyboard meanderings.

As if recorded in a dead end Mexican border town, *Together Through Life* has no need for the contrived digital details of modern day record making. From *Time Out Of Mind* onward, Dylan has been a one man preservation society highlighting the popular song tradition that slammed shut around 1962, which was both the time of Bob's first album and the year before the Beatles ushered in a new wave of rock and roll pop music that aided and abetted Dylan's commission of homicide on Tin Pan Alley. Bob Dylan and the Beatles almost singlehandedly invented the concept and artistic genre of singer songwriters and put an end to the process of music recording whereby professional studio instrumentalists were brought in to make songs written by professional songwriters pop. From 1997 to the present Bob Dylan almost seems to be making amends for this crime of involuntary manslaughter, a gesture which befittingly, perfectly, and conveniently fits the mold of the outlaw role that he and his band personify onstage.

Together Through Life features battered singing, caustic and stinging guitar fills, spontaneous kinetics, and perilous lyrics emanating from a carefree band sounding as though it were nonchalantly roaming along the Rio Grande in south Texas. Produced by Jack Frost, Bob's pseudonym, the mere 45 minutes of music is comprised of 10 songs, 9 of which were written in collaboration with Grateful Dead lyricist Robert Hunter.

Compared with its predecessor *Modern Times*, *Together Through Life* lacks thematic unity and heaviness. It speaks of the enduring power of romance, without which life is hard, but other than that is teeming with contradictions, frayed ends, and crossed signals. Although rich and deeply striking at moments, *Together Through Life* also lacks the aura of an instant classic like *Modern Times*, *Love and Theft*, and *Time Out Of Mind*. Dylan's wheezing and croaking comes off like the growl of a seasoned blues journeyman, not an old fart who wrote and sang on *Highway 61 Revisited* and *Blood On The Tracks*.

"Oh, well, I love you pretty baby", Bob declares emphatically in the opening track, **Beyond Here Lies Nothing**, a swampy blues rock samba instant classic, if there is such a thing. A play off the melody of **Unchain My Heart**, **Beyond Here Lies Nothing** is at moments a throwback to the whirling dervish fiddle of Scarlet Rivera on *Desire* and at others Hidalgo's accordion sounds like it is echoing in the mariachi chasms of Plaza Garibaldi in the historic heart of Mexico City. It has enjoyed a somewhat consistent presence on live show set lists since 2009, sometimes re-worked as a simmering mambo to quite enthusiastic hip-grinding crowd response.

Bob bites down gently on each syllable on the love-struck ballad **Life Is Hard** as he eagerly croons, "Life is hard without you near me." Recile's soft-shoe drum brush strokes and Herron's weepy peddle steel and old-school mandolin doodling create a 1940s Sinatra-esque romantic fantasy that is obviously alluring to even Bob himself. His vocals are honest and believable on **Life Is Hard** as well as throughout *Together Through Life*.

My Wife's Home Town is melodically a transparent rip off of Muddy Water's version of Willie Dixon's **I Just Want To Make Love To You** with completely new lazy lyrics grafted onto Muddy's version with the aid of Robert Hunter. Bob is loose and laughing it up in this comedic portrayal of the henpecked husband archetype.

"If you ever go to Houston, you better walk right", words sung on the **Midnight Special** recording on which Bob played harmonica for Harry Belafonte in 1961, are stolen verbatim on **If You Ever Go To Houston**. Hidalgo's loping accordion and Herron's livening pedal steel make Texas feel like it's only about a mile from New Orleans as Bob warns wayward travelers to repent their drunken outlaw ways. **If You Ever Go To Houston** might have fit pretty well onto Dylan's lovely, captivating soundtrack for the 1973 film *Pat Garret and Billy The Kid*. Don't ask me where I come up with this stuff. Look into it, see what you think, and ABSOLUTELY let me know.

Forgetful Heart might take the cake for master songwriting on *Together Through Life*. Laced with elegantly merged chords and longing, aching lyrics, it has remained a consistent staple in Dylan's live concerts over the ensuing years, receiving multiple re-workings accentuating whimsical keyboards, each one better than the rest. "The door has closed forevermore, if indeed there ever was a door," ominously introduces a wonderful fade.

Jolene, first of all, is a play off of Mink DeVille's **Return To Magenta**, Little Richard's **Lucille**, and Chuck Berry's **Nadine**, artfully conjuring up a cast of lustful characters encased in a tough juke joint. **Jolene** gets its hooks in early and refuses to let go.

This Dream Of You once again features Donnie Herron's Scarlet-Rivera-on-*Desire*-like fiddle stalked by a mariachi band in the form of Hidalgo's accordion. On his only entirely self-composed contribution to *Together Through Life*, Bob croons, "All I have and all I've known is this dream of you I have that keeps me livin' on and on." In Dylan's old age, he has not aged ungracefully into a romantic cynic. Rather, he speaks of moons, shadows dancing on walls that seem to know it all, defending himself to his dying breath, and being lost in the crowd devoid of tears. If anyone is "forever young" in his seventies, it is the author himself. You've got to hand it to him. His 1960s intuitively spot on, yet guarded heart seems blown wide open in his seventies.

Shake, Shake, Mama is a light-hearted flirty blues rocker that would not have fit in at all on *Modern Times*, but aptly suits *Together Through Life* just fine. It stands in stark contradiction to the earnestly delivered songs preceding and after it, **This Dream Of You** and **I Feel A Change Comin' On**. Bob again drives home his rockabilly hook early and won't let go.

I Feel A Change Comin' On is yet another masterpiece in the elder masterwork era of Mr. Bob, which commenced with *Time Out Of Mind* and has never looked back. Probably an homage to Sam Cooke's **A Change Is Gonna Come**, this is an instant classic in the tradition of **Lay, Lady Lay**. "I'm reading James Joyce, some people tell me I got the blood of the land in my voice" is the line from *Together Through Life* that may just best stand the test of time.

It's All Good is the song Bob wrote for Dahan's film *My Own Love*, a bayou boogie that would have made John Lee Hooker proud. It paints a portrait of an ugly America that devolves into bare-knuckle Darwinism survival of the coldest and most cruel, all of which Bob shrugs off with a cold shoulder of his own. **It's All Good** brings *Together Through Life* to a wicked finish. If a song can be apocalyptic and cheerful simultaneously, this is it. The irony permeating the air is that Bob Dylan knows damn well it is NOT all good, yet his charming sarcasm has you dancing all the way to fires of hell.

Thus, there you have it, another album that sonically fits right in with Dylan's other 2000 era albums, fixated on pre-rock and roll American music, stretching across his own mythic picturesque America from its hazy past to its barbed present. Impulsive, caustic, and sentimental, *Together Through Life* takes Tin Pan Alley rhymes and oft-used melodies to memorialize an America that is heroically struggling for dignity in an uncaring world. This album is nowhere near as simple as it sounds on the first listen. The pain of its perilous lyrics can get lost in its humor and a band that sounds like it is having a gas, riot, and hoot all at the same time.

As for Bob, he himself might be coasting a bit, but that beats flailing aimlessly as he did on much of *Empire Burlesque, Knocked Out Loaded*, and *Down In The Groove*, let alone not giving a hoot which was the case on *Self Portrait*. Those horror shows left us all still and permanently shell-shocked and in need of PTSD therapy. Every time a Dylan album comes out, I honestly will always fear the worst. That's just how it is with trust. It's a fragile thing. Even though Bob's old man era appears bulletproof up to now, you just never know, man.

Together Through Life takes us on a messy, merry, mischievous escapade through the United States of Americana with masterful readings of 20th century folk music, ultimately pulling off neither masterpiece nor accomplishing disaster.

Dylan June 26, 2010 at the Azkena Rock Festival in Vitoria-Gasteiz, Spain.
Photo taken by Alberto Cabello.

#55

Christmas In The Heart

In the spring of 2009 the director of public relations for Feeding America, Inc., who happens to be one of my three beautiful nieces, received a phone call from a man who introduced himself by saying that he was with Bob Dylan. "Yeah, right, you're with Bob Dylan, and I'm Madonna," she thought. However, the guy went on to say that Dylan was recording an album of Christmas carols and popular hymns and that Bob desired that 100% of the profits from U.S. sales be donated to help feed the hungry in America (international sale profits were, in turn, contributed to Crisis in the U.K. and World Food Programe). Turns out the apparent hoax was for real. Ladies and gentlemen, please welcome Bob Dylan's latest musical version of his penchant for rabbit-in-his-hat chicanery, *Christmas In The Heart*. If stupefied, you are forgiven, and a little historical context might be in order.

Born and raised Jewish, in Dylan's Hibbing childhood he attended a rather scrawny, humble synagogue on a residential side street just off 1st Avenue, where Bob's maternal grandmother operated the only movie theater in town. Dylan has always insisted that he never felt left out of Christmas as a Jewish minority in a primarily Christian town.

In fact, the two story stucco where the Zimmerman's resided was and still is right across the street from the largest of the two Catholic churches in Hibbing. A German Catholic parish was a mere ¾ of a mile away, and the Irish Catholics were a stone's throw away. A handful of smaller Protestant churches pepper the grid-like boulevards and meandering residential thoroughfares designed in the 1920s when the Oliver Mining Company, a subsidiary of U.S. Steel, re-located the whole town of Hibbing two miles south in order to access the world's biggest iron ore mine on the Mesabi Iron Range. Growing up in a remote, god-forsaken, hardworking mining community in one of the few Jewish families within miles, Dylan somehow picked up on the universality of the Christmas spirit.

On *Christmas In The Heart* it is apparent that Bob personally very much relates to the music he is interpreting and that he seeks for all his listeners to relate to it in their own way. So far as Christmas is for kids, a 68-year-old little boy who hung out in Hibbing comic shops on Main Street and adolescent who formed a Little Richards cover band called the Golden Chords while attending nearby historic Hibbing High School certainly comes out to play on *Christmas in The Heart.*

The moniker Bob Dylan followed by the oxymoronic term Christmas album invited all sorts of sarcastic hyperbole to which Dylan paid no, as in zero, attention. Those who would think it ironic that Bob would record a slate of 15 holiday season traditionals are critics on the outside looking in, have no gut level understanding of Dylan or his work, do not fathom what he is capable and not capable of doing, and never have, still don't, and probably never will know what to make of him.

Christmas In The Heart just might represent the most miraculous accomplishment in Dylan's career of artistic wonderments. For, in overcoming the Mt. Everest of skepticism surrounding this philanthropic project, the album manages to achieve a number of milestones, including, but not limited to the following.

First, it received generally favorable reviews from critics and fans alike. Second, it brought a breath of fresh air into classic carols we have all heard a thousand times. Third, Dylan holds tight to a mood of levity while upholding the highest of improvisational and audio standards in a genre usually amounting to no more than an artistic wasteland.

Fourth, he proved how much life there is still left in these hallowed hymns after centuries of tired and pedestrian secular and religious renditions. Fifth, the wide variety of band arrangements utilized on *Christmas In The Heart* resulted in a choice repertoire of seasoned tunes that genuinely sound modern while avoiding cliché predictability. Finally, Dylan reminded every woman and every man in every nation how much other artists have succeeded in butchering some of the most terrific music that has ever been written.

Plus, he did it for a good cause, raising, according to my beloved niece, in the neighborhood of 1 million smackers for food pantries, depositories, and soup kitchens all across the sweet land of liberty, not to mention overseas profits, which likely far surpassed domestic proceeds. My man!

Backing Bob in a Santa Monica recording studio were a coed choir of seven, his touring band and *Together Through Life* rhythm section of bassist Tony Ganier and drummer George Recile, Donnie Herron on steel guitar, mandolin, trumpet, and fiddle, and David Hidalgo back on accordion. Brought in for this project were Patrick Warren on keyboards, and on lead guitar, veteran session man and star in his own right, Phil Upchurch. If these guys do not sound like they are having fun playing music they know and love well, I will give you a complimentary copy of this here book.

Here Comes Santa Claus starts off the proceedings with some Christmas bells ringing in a jumping romp reminiscent of pre-Vatican II chimes I heard at the roughly 2,000 Catholics masses I attended by age 12 at St. Patrick's, a grey gothic monolith towering over downtown Decatur, Illinois. On **Do You Hear What I Hear** I hear a crack band with some f-ing soul.

Winter Wonderland features Tony's bouncing bass making it all but impossible to bob your head back and forth. **Hark The Herald Angels Sing** again finds Tony in the driver's seat via his double bass bow while Bob strains to find a couple high notes with credibility nonetheless.

I'll Be Home For Christmas brings home Bob's sincere, completely disarming sweetness.

George's military march snare drum rolls on **Little Drummer Boy** and Bob's hushed vocal paint a civil war landscape behind a sweet treatment of an all-time favorite. R and B sensibilities drip from **The Christmas Blues** on which Bob introduces a juicy little harmonica filler. Bob sings the first verse in Latin on **O' Come All Ye Faithful,** while the choir and Hidalgo's accordion lightly lift consciousness vibes to the heavens above.

Donnie's mandolin in the intro to **Have Yourself A Merry Little Christmas** sets the stage for another delightful vocal and stellar choral backing. **Must Be Santa** highlights Hidalgo's accordion runs and a snare back beat from George in an audio recording that was made into both a most bizarre music video as well as a video e-card in which Dylan appears with Santa at the end after a fight and escape scene provide the requisite dilemma and conflict resolution plot. The sublime **Silver Bells** tells of sparkling Christmastime in the city, and my 2013 December sojourn to Hibbing certainly was filled with such neon lit icy street scenes, not to mention being treated, in the absolutely ornate high school auditorium where Bob legendarily performed as a youth, to a junior/senior high holiday concert, to which the whole town of Hibbing seemingly turned out.

On **The First Noel** the choir and Donnie's fiddle support Bob's strong, committed, heartfelt caroling. Hawaiian pedal steel guitar unapologetically twangs throughout and never looks back on **Christmas Island**, compliments of Donnie, who pretty much steals this show, with some perty Nashville cat licks thrown in by Upchurch. **The Christmas Song** finds Bob roasting his chestnuts while simultaneously doing his best Andy Williams or Bing Crosby or Johnny Mathis or Frank Sinatra or Dean Martin, you tell me. **O Little Town of Bethlehem**, a most fitting closer, brings it all back home (pun intended) by scoring the winning run with two outs in the bottom of the ninth as the choir, Bob, and all the boys take us on a pilgrimage back to that fateful night so long ago when the stars aligned with three wise men and a babe wrapped in swaddling clothes.

Dylan has stated that earthly hunger is a solvable problem and each ought to pitch in. 12 of the 35 million Americans who don't know where their next meal is coming from are children. *Christmas In The Heart* comes straight from the heart of the little boy in Bob Dylan, so the only way to play these songs is straight – without the irony that some expected from Mr. Shape Shifting Shuck and Jive Persona. Christmas carols from the heart never fail to reach the heart anyway, no matter critiques from on high.

Just go to historic Hibbing High School next December the week before Christmas and see for yourself. The National Register of Historic Places has recognized this architectural behemoth, for its elaborate, glamorous, gaudy, gorgeous, glistening, gilded theatrical palace represents the town's crown jewel. One block from Bob Dylan's boyhood residence, the spirit will be so thick you can cut it with a knife, whether Jew, Gentile, rock star, or little kid who saw the ornate Belgian handmade cut glass chandeliers hanging from those rafters and thought, "I'm gonna be big, real big."

Chandelier of handmade Belgian glass in the rafters of the
auditorium in Hibbing High School. Photo by author.

The Zimmerman home in Duluth, Minnesota where Bob lived
from birth to age 7. Photo by Jonathunder.

7th Avenue Zimmerman house in Hibbing, Minnesota where
Bob lived from age 7 to 18. Photo by author.

#56

Bootleg Series Volume 9/The Witmark Demos 1962-1964

Here we have a raw, solo acoustic, wide-angle-lens two-disc release which both immortalizes the pre-electric Dylan and humanizes him at the same time.

On October 19, 2010 Columbia let go of another early 60s official bootleg release, *Volume 9 The Witmark Demos 1962-1964*, which both towers over and falls short of the *Philharmonic Hall, Carnegie Hall*, and *Gaslight* bootlegs in 2004 and '05 for a variety of reasons. Although this compilation provides a rare glimpse of less than perfect studio recordings that portray him as more mortal and less accomplished than one might imagine, here serious students of Bob Dylan are given a unique opportunity. This collection does not solely capture a concert recording representing a snapshot of a stage of Dylan's evolution on a given day at a given time. It is far more than that. Where else, on just one album, can authentic Dylanologists monitor Bob's early 60s songwriting progress over an entire two year span during which his budding development as a virtuoso composer and performing talent was accelerating at a velocity that was nothing short of conspicuous, outlandish, glaring, peculiar, and eccentric, to say the least? More to the point, what designates the Witmark demo release such a noteworthy treasure is that it covers the entire 1962 to 1964 time period, not just a 60 or 90 minute flash, wink of the eye, momentary splice, and/or millisecond in the scheme of Dylan's solo folk trajectory, which red flags it as a prime audio source for historians on the matter.

Well, nowhere, I am here to tell ya. Over the course of a whopping 47 tracks, 15 of which represent songwriting that the planet earth did not know existed, we are exposed to Bob laying down somewhat casual demos for publishers M. Witmark and Son and Leeds Music in a cramped 6' by 8' studio. 39 of these tracks were recorded for Witmark and 8 were recorded for Bob's first and fleeting music publisher, Leeds.

Both companies would use reel-to-reel tape just to get rough demos in order to help push sales of Dylan's songs to other artists. Basically, a Witmark or Leeds copyist would transcribe lyrics and music onto song sheets that got mailed to recording companies far and wide, who would subsequently request an inexpensive plastic acetate if one of their artists expressed interest, which was, in turn, sent to the prospective aspiring cover artists for preview purposes.

In this manner, Dylan became a millionaire practically overnight from Peter, Paul, and Mary's version of **Blowin' In The Wind** alone. Prior to this, it only took $1,000 from Witmark to persuade Leeds, Dylan's brief music publisher for less than a year after his first album, to let go of its rights to his original music. Ouch, and (editorial comment) Lou Levy of Leeds, who was the principle dupe swindled (albeit legally and fairly) by Albert Grossman in this deal, has got to personify Webster's dictionary definition of the concept of regret. Suffice it to say, and more to the point, however, Bob Dylan caught the songwriting bug as soon as he penned his name to that Leeds contract in the first week of January 1962, and he never looked back. Off to the races was the heir apparent to not just Woody Guthrie, but Stephen Foster, George Gershwin, Richard Rogers, Irving Berlin, Jerome Kern, and Hoagy Carmichael, to name a few.

On most of these Witmark demos it is obvious that Bob is understandably not giving it his best shot, yet this more often than not comes off as fascinatingly relaxed and most compelling. Even though these versions of the 33 previously released songs are not up to par with the studio renditions we all know and love (I guess we're ALL human), what legitimizes this album as indispensible are the 15 ditties that further document the wealth, in terms of both quantity and quality, of potentially commercially viable music which Dylan discarded into the ole circular file during his early songwriting days. Well, let's just say that here we have 15 more original songs which got recorded but never graced a studio album set list.

Unearthed and brought to the light of day are no less than 11 compositions which range from forced and/or mediocre in a few cases to stunning in a sensational sense, namely **Man On The Street, Poor Boy Blues, Ballad For A Friend, Long Ago, Far Away, Bound To Lose, Bound To Win, All Over You, I'd Hate To Be You On That Dreadful Day, Long Time Gone, Farewell, Gypsie Lou, Ain't Gonna Grieve**, and **Guess I'm Doing Fine**. Come on dude, we knew you were on fire throughout the 60s, but your inner bonfire was blazing far, far more than we ever knew. Of course, that last sentence became the understatement of the 21ˢᵗ century four years later when *The Complete Basement Tapes* was released, but you get the drift.

Broadly speaking, casual fans have no business either spending money on or attempting to listen to this album. They won't give it the time of day anyway. Trust me. Still, academics in the field of Dylanology and deeply genuine songwriting musicians owe it to this slightly sloppy treasure and themselves to carefully monitor these rather off-the-cuff, captivating, compelling, quite carefree, and mostly killer takes.

In 2010, for the record, yet another absolutely redundant and commercially motivated album was released under Columbia's series known as legacy recordings, *The Original Mono Recordings*. This consisted of all of Dylan's first 8 albums as they were originally recorded and intended to be heard in mono, as opposed to stereo sound. Can you say, "Columbia stole this idea from the Beatles' empire having profited greatly from its 2009 similar scheme?"

Alrighty then, no need to waste breath on that nonsense.

#57

In Concert Brandeis University

A bonus disc to *The Witmark Demos 1962-1964*, *In Concert At Brandeis University*, was temporarily offered with all Amazon online orders. Six months later on April 12, 2011 it was officially released on its own right, yet not as part of the official bootleg series.

The concert took place May 10, 1963, when Bob was still so unknown that college campus concerts were considered the big time to him and his new manager, Albert Grossman. Unbeknownst to Dylan, the performance was recorded on a single reel-to-reel tape recorder patched into the PA system in the gymnasium at Brandeis, a last minute campus venue change due to severe winter weather throughout New England, the second week of May, no less!

Right from the department of who would've thunk, the Brandeis tape was inadvertently found more than forty years ex post facto in the basement of the first ever full-time jazz and pop music critic at an American newspaper, Ralph Gleason, who after abducting the original tape reel in '63 would go on to co-found a little magazine called *Rolling Stone*. This unlikely discovery was, catch this, a full 30 years after Gleason's death in San Francisco. Go figure. When this was brought to the attention of Dylan's people, a financial transaction was quickly arranged by Jeff Rosen, and the rest is history, as they say. The fact that this recording existed in the first place was a secret to all except Gleason himself, but on it a relaxed and unfettered Bob banters with the crowd and delivers three songs as well as three outtakes off his just-released *Freewheelin' Bob Dylan* and the first public unveiling of **The Ballad of Hollis Brown**. Although we only get 38 minutes and 7 songs, and the opener is not patched into the reel-to-reel until halfway through, *In Concert At Brandeis* certainly finds Dylan at the top of his live performance game in between the October 1962 Gaslight and October 1963 Carnegie Hall shows.

Incidentally, the day might or might not come when Columbia eventually releases the New York Town Hall show (one month before the Brandeis show) from April 12 of 1963, which has partially found its way to the Internet in bits and pieces. From what little I've heard of this stuff (on which Dylan sounds even more gripping than he did a month later at Brandeis), I'm guessing the acoustic voltage from a Dylan concert just six weeks prior to the release of *Freewheelin'* would potentially tower over the Gaslight, Brandeis, Carnegie, and Philharmonic Hall recordings. And who knows, perhaps, unlike at Brandeis, somebody at the Town Hall gig actually plugged Dylan into a tape recorder before he was halfway done with his set list! Such an official bootleg would definitely promise to be yet another stunning display of the early Dylan raw magic. How gratifying the day!

The following chronological history lesson bears repeating, for those of you paying attention. The order of the most renown early 60s Dylan concerts/material that later became commercial releases: Gaslight October '62, Town Hall April 12, 1963 (still not commercially/formally released), Brandeis University May 10, 1963, Carnegie Hall October 26, 1963, and Philharmonic Hall Halloween 1964. Again, the Witmark demos range from 1962-64. And, again again, these recordings have been released so haphazardly that it is almost impossible to keep sequential track.

On a snowy New England day in May of 1963 at Brandeis University, still not quite yet on anybody's pedestal outside Greenwich Village, Bob Dylan was on the verge of becoming a cultural icon named Bob Dylan as a result of *The Freewheelin' Bob Dylan*, which was released two weeks after the recording of *Concert At Brandeis University*. Funny thing is, due to John Hammond's laudable patience, Columbia took so much time releasing *Freewheelin'* that by the time it came out, Dylan had already traveled light years beyond it, even though it was light years ahead of its time.

Right, it makes no sense. Go figure, my friend, go figure. In his time, could anybody explain Mozart?

Yes, I said that.

#58

Tempest

As for life as a senior citizen these days, resting on one's laurels is NOT only NOT an option for our friend, but in his vocabulary it is a concept which is non-existent. Don't you dig triple negatives that are still grammatical?

Here we find our latter-day Bob, having written what he surely realizes are a bunch of killer songs, each one more sinister than the rest, reveling in recording studio horseplay in Jackson Browne's Santa Monica Groove Masters like a little kid in a toy shop. Having apparently just had the time of his life, 71-year-old Bob Dylan released *Tempest* to once-again widespread critical acclaim on September 10, 2012. Nine of these ten scorching, spellbinding numbers are self-composed, with the opening track, **Duquesne Whistle**, receiving lyrical support from old pal Robert Hunter. Now more than comfortable in his late-career role as self-producer Jack Frost, Dylan gives birth to ten out of ten non-duds that each merit another listen the moment they end.

Tempest continued the late Dylan era CD custom of including no printed lyrics and minimal credits to contributing personnel. The album cover art features a dark red duotone photograph of a statue located at the base of the Austrian parliament building in Vienna, and a deluxe edition included a 60-page notebook of vintage magazine covers with rare photographs of Dylan over the decades.

The release of *Tempest* was first announced on Bob's official web site on July 17, 2012, and the album's only single, **Duquesne Whistle**, was put to an odd, grotesque promotional video directed by Nash Edgerton in which Dylan is seen stalking a neighborhood of urban neon night lights while seemingly safeguarded by a posse of misfits, when suddenly a tone of Charlie Chaplin-inspired light comedy takes a dark turn and some pitiful bastard gets bloodily pummeled by a gang of heartless thugs. What the subject matter of this short horror film has to do with a song about a mythical jubilee train in the gospel legend tradition is anybody's guess. However comma, my suggestion is that you don't bother asking Senor Bob lest you be taken on one of his highbrow balderdash shuck-and-jive-now-you-see-me-now-you-don't-I'm-making-a- point-or-did-I-circular-ever-evasive-non-answers to your dead-in-the-water in-the-first-place inquiry. On the topic of Bob Dylan, whenever in doubt, best to just go figure, or else!

Back to the record at hand, *Tempest*, which is, and if this is not a mouthful, I don't know what is, conceivably, make that surely, the single darkest disk in Dylan's catalogue. Whew, just typing that last sentence was exhausting. Yet, between the thousands who meet their makers in the sinking of the Titanic in 1912 in the title track **Tempest**, the deplorable, hideous violent assassination of John Lennon which is touchingly lamented in the closing track, **Roll On John**, and the various and sundry mayhem and murder references meandering throughout **Pay In Blood** and **Scarlet Town**, there is more haunting and haunted death in these 68.5 minutes of dark ruminations than any other Dylan album, period.

Dylan is purportedly to have intended *Tempest* to be a religious album, whatever that means in the Bob Dylan context. On it he quotes historical figures and artists of every conceivable genre like a rapper on fire, once again giving we the listeners the impression that he has an infinite supply of lyrics and verses that simply do not stop and will not cease. He somehow scores a bull's eye as for his religious aspiration by repeatedly underscoring a theme of unmerciful, relentless, and pitiless testing of human spiritual trust in extreme predicaments. Individually and collectively, the songs capture humanity in its flawed glory at every turn. Once again, we find Bob Dylan at another towering summit in his non-rational but not irrational game.

The musicians backing Bob are essentially his touring band, now more consummate than ever with the return of gee-tar ace Charlie Sexton and another cameo appearance by Los Lobos accordionist, David Hidalgo. Look, by the way, for this to possibly be the last recording invitation to Hidalgo from Bob due to David's loose lips about the forthcoming release of *Tempest* prior to Columbia's official communiqué.

Like on all four of the records leading up to *Tempest*, traditional American root music forms are drawn onto themes of love, struggle, and death. Easy-to-miss subtle allusions to Louis Armstrong and the Isley Brothers pop up here and there, as does more ubiquitous regard shown for the music of Ireland, Scotland, Appalachia, Chicago, and New Orleans.

On *Tempest* Bob Dylan has arrived at an artistic crest upon which he personifies the master storyteller archetype and explores various strands of early American roots music, which he gradually internalized as he ripened, fertilized, and matured in his unparalleled, lone-ranger, head-strong manner. No American writers, except Twain, have achieved eloquence and consistency at the steady, honest clip of Bob Dylan. Unlike Twain, who in old age sort of became a relic and one of the world's first popular culture celebrities, Dylan seems bent on remaining true to the call of a creative wellspring within which he's always refused to abdicate, no matter what. What others think of him in the public eye just isn't any of his business.

For 5.5 decades, his pervasive influence on artists of all walks of life has essentially resided in his own fabrication of the impression that he possesses a charismatically compelling power and glory derived from making up things from scratch. At 74, from the apex of Mt. Tempest, if you will, Dylan stands not only peerless, but with his eagle eyes vigilantly fixed inward on a horizon of infinite anticipation of what he will come up with next, which will indubitably be on his terms and his alone.

Trains…how much can be channeled through a simple sound and sight. **Duquesne Whistle** is one of those railroad songs that evokes the whole range of emotional touchstones and spiritual images that only trains can. Its deceptively gentle old-timey introductory passing verse is the perfect opening to an album which delivers sudden juxtapositions and impromptu mood shifts within songs, between songs, and even within verses. From a bygone-day, 1920s-sounding genesis we are abruptly swerved 180 degrees forward by George's brush sticks on his snare drum into an understated jump blues that Bob, for a time, transformed into quite the rocker in the number 6 slot in his fixed set list on the never-ending tour. Is the sound of this train a lover or the divine itself? Whatever the case, it has unquestionably swept Bob's joyful heart away. Such a lovely, light commencement to a record which, unbeknownst to the innocent listener, will ultimately, albeit gradually, take some of the most somber and shadowy turns of any Bob Dylan record we have ever heard.

Song two, **Soon After Midnight** puts on the brakes just a touch with an easy tempo waltz sketching a portrait of a midnight romantic rumination. Donnie's pedal steel and George's brushes provide the needed simple acoustic instrumental arrangement to a little ditty that a powerhouse songwriter like Bob can write blindfolded. What we do not yet realize is that **Soon After Midnight** is really nothing more than a transition number on a record that is about to narrate one tragic episode after another in a musical version of an elaborate, fully-consummate novel, much as *John Wesley Harding* and *Blood On The Tracks* were back in the day.

Narrow Way pierces our eardrums by means of a mean and nasty slide riff ripping out of what is surely Charlie's hollow body Gibson, the appropriate instrument (indeed) to impart a pre-rock 1940s sentiment on what ironically constitutes Dylan's most potent rocker in years. This little 7 minutes of wrathful grinding blues sinks its hooks in early and refuses to let go, a strategy Bob utilized to celebrated success over and over again on *Together Through Life*. Charlie's scalding guitar circulations hearken back to Muddy Waters at his best, and Bob slips in a clever rip off from the chorus of a Mississippi Sheiks 1934 blues line, "You'll work down to me someday."

Long and Wasted Years offers up soulful guitar lines as a backdrop to an instance of Bob's uncanny ability to interpret a song like no other, despite his shredded voice. Although **Long and Wasted Years** incrementally builds in tone toward a vengeful mood, Bob's husky, lusty, and robust singing is mournful and deeply nostalgic. He toys with the phrasing of each line in order to tease every bit of hurt out of this tale of love gone wrong. In the midst of poetic references to **Twist and Shout**, broken family connections, hiding behind dark sunglasses, mythological trains, and shedding tears of grief on winter mornings, somehow one can make out the talking melody and loping verses of **Three Angels** on *New Morning* a full four decades prior. **Long and Wasted Years** would go on to evolve into a show stopper on the never-ending tour. Just ask the Japanese and Australians who were there in 2014.

The grim, wrathful, tenacious **Pay In Blood** commences an incredibly shadowy turn for the somber. As if raging evil is being delivered in snarling vocals, Bob's phlegm can be heard in his close-miked, shameless, remorseless, unapologetic, biting lyrics. A vaguely menacing chord sequence with a Tex-Mex swagger and Kieth Richards guitar licks from Senor Sexton shoulder palpably-rising anger in chorus lines such as, "Man can't live by bread alone, I pay in blood but not my own." Dylan has not spilled rage into a song like this since **Idiot Wind** and/or **Like A Rolling Stone**. "I'm sworn to uphold the lives of God, you can put me in front of a firing squad" sounds like something right out of the mouths of Satan's lower legions. By upping the ghastly ante of unnerving gruesomeness, **Pay In Blood** stands in unspeakably dark contrast to much of Dylan's eerily uplifting songwriting laced with spiritual references such as **Man In The Long Black Coat** and **Gotta Serve Somebody.**

Scarlet Town, reminiscent of the haunting *Modern Times* closer **Ain't Talkin'**, draws on verses from 19th century poet and abolitionist John Greenleaf Whittier. Donnie Herron's haunting fiddle and banjo, which deceptively lead the hypnotic melody until the guitar lead from Charlie rises out of a fog, sketch a ghostly portrait of a village suitable for the setting of **Pay In Blood**. Bob's tender delivery somehow softens the blow of the bloody, murderous mischief brooding amidst the goings on in the streets of the 21st century Scarlet Town of Americana.

Can you say **Mannish Boy**? **Early Roman Kings** is an outright, blatant, but deferent utilization/rip off of this standard and iconic Muddy Waters blues riff (with a melodic twist, unlike his **Rollin' and Tumblin'** Muddy salute on *Modern Times*) and a temporary light interlude in the abject detour into doom and gloom that *Tempest* has now taken. "I ain't dead yet, my bell still rings," Bob snarls to let us know that *Tempest* is no career swan song, despite idiotic (well, let's just say incorrect) interpretations of William Shakespeare's final work, *The Tempest*, as a clever clue from Bob that *Tempest* would be his final album effort. Besides, as Bob himself has clarified when questioned on this issue, his album title lacks Shakespeare's definite article. "They are two different titles," he properly points out.

The last three songs on *Tempest* are an ambitious run, indeed. A Shakespearean body pile resulting from a lovers' triangle is the eventual upshot of **Tin Angel**, another hypnotic bluesy narrative reminding one and all that at the age of 71 Bob Dylan still has an endless supply of verses and lyrics laced with whimsical wordplay. **Tin Angel** is another shadowy, silhouetted gem in the dramatic syncopated veins of **Man In The Long Black Coat** on *Oh Mercy* and **Long Black Davey** on *Good As I Been To You*. Songs like **Tin Angel** in the late Dylan era silence any doubts, if they exist, that Dylan is still at the top of his game.

Here we come to the title track, **Tempest**, a meandering, hypnotic, eleven-minute, forty-five-verse epic saga that retells the 1912 sinking of the Titanic with slightly more than slight poetic and artistic license here and there. Perhaps a metaphor for mankind heading unknowingly toward an unfortunate fate, Dylan illustrates an historically factual tale whereby whenever helpless humans are put to the ultimate test, both noble and pathetically horrible reactions are to be expected. An Irish-sounding folk melody is supported by fiddle from Donnie and David's accordion, a perfect musical backdrop on which Bob depicts a series of horrifying scenes presented in touching contrast to acts of bravery. This long, unwinding waltz is nothing short of a teary-eyed latter day **Desolation Row**.

Beneath the biting humor and hideous mayhem swirling about in **Tempest**, sexual and political metaphors point to truths about human nature, twisted morals, pre-destined fate, and mortality. All the while, Bob orchestrates a marriage of words and music channeled from a bard's ear and a poet's pen. Not to minimize the other nine non-duds on the album *Tempest*, the song **Tempest** singlehandedly makes a convincing case for the theory that Dylan's 1960s musical magic is evenly matched by the quality of his commercial output since he turned 56 and sprang *Time Out Of Mind* on us. Unlike the watchman on the Titanic, Bob's seasoned eyes are 360 degrees wide open to each and every musical influence and literary inspiration known to mankind as he incomprehensibly still finds ways to surprise even his most experienced and understandably jaded listeners. Hey, I resemble that comment!

Just when one might think Dylan has concluded another LP with an epic narrative, **Roll On John**, a heart-wrenching belated tribute to John Lennon, is saved for a finale. The song is more of a prayer from one unstoppable, committed, and visionary artist to another than a eulogy as well as a reminder that it is this personification, or version, of Bob Dylan on *Tempest* that now stands virtually alone among his 1960s peers. Throbbing with survivor's guilt, **Roll On John** is at times charmingly clumsy, but extraordinarily moving nonetheless. It veers in and out of biographical elements and Lennon song quotations from **A Day In The Life** and **Come Together**, offering an unobstructed glimpse of the oft-overlooked soft side of Bob Dylan. The song comes as emotional relief after the terrible beauty that most of the rest of *Tempest* is. Donnie's mandolin and Tony's bass indicate utter reverence being paid to their beloved band leader, whose own final act, a thing to behold, rolls on while he pours out his loving heart to his fallen friend, "Shine your light, move it on, you burned so bright, roll on John." Thirty two years after Lennon's fatal fall from earthly existence at the hands of fanatic fan Mark David Chapman, finally a fond farewell befitting Bob's fellow fearless free spirit.

When all is said and done, *Tempest* continues Bob's rich vein of late-career form, surpassing *Together Through Life* and *Modern Times* on sheer lyrical power and vocal punch alone, while managing to stretch his familiar old timey sonic palette in all sorts of unexpected directions. Bob comes off as still inspired by the infinite possibilities of language, snappy idiomatic jokes, spookily dark if not evil ruminations, powerfully vivid sketches, and philosophical asides. The record is a distillation of jump blues, railroad boogie, archaic country, and lush folk. If that is not enough, various musical curveballs are sprinkled in on *Tempest* often enough to camouflage its transparent musical antecedents.

How Dylan comes up with this stuff is and has forever been beyond me. Am I here all alone? I am most curious how some of this stuff is hitting you. Last time I checked, I don't know everything.

Delivering the goods at 71. One must wonder who, other than you can call me Archie you can call me Ray could have ever pulled off such a preposterous, improbable trick. With all due respect to the dead and buried, not Sinatra, and not B.B. King. Not McCartney, Young, Townsend, or Clapton, at least yet. None of these or any other still active musical artists from the 60s have remained as relevant, compelling, prolific, productive, just plain active, cutting edge, or successfully creative into their seventies. What's really weird is that 30 years ago all these fabled Dylan contemporaries were twice as awesome as they are now, whereas Dylan 30 years ago was half as good as he is now! How does that work?

So, no matter what you say, you STILL gotta give ole Bob a well-deserved standing "O". Bravo, my friend.

59

Bootleg Series 10/Another Self Portrait

The August 13, 2013 release of the mind-boggling *Bootleg Series Volume 10 Another Self Portrait* cast a whole new light on not just the *Self Parody/Portrait* double album debacle of 1970, but the entire 1969 to '71 *Nashville Skyline* and *New Morning* phases as well. Deluxe edition packages threw in complete Isle of Wight and re-mastered *Self Portrait* discs to boot. Just hearing *Self Portrait* without obnoxiously loud back-up harmonies alone is enough to heal the post-traumatic stress disorder that the original vinyl recording perpetrated on millions of members of the human race for four ghostly decades. Except, I forgot, nobody listened to it more than once, or even to its finish, so it wasn't THAT bad. Please forgive. It is soooo unlike me to exaggerate.

Anyhoo, just sit back a spell on your front porch rocker, take yer shoes off, and take in this confoundingly complex assortment of live tracks, alternate takes, demos, and unreleased original compositions and covers spanning three easy-to-misconstrue studio albums. Whatever beliefs or non-beliefs, which of course are actually beliefs, you once held about whatever Dylan was doing from 1969 to 1971, while the rest of his generation was obsessed with revolutionizing this planet, well, you might as well let them go. Once you get done hearing this stuff, they will just become distant memories anyway.

It all starts with a booklet containing rare period photos of Dylan by John Cohen and Al Clayton. Then, there are the extensive essay by journalist Michael Simmons and favorable review liner notes by Greil

Marcus, the coiner of, "What is this sh**?," in his Rolling Stone review of *Self Parody* back in the day. Boy, has Greil changed his tune. And understandably so.

When all is said and done, clearly the right song/recording selections were made on *New Morning*. On the other hand, *Another Self Portrait* delivers compellingly interesting alternate versions, complete with **Got To Get You Into My Life** brass rocket overdubs to the moon on **New Morning**. As for *Self Parody*, several (if not countless) errors in song selection and production are rectified on *Another Self Portrait*. As for the just two *Nashville Skyline* re-workings, bottom-of-the-barrel pleasing discoveries rise to the surface, raising perplexing riddles as to why Dylan did not share this stuff upon its initial marinade (Did you know that marination is not a word? Thank God above for those squiggly red lines on word programs!). Lucky are we, nevertheless, that, like cold two-day-old leftover lasagna at 1:30 in the morning, Dylan's country music gets better and better with age. Invigorating Bromberg grooves, peerless vocal performances, and unending discoveries of greatness litter this coherent, indispensably important, and perhaps most fulfilling Dylan album release of all time.

First and foremost, thank God almighty for resuscitations of **Little Sadie**, **Alberta #3**, and **All The Tired Horses**, only this time the horses are full of piss and vinegar. Both discs are completely re-invigorated and find Bob's vocal chords more un-gripped than was the case on the 1970 release of *Self Parody*. We also get George Harrison ripping a hot lead on **Working On A Guru**, a new-and-improved **Copper Kettle** on the back porch at sunset, the traditional **Bring Me A Little Water** featuring soulful 88s and grab-you-by-the-throat vocals, full orchestra overdubs on **Sign On The Window**, a more folkie and less jazzy **If Dogs Run Free**, a **Time Passes Slowly** without Leon Russell (but you could have fooled me), a sublime, unpretentious **Spanish Is The Loving Tongue** on keyboards, recently deceased Dave Van Ronk's confiscation and signature arrangement of the traditional **Tell Ole Bill (This Evening So Soon)**, Eric Anderson's Dylan wheelhouse **Thirsty Boots**, Eddie Noack's Johnny Cash gospel favorite, **These Hands**, and last, but taking the f***ing cake, an exalted, stately **When I Paint My Masterpiece** on the 88s all by Bob's lonesome.

In the end, it's all just one word. Fascinating! Make that three because for the listener it's gratifying and consoling, too. As for Bob the country music mad scientist, it is outright redeeming as hell. And I mean hell as in the hellish nightmares induced by the 1970 *Self Portrait/Parody* debacle, which, for some of us, were not only cause for doubt of our friend Bob, but which had persisted as potential recurring horror shows every time our heads hit the pillows for some 16,060 days and nights. Did I exaggerate? Again? What has gotten into me?

So, whether rocking barefoot on the porch, sitting by the campfire, or Sunday rural driving, this must-of-a-Dylan companion will absolutely deliver the goods on time and right when needed. Jeff Rosen and Steve Berkowitz, bravo again. This is getting to sound familiar with all these official bootlegs, man. Someday perhaps these guys (along with Tony Ganier) will have a memoir or two of their own to share, from the inside, a glimpse of the inner circle of Bob Dylan, Mr. Musical Americana. Not real likely, but until then, keep these boots coming, dudes.

How did you two geniuses ever take this mess and turn it into a musical memorial mumbo jumbo masterpiece?

#60

The Complete Basement Tapes

The Complete Basement Tapes was released in November 2014, but, of course, was recorded in 1967 in the Red Room of the Dylan home and the basement of Big Pink near Woodstock, New York. See album #9 for a historically chronological description and brief analysis of the highlights of this staggering, 6 disc, 138-track monster.

Now that it is out, *The Complete Basement Tapes*, like any number of other Dylan albums, conceivably deserves yet another full book treatment to follow up on and amplify what has already been interpreted, suggested, and documented. And don't look at me.

Mind-boggling stuff, man.

#61

Shadows In The Night

*S*hadows *In The Night* is not so much a Bob Dylan album as it is a Frank Sinatra LP by Bob Dylan. Dylan had been subtly hinting at a Sinatra tribute album ever since *Love and Theft* in 2001 with songs such as **Bye And Bye, Floater (Too Much To Ask), Moonlight**, and **Po Boy**, and on February 3, 2015 *Shadows In The Night* finally put out of our misery those of us who couldn't wait for something of this ilk.

Surprised? Think again. That'll teach you to ever put Bob Dylan into a confined, narrow-minded box.

American standards were not only a major part of the 100 episodes of Bob's *Theme Time Radio Hour* on Sirius (satellite) radio from 2006 to 2009, but the throwbacks **Nettie Moore** from *Modern Times* and **Soon After Midnight** from *Tempest* were further 21st century tips of Bob's ole hat to the pre-rock bygone days of timeless songwriting. Furthermore, as far back as 1970, **Blue Moon** on *Self Portrait (Parody)* and **Tomorrow Night** on 1992's *Good As I Been To You* provide evidence enough that Dylan holds great reverence for straight standards, as opposed to, say, **Corrina, Corrina** on *Freewheelin'*, which falls in the traditional folk standard category, as does pretty much all the material on *Good As I Been To You* and *World Gone Wrong*.

Two big ole however commas are in order. First, none of the above stopped millions of casual musical onlookers from being surprised, if not shocked, by the throwback, if not archaic, content of Bob's new record, but that is certainly nothing new and to be expected. More importantly, on *Shadows In The Night* Bob unshackles himself from any hint of folk, rock, or even, god forbid, upbeat 4/4 tempos, as pedal steel man extraordinaire Donnie Herron provides a one man string section on asymmetrical jazzy arrangements spanning the 1920s to the 1950s. In the process, Dylan tenderly croons ten melodies Sinatra helped make classics.

Bob simultaneously not only digs up the graves of these gems, but he rights the wrong of their having been trashed by the fickleness, forgetfulness, and unfaithfulness of time. Speaking of time, in fact, on *Shadows In The Night* that ugly monster in the English language referred to as time is rendered pointless, out of place, and impertinent. These wonderful ditties are beyond the confines of words and time. They bypass the mind, and without passing go, they gently pierce the heart. Partly inspired by Willie Nelson's 1979 *Stardust, Shadows In The Night* gives Dylan plenty of latitude to scale the mountainous heights Sinatra set for standards. As a matter of fact, to Dylan, Frank Sinatra has always been, is now, and forever shall be the mountain itself.

The everlasting hip summit of Mt. Sinatra is a towering pinnacle. Frank delivered each sound, syllable, phrase, and word with his unique, uncanny, intuitive skills as a trustworthy Thespian who was not pretending. It is no accident that the number of Hollywood films Sinatra acted in slightly exceeds his LP discography total (both are in the neighborhood of 60- something). His acting versatility spanned the arenas of comedy (*Robin and the 7 Hoods* in 1964) to the darkest Shakespearean drama imaginable (*Suddenly* in 1954). The best singers, of which there are very few, are authentic, not because of their vocal box versatility or scale range necessarily, but due to their portrayal of themselves, if you will. Sinatra the singer was always some genuine version of his own complicated self. That's why we believe him.

That Bob Dylan lacks the choir boy vocal box pipes of his buddy and mentor, I think we can safely assume that we all agree. Can I have an, "Amen?" What Dylan does achieve on *Shadows In The Night* is a step beyond that incredibly disarming sweetness on *Christmas In The Heart*, for instance, that we already knew lurks somewhere inside him. He manages to reach inside his soul, like James Dean in *Rebel Without A Cause* or Marlon Brando in *On The Waterfront*, and, rather than putting on any pretenses, Bob Dylan sings to you, not at you. This is no small feat on a CD, which is only an audio format. It reminds me of the two dozen or so precious chances I have had at Dylan concerts to stand within eight feet of Bob, with an unobstructed view for a couple hours, and visually witness what I consider the finest Hollywood performances I've ever witnessed with my own eyes. Therefore, when I listen to *Shadows In The Night*, I cannot help but see with my mind's eye what I am hearing. All credit where credit is due to Bob Dylan in his early 70s. When it comes to vocalists, only the greats are able to paint elaborate visual images in the minds of listeners without video formatting.

As sad as this collection is in terms of the quest for eternal love, it is more disturbing still to consider that sensational songs like these were buried by the advent of rock and roll and its various offshoots. Nothing against the rightly-celebrated Chuck Berry, Buddy Holly, and the like, but the unintended consequences they wrought onto civilization are, admittedly, nothing short of a modern day tragedy the likes of *Romeo and Juliet*. What about the loss of classical songs about loss? Can we all please take a moment to grab hold of our personal and collective grief over the (for all practical purposes) death of countless long gone and all but forgotten pre-rock classical ditties? And wipe away our tears? And thank Bob Dylan for reminding the human race on *Shadows In The Night* of this involuntary manslaughter? And let's, in full disclosure, and while we're at it, do the same for Paul McCartney's equally wonderful 2012 jazz cover LP, *Kisses On The Bottom*. Thank you, gentlemen!

Shadows In The Night musically features lots of asymmetrical gliding pedal steel and tremulous, foreboding lovesick lyrics centered around romantic separation and heartache, much like Sinatra's albums *Where Are You* (1957) and *No One Cares* (1959). Dylan's band even returned to Capital Studios in Los Angeles, where in the late 50s Sinatra recorded what he referred to as suicide songs in studio B with the aid of a couple of musical prodigies in their own rights, conductor Nelson Riddle and arranger Gordon Jenkins.

Not so parenthetically perhaps, the songs themselves, while bluesy, are jazz standards that come from an age gone by when the straight blues were looked down upon as lesser than and/or too dark for prime time. Guys like Sinatra (who dipped his toes into the blues while still couching it in jazz sensibilities) and Ray Charles (who elevated black, then Negro, R and B into mainstream white culture) and, arguably, even Dylan himself, eventually helped put an end to such highbrow snobbery. More but not entirely parenthetically, the original king of musical crossing over, Ray Charles and his big band of renown, did a similar favor for country music, a feat that surely did not go unnoticed by Dylan, who is widely regarded as the most influential artist to ever cross over into country music. Well, guess where Mr. Bob got THAT idea! No wonder Dylan's passion for the music of those who preceded him stands front and center now that he is, well, an old man.

All this jazz/blues/country hybridization stuff always seems to boil down to the indisputable fact, "It's all rock and roll to me!"

Back to the spring of 2014, when Bob's touring band went into that room where Sinatra recorded half of the songs on *Shadows In The Night*. Old fashioned analog signal techniques, so if you turn up the volume at the end of some of the tracks, tube amplifiers can be heard hissing. Without headphones or visible microphones, other than the one Dylan sang into, 23 songs were attempted and 10 are on the record, so somewhere you gotta figure there are 13 outtakes which may or may not see the light of day at some point.

Shadows In The Night is also highlighted by Tony Ganier's sympathetic bass lines, but due to lack of necessity, it is almost devoid of George Recile's percussion and Stu Kimball and Charlie Sexton's guitar accompaniment. It is all about pedal steel, double bass, and Dylan's, believe it or not, velvety voice. Gone is Bob's, if you will, old man sounding like a monster vocal that has plagued far too many 21st century Dylan live shows going back to roughly 2003 (when Bob turned 62), particularly in open air outdoor arenas where Bob has strained to be audible over the five other instruments in addition to his piano. Now well into his 70s, Bob realizes his voice is now best suited for either the hushed recording studio sonics of *Shadows In The Night* or else indoor live performance venues with superb acoustics where, with the aid of expert audio technicians working the soundboard, from the upper balcony one can, as they say, hear a pin drop onstage.

The back cover art, interestingly, shows Dylan in formal black tie, white jacket attire and accompanied by a masked woman in black, possibly a reference to a pinnacle in New York social history, the 1966 black and white masquerade ball hosted by Truman Capote at the Plaza Hotel, which Sinatra attended with Mia Farrow. The front cover showcases a contemporary photo of Dylan behind black bars reminiscent of jazz artist Freddie Hubbard's 1962 LP *Hub-Tones*. As on other albums in Dylan's later years, there are no printed lyrics and minimal credits.

The history behind the treasures found on *Shadows In The Night* is not a topic on which I can claim to be an expert. Even finding data on some of these songs is not easy to do these days. Nevertheless, brief, albeit amateurish, bio-analysis of their outstanding composers and descriptions of Dylan's treatments of them are in order.

The album commences with **I'm A Fool To Want You** and Herron's sliding pedal steel guitar mimicking a Hawaiian guitar riff, which is immediately followed by Tony Ganier providing the downright bluest note on *Shadows In The Night* with his double bass bow. With this 1951 composition by Jack Wolf and Joel Herron, Dylan makes it clear he is taking this business most seriously. We have never, as in never, heard Bob Dylan croon with such care and beauty. Sweet, subtle, indispensible brass backing is practically imperceptibly provided by Andrew Martin and Francisco Torres on trombones and Dylan Hart on French horn.

Next, **The Night We Called It A Day** is a 1941 tune written by Matt Dennis. Here we are again treated to a brass section of Alan Kaplan and

Torres on trombone and Joseph Meyer on French horn. Sort of in the tradition of the oddly violent video for **Duquesne Whistle** on *Tempest*, a video was made for **The Night We Called It A Day** in which Bob gets away with murdering a woman after she herself murders some thug Bob encounters in a bar. What is it with Bob's penchant for needlessly interspersing graphic violence into what are otherwise sensually pleasing, civil film plots? Although well done, the film's connection to this song is, at best, a stretch even if a wide berth is granted for artistic license. On the other hand, as usual, that's just me, and that is definitely merely Bob Dylan's calling card – expect the unexpected.

Stay With Me is from a 1963 film, *The Cardinal*, about a young Boston Catholic priest fighting Nazism and his own demons. Written by Jerome Moross and Carolyn Leigh, it concluded many of Dylan's fall 2014 live shows in the U.S., while Bob crooned away while sitting at a baby grand. On *Shadows In The Night*, however, he plays no piano on this song or any other. Rather, true to Sinatra form, he carefully bites down on each line, syllable, and jazzy adventure as if to salute the vocal and phrasing master that Frank was.

Autumn Leaves was originally written in 1945 by Joseph Kosma with French lyrics by Jacques Prevert, but the English lyrics were penned by the great Johnny Mercer in 1947. Dylan's treatment is the spookiest vibe on *Shadows In The Night*, which, my friends, is saying a lot, indeed.

Why Try To Change Me Now, written by Bronx child prodigy Cy Coleman and Joseph Allan McCarthy in 1950, is next. Coleman was paid tribute at the 2009 Grammy award ceremony for his contribution to jazz-accented songwriting. Of all the songwriters on *Shadow In The Night*, Coleman is historically the youngest and lived until 2004, well into the modern age of digital recording, hip hop, and the latter period of Dylan's work. How befitting that Bob took the opportunity to record a song composed by a guy that Tony Bennett considers one of America's greatest songwriters.

Some Enchanted Evening from South Pacific in 1949, *Shadows In The Night's* most recognizable song, is perhaps Richard Rogers and

Oscar Hammerstein's most beloved and famous song. Could it get any more appropriate?

Full Moon And Empty Arms is a 1945 Buddy Kaye and Ted Mossman composition based on Sergei Rachmaninoff's **Piano Concerto No. 2**. It exemplifies astute music from Sinatra's catalogue that Dylan consciously selected with imaginative discernment. **Where Are You**, written by Harold Adamson and Jimmy McHugh for a 1937 film *Top Of The Town*, was also the title of one of Sinatra's darkest records in 1957. **What'll I Do**, which gets my vote for most stunning melody of the bunch, is a 1923 Irving Berlin work that was woven into the musical theme of Nelson Riddle's 1974 score for *The Great Gatsby*.

That Lucky Old Sun, the closest thing to a folk spiritual on *Shadows In The Night*, was written in 1949 by Beasley Smith and Haven Gillespie and made a hit by Sinatra the same year. What a closer! Bob actually pulled this one out of the woodwork back in 2000 at a live concert in California, which worked out real well, but this studio rendition puts that one to shame. Daniel Fornero and Larry Hall on trumpet and Andrew Martin on trombone softly support one of Dylan's most affected vocal deliveries since 1961, and, thus, *Shadows In The Night* is over, just as it seems to be gathering steam. Who wants this to stop?

In 1995, as much as Sinatra seemed enraptured, if not pleasantly shocked, by Dylan's delivery of **Restless Farewell** at his 80th birthday party at Madison Square Garden Theater, he surely would be moved to tears by *Shadows In The Night* were he still around to take it in. Yet, one gets the feeling that Bob did not make this record for Frank. As much as he made it for us, without a shadow of a doubt, he paid this homage for himself. Bob will die with a more satisfied mind (pun intended from the opening tune on *Saved*, in case you forgot).

If you ever want to satisfy your mind by getting out of your head and into your heart for 35 minutes, *Shadows In The Night* is the ticket. There is not one false word on these songs. They are genuinely, and eternally, the real audio deal.

Author's Note

These days I am a songwriter, recording artist, educator, writer, devoted reader, comprehensive addictive personality, old-timer athlete, kindergarten yoga practitioner, advanced certified yoga instructor, nut, and idiot. There you have it. That's a lot of boxes that don't even fit. Did I leave anything out? Probably. Make that no doubt, but you get the drift.

Try fitting all THAT onto one website. I once rejected the concept as inadequate, lame, belittling, and unnecessary. Friends experienced in marketing (not my bag, dude) convinced me otherwise, so www.BobShiel.com is now up, running, and being developed. Direct communication is the only way to go. I <u>AM</u> on **Facebook**, and old fashioned **bobshiel@hotmail.com** also works wonders.

What qualifies me to arrogantly write, and even more audaciously consider that others might read, what my right brain is compelled to ejaculate concerning the music of Bob Dylan?

Well, first, of all, what gave Robert Zimmerman the right to abandon his hometown, childhood, parents, and earthly karma and proceed to re-invent his persona, legal name, metaphysical trajectory, popular music as we once knew it, and notions of cool in any number of genres of arenas including but not limited to dress, hairstyle, sunglasses, footwear, trumpeting a voice for the downtrodden, album covers, film, literary prose, poetry, intellectual eccentricity, artistic vogue, provocative spiritual quirkiness, absurdist humor, social mockery, political satire, cultural icon evasion, racial relations, and crossbreeding country, folk, jazz, gospel, bluegrass, rock, and blues, for starters.

I apologize. I just have always wanted to write a sentence with exactly 100 words. But don't you dare go back and count 'em, or else I will ascertain that you are just as anal as yours truly. Join the club.

As for Dylanologists. What makes me any more fit to tackle 61 LPs than any of them? Get ready. 116-word sentence incoming.

There are those who have attended dozens of Bob Dylan concerts, followed his music and life to varying degrees of obsession or casual observance, personally grounded themselves in and even recorded hundreds of Dylan compositions, tracked multiple Dylan web sites and blogs going back to the dawn of the Internet, subscribed to *On The Tracks* or *Isis* or some of the other Dylan fanzines, collected libraries of printed material, books, magazine articles, photographs, films, concert footage, bootleg CDs, t-shirts, logo clothing, trinkets, and wall posters, performed his songs as professional musicians, read biography after biography and/or any of the litany of Dylan-related publications that have turned into a virtual cottage industry for writers and book publishers, and a very few who have even done all of these things.

So, what makes me any more qualified than any of these loveable weirdos? In the scheme of things, absolutely nothing. You got me there! On the other hand, I AM, admittedly, one of them.

Still, being a weirdo is no qualification to take on such a massive topic as 61 Bob Dylan albums. Guilty as charged! Let's just say I'm a Dylan nut who suddenly found myself retired last summer, and the first and best thing to do seemed to be to write something about something I love. Where in the heck did I get THAT big idea?

Well, if you'll hang in there for a moment, I'll gladly explain.

The whimsy to write something major about Dylan's records crept into my conscious mind around 1997, around the time of *Time Out Of Mind*. I guess I just couldn't contain my relief and glee that Bob had not actually died, as feared, from histoplasmosis. For some odd reason, the idea first occurred to me while reading the fall 1997 cover story on Dylan in *Newsweek*. Of course, I was consumed by and with a marriage, two step-children, and work, so there was no time for such frivolous sub-conscious clowning around.

Then, in 2001 a Schererville, Indiana Borders Bookstore displayed a promotional-only poster for *Love and Theft*, which on one side had a black and white head shot of Bob and on the other a beautiful array of every Dylan album cover going all the way back, many of which, as we all well know, are totally stand-alone works of art. Looking back, and I do this occasionally even though Dylan told us not to, this is when things really started taking root and getting out of hand.

Although the corporate global monster Borders refused to sell one to me, on legal grounds (no wonder they've gone bankrupt!), a Massachusetts woman on one of the Dylan internet chat lines graciously responded to a request for help I posted, and after exchanging a handful of friendly e-mails with her, she graciously shipped me the poster, a collector's rarity, at no charge. I instantly framed it myself, with slight professional assistance. First of all, how she got a hold of it I will never know, but this was a typical case of the spirit of generosity I have encountered for decades in the Bob Dylan international network. For this, I shall go to my grave grateful (and dead).

Having enjoyed the most inspiring aesthetics of said poster now for 14 years, in 20/20 retrospect I realize that blame can be placed on that poster for sub-consciously planting mustard seeds which will be harvested when folks start reading *61 Highways Revisited*. I have been visually surveying Dylan's studio album covers in chronological order in my home recording studio since 2001. For 14 years, every time I consciously look at that poster, I think, "That's a book." So, thanks to my anonymous lady friend from Massachusetts, whose name I do not recall and with whom I have lost contact. Nevertheless, all I can say is, it's HER fault.

Fast forwarding, it was not until 2014, when I abruptly retired (I'll go with re-**F**ired) from my 27-year teaching position at City Colleges of Chicago, where I had the enlightening pleasure of working with roughly 8,000 nothing short of heroic college-tracked international students of English As A Second Language, that a lucid poetic fantasy for *61 Highways Revisited* was chiseled in the inner landscapes of my mind. What would I do without fear, or even concern, about money and my new-found, lavish luxury of time? The prospects were rousingly and exhilaratingly intimidating. As an artist of sloth who wears it well, what would ample leisure call me to undertake, fabricate, and/ or otherwise do with myself?

Well, my most recent track record concerning idle hours had been incredibly productive. In 2010 I spent the best $250 of my life on an amazing stand-alone portable 8-track digital audio recording device, complete with all the bells and whistles needed to cut multi-track music in the confines of my home. Four years and thousands of hours later I am in possession of roughly 16 hours of original and cover songs on my iTunes, including 32 renditions of Dylan songs on the double CD audio companion to this here book, *61 Highways Revisited*.

Actually, writing *61 Highways Revisited* has brought all that music recording to a virtual standstill. Playing music has still been a daily endeavor while writing *61 Highways Revisited*, but just enough to blow off steam in order to return to the book. One creative project at a time is my mantra. However, sometimes I cheat in this regard, as I did write a song during a March 2015 month-long trip to Brazil while editing this here book, and upon returning to Chicago, recorded it in true Dylan fashion by borrowing the riff from **Mannish Boy** as Bob did on **Early Roman Kings**!

Point being, when I decided to retire, my domestic music muse apparently wanted to take a hiatus to transcribe an esoteric trumpet in my head that evidently had 104,000-plus words to express about Dylan's albums. My music muse was replaced by a voice inspired to finally write about Dylan's albums in full length. I immediately found that voice September 2, 2014, the day after Labor Day, though the tongue transmitting *61 Highways Revisited* is indubitably not really me. It is a voice of another character that has always emerged if, and only if and when the topic is the music of Bob Dylan, not Bob Dylan. Otherwise, I'm sure you'll find me to be a completely different character, still but not as incessantly off the wall.

Am I a sick Dylan worshiper? I care little about Bob Dylan the fallible and gifted human being. That is another book that I will not write. A mere fundamental grasp of Bob, which mind you is no piece of cake, is inherently sufficient to miscomprehend his music, given that understanding his music is not even relevant to the conversation.

I cannot explain why a fire has always been lit under my ass by Bob's music. Even on buses to high school tracks meets, I vividly recall singing the "pencil in your hand" verse of **Ballad of a Thin Man** to calm my nerves and goad myself into swiftly tripling my heart rate by sprinting 880 yards in 2 minutes flat on a cinder track. Now, what's that about?

It was not until 1997 or '98 that I stopped feeling disconnected from all things Dylan. The Internet is to thank. At Dylan concerts I began meeting folks in the form of Dylan nuts and staying in touch online. I did not feel so alone anymore. Bob used to come into town like a stealth rock star, and I would find out three days before show time. I mean, in the mid to late 80s albums would sit in record stores for weeks before I would stumble across them. Those days are gone.

Technology has conspicuously never managed to lessen the 21ˢᵗ century 24/7 doses of stress with which human evolution has not managed to keep pace. That previous sentence is one of the handful of broad possible areas of subject matter for my next book. On the other hand, I will say this in defense of the Internet. It has most gratifyingly displaced the distended disconnect between this here two-legged and America's Secretary of the Department of Artistic Vision Defense. Shy superstar. Reluctant poster boy of the left. Dark beam of salvation. Sincere or not social activist. Distinctive poet. Reclusive rebel. Unlikely pop icon. Goofy logic prophet. Hillbilly voice for acid humor. Disarming sweetness. True patriot. Intellectual irony. Colors of hope. Vigilant vision. Bob Dylan.

So, we'll see you on **Facebook**, e-mail, your preferred format, your living room or mine, or any venue where two or more of us may gather. This conversation has a life of its own, beyond the music and out of range from our tireless troubadour. When (think *Shot Of Love*) our hearts of stone are touched, it is not (think **Precious Angel**) spiritual warfare to which we are called, but the mystic chords of the better angels of our natures which are recalled.

Epilogue

What does the future hold for Bob Dylan? At 74, he may have one, ten, possibly 20 years to live. Will he still be doing Super Bowl commercials for auto makers at 89 in 2030? If B.B. King was able to do it, never underestimate the realms of possibility. How many times, and let's get rigorously honest dude, have we all figured Dylan was done? It's happily, and fortunately, embarrassing.

All indications, health-wise, do not point to Bob's lease on mortality running out before 2025. How long can he maintain this lunatic-in-a-good-way never-ending tour pace of 100 plus shows annually on three or four continents? Well, actually it has already slowed slightly. 2014 saw a mere 93 concerts (you try that at 73, dude), and in 2015 only 76 or so are scheduled (as of this spring 2015 writing), with roughly half of those in Europe and half in the U.S., which is the biggest drop in tour dates in 27 years. However, it is likely that 76 number will only go up a hair as dates are typically added as the time gets closer. Never a betting man, I would venture that this downward trend will continue, but I do not foresee an end to Dylan's touring any time soon. His cultural vibrancy and popularity in 2015, some 54 years into his storied career, was evidenced by a much-ballyhooed appearance on Letterman's second-to-last show, where he was aptly introduced as the greatest songwriter of modern times. The point merely being that public demand yearns for more and Bob shows no signs of slowing down. You can draw your own conclusion(s).

Will future official bootleg releases give us something right off the soundboards from 1997 to 2002? The 1992 Bromberg recordings in Chicago? Outtakes from *Tempest, Together Through Life, Modern Times*, or *Shadows In The Night*? The fall 1980 gospel tour? The 2014-15 live set list written in stone? God only knows.

Can we safely expect more albums with original songwriting? My instincts on this are abso-certain-sure-definitely. Just listen to *Tempest*. If *Shadows In The Night* were to end up being Bob Dylan's last album, how fitting it would be. On the other hand, don't bet on it. Its pre-rock Sinatra stuff is the best fodder for any songwriter because back then, they actually wrote intelligent, simple melodies inside which other melodies can be heard and superimposed. Dylan himself will tell you that. In fact, that is precisely what he **told** us on *Theme Time Radio Hour*. All in all, short of a heart attack, this guy ain't done, dude. Plus, if that 1993 ten-album deal with Colombia still stands, I figure he still owes them four more LPs. End of conversation.

The same goes for more exhibits of three-dimensional metal work sculpture, television commercials, film projects of one sort or another, paintings (if you want to be shocked at how well Dylan paints, check out the coffee table must, *Bob Dylan, The Brazil Series*), forthcoming memoir volumes of *Chronicles*, and the inevitable receipt of awards such as, incidentally, being crowned the greatest songwriter ever by Rolling Stone this year. Will the folks in Stockholm ever grant Bob a Nobel Prize in Literature, not that he gives a hoot? I'm not sure I want to know, or give a crap. All this dim-witted nincompoop can say is that it's starting to look like it. Then, I have no idea what I am doing tomorrow morning, so there you go. Who would have thunk Obama would give the once reluctant, mislabeled, and misconceived counter-cultural icon Bob Dylan a presidential medal of freedom? This surrealistic phenomena really took place in 2012. Truth trumps fiction, man.

I reckon Bob will end up surrounded by family and friends who love him. He is by all accounts pretty much adored by his former wives, five biological offspring, one step-child, several grandchildren, and inner circle of professional collaborators, for lack of a better term. This is not to mention the hundreds of millions of fellow pilgrims touched by Bob's humanity and genius all at once. His death, appropriately, will hearken a new beginning. Many, trust me, though not yours truly, will be taken aback by their sense of loss, love, gratitude, and remembrance. I am fearlessly anticipating this. Bob Dylan has touched and changed the world collectively and billions personally. When he's gone, he will be gone. But will he? Not really.

Interest will soar. I see myself fulfilling a collectively sub-conscious demand for education and entertainment. Picture an audience. A laptop and projector. My guitar and an assortment of musical instruments. 61 albums. This book. My double CD audio companion to *61 Highways Revisited*, by the same title, containing 32 songs which Dylan either wrote or covered. In addition, roughly 60 and counting additional completely self-recorded multi-track electric and acoustic cover renditions of the Dylan material you have been reading about. Your living room. Or mine. A nightclub. A community college. A music school. A church basement. Raising money for a good cause. The audience, upon request, selects an album. Discussion commences. Questions are formulated. Live music happens. Somebody reads an excerpt from *61 Highways Revisited*. Q and A unfolds. We google questions that stump us. We learn, so we have fun. Letting go of all that stuff in the way, those obstacles to thoughts we have never had before. Everybody wins because we go home feeling better.

Interested? I do road trips. Again, contact me at **bobshiel@hotmail.com** or on **Facebook**, and we will conspire. Have audience, will show up. Guaranteed entertainment and education. If you don't have all 61 albums, I do.

That's it, ladies and gents. 104,204 words, one fun journey without a destination, and not one single dent in the T-bird. However comma, Daddy's T-bird has, for now, been taken away. Now, I am the one who has to live with the scary thought that I'll think of something which should have been put in this here book, but wasn't, every day for the rest of my life.

Relax! The fun, fun, fun doesn't stop here! I hear Mommy and Daddy are staying home next Saturday night, and Daddy says I can use the T-bird to go to the Bob Dylan concert as long as I stay forever young. I say that's a deal I can't pass up!

Take it easy, but take it. I think Woody Guthrie said that. I'll let you be in my dream if I can be in yours, and Bob Dylan said that.

Printed in Great Britain
by Amazon.co.uk, Ltd.,
Marston Gate.